PLEASE UNDERSTAND ME

PLEASE UNDERSTAND ME

CHARACTER
&
TEMPERAMENT
TYPES

DAVID
KEIRSEY

MARILYN
BATES

DISTRIBUTED BY **PROMETHEUS NEMESIS BOOK COMPANY**
Post Office Box 2748, Del Mar, CA 92014

Fourth Edition

ISBN 0-9606954-0-0

TABLE OF CONTENTS

DIFFERENT DRUMS AND DIFFERENT DRUMMERS

If I do not want what you want, please try not to tell me that my want is wrong.

Or if I believe other than you, at least pause before you correct my view.

Or if my emotion is less than yours, or more, given the same circumstances, try not to ask me to feel more strongly or weakly.

Or yet if I act, or fail to act, in the manner of your design for action, let me be.

I do not, for the moment at least, ask you to understand me. That will come only when you are willing to give up changing me into a copy of you.

I may be your spouse, your parent, your offspring, your friend, or your colleague. If you will allow me any of my own wants, or emotions, or beliefs, or actions, then you open yourself, so that some day these ways of mine might not seem so wrong, and might finally appear to you as right—for me. To put up with me is the first step to understanding me. Not that you embrace my ways as right for you, but that you are no longer irritated or disappointed with me for my seeming waywardness. And in understanding me you might come to prize my differences from you, and, far from seeking to change me, preserve and even nurture those differences.

The point of this book is that people are different from each other, and that no amount of getting after them is going to change them. Nor is there any reason to change them, because the differences are probably good, not bad.

People are different in fundamental ways. They *want* different things; they have different motives, purposes, aims, values, needs, drives, impulses, urges. Nothing is more fundamental than that. They *believe* differently: they think, cognize, conceptualize, perceive, understand, comprehend, and cogitate differently. And of course, manners of acting and emoting, governed as they are by wants and beliefs, follow suit and differ radically among people.

Differences abound and are not at all difficult to see, if one looks. And it is precisely these variations in behavior and attitude that trigger in each of us a common response: Seeing others around us differing from us, we conclude that these differences in individual behavior are but temporary manifestations of madness, badness, stupidity, or sickness. In other words, we rather naturally account for variations in the behavior of others in terms of flaw and affliction. Our job, at least for those near us, would seem to be to correct these flaws. Our Pygmalion project, then, is to make all those near us just like us.

Fortunately, this project is impossible. To sculpt the other into our own likeness fails before it begins. People can't change *form* no matter how much and in what manner we require them to. Form is inherent, ingrained, indelible. Ask a snake to swallow itself. Ask a person to change form—think or want differently—and you ask the impossible, for it is the thinking and wanting that is required to change the thinking and wanting. Form cannot be self-changing.

Of course, some change is possible, but it is a twisting and distortion of underlying form. Remove the fangs of a lion and behold a toothless lion, not a domestic cat. Our attempts to change spouse, offspring, or others can result in change, but the result is a scar and not a transformation.

The belief that people are fundamentally alike appears to be a twentieth century notion. Probably the idea is related to the growth of democracy in the Western world. If we are equals then we must be alike. Freud believed we are all driven from within by Eros, and that what seem to be "higher" motives are merely disguised versions of Eros. His colleagues and followers took issue with him, though most retained the idea of singular motivation. Adler saw us all seeking power (and later other things). Sullivan took up the later Adlerian theme and put social solidarity as the basic instinctual craving. Finally, the Existentialists—eg. Fromm—had us seeking after Self. Each appealed to instinct as purpose, and each made one instinct primary for everybody.

In 1920 Jung disagreed. He said that people are different in fundamental ways even though they all have the same multitude of instincts (archetypes) to drive them from within. One instinct is no more important than another. What is important is our preference for how we "function." Our preference for a given "function" is characteristic, and so we may be "typed" by this preference. Thus Jung invented the "function types" or "psychological types."

In 1907 Adickes said man is divided into four world views: dogmatic, agnostic, traditional and innovative. In 1920 Kretschmer said abnormal behavior was determined by the temperament similar to those of Adickes: hyperesthetic, anesthetic, melancholic and hypomanic. Thus some people are born too sensitive, some too insensitive, some too serious, some too excitable. Around 1920 Adler spoke similarly by pointing to four "mistaken goals" people of different make pursue when upset: recognition, power, service and revenge. Also in 1920 Spranger told of four human values that set people apart: religious, theoretic, economic and artistic. So the early twentieth century saw a brief revival of a view presented almost twenty five centuries earlier by Hippocrates, who, in trying to account for behavior, spoke of four temperaments clearly corresponding to those of Adickes, Kretschmer, Adler and Spranger: choleric, phlegmatic, melancholic and sanguine.

By 1930 the views of Jung as well as those of Adickes, Kretschmer, Adler, Spranger and Hippocrates had all but been forgotten, replaced as they were by so called "dynamic" psychology on the one hand and "behaviorist" psychology on the other. Behavior was now to be explained as due to unconscious motives or to past experience or both. The idea of temperament was abandoned.

A revival of the idea of temperament in the 1950s was acciden-tal. Isabel Myers dusted off Jung's book on psychological types and with her mother Katheryn Briggs devised the Myers-Briggs Type Indicator, a tool for identifying sixteen different patterns of action. The test was used so widely that it created interna-tional interest in the idea of types of people and revived interest in Jung's theory of psychological types. But it also revived interest in the ancient theory of four temperaments because the sixteen Myers-Briggs types fell neatly into the four temperaments of Hippocrates, Adickes, Kretschmer, Spranger and Adler.

Suppose it is so that people differ in temperament and that therefore their behavior is just as inborn as their body build. Then we do violence to others when we assume such differ-ences to be flaws and afflictions. In this misunderstanding of others we also diminish our ability to predict what they will do. Likewise, we cannot even reward others should we want to, since what is reward to us is, very likely, a matter of indif-ference to the other. To each his own, different strokes to different folks. To achieve the intent of these sayings will take a lot of work in coming to see our differences as something other than flaws.

The payoff of such work is that you can look upon your spouse, for example, as a DIFFERENT person—someone you don't quite understand, but someone you can, with a sense of puzzle-ment perhaps, gradually come to appreciate. Similarly, you can gain an appreciation of your offspring, parent, superior, sub-ordinate, colleague and friend. Much to gain, nothing to lose.

But first it is necessary to study yourself. If you don't have yourself accurately portrayed, no way can you portray any-one else accurately. The best way at present to do this is to take the Myers-Briggs Type Indicator test. This can be done by attending a workshop on the Myers-Briggs types or by going to a counselor or psychologist who is authorized to administer this test. In the meantime it may help you to read this book with more personal involvement than otherwise to answer the questions on pages 5 through 10. An answer sheet is provided on page 11, with additional copies to be found in the back of the book. Decide on answer **a** or **b** and put a check mark in the proper column of the answer sheet. Scoring directions are provided at the bottom of page 11. There are no right or wrong answers since about half the population agrees with either answer you choose.

The Keirsey Temperament Sorter

1. **At a party do you**
   - (a) interact with many, including strangers
   - (b) interact with a few, known to you

2. **Are you more**
   - (a) realistic than speculative
   - (b) speculative than realistic

3. **Is it worse to**
   - (a) have your "head in the clouds"
   - (b) be "in a rut"

4. **Are you more impressed by**
   - (a) principles
   - (b) emotions

5. **Are you more drawn toward the**
   - (a) convincing
   - (b) touching

6. **Do you prefer to work**
   - (a) to deadlines
   - (b) just "whenever"

7. **Do you tend to choose**
   - (a) rather carefully
   - (b) somewhat impulsively

8. **At parties do you**
   - (a) stay late, with increasing energy
   - (b) leave early, with decreased energy

9. **Are you more attracted to**
   - (a) sensible people
   - (b) imaginative people

10. **Are you more interested in**
    - (a) what is actual
    - (b) what is possible

11. **In judging others are you more swayed by**
    - (a) laws than circumstances
    - (b) circumstances than laws

12. In approaching others is your inclination to be somewhat
    (a) objective   (b) personal

13. Are you more
    (a) punctual   (b) leisurely

14. Does it bother you more having things
    (a) incomplete   (b) completed

15. In your social groups do you
    (a) keep abreast of other's happenings
    (b) get behind on the news

16. In doing ordinary things are you more likely to
    (a) do it the usual way   (b) do it your own way

17. Writers should
    (a) "say what they mean and mean what they say"
    (b) express things more by use of analogy

18. Which appeals to you more
    (a) consistency of thought
    (b) harmonious human relationships

19. Are you more comfortable in making
    (a) logical judgments   (b) value judgments

20. Do you want things
    (a) settled and decided   (b) unsettled and undecided

21. Would you say you are more
    (a) serious and determined   (b) easy-going

22. In phoning do you
    (a) rarely question that it will all be said
    (b) rehearse what you'll say

23. Facts
    (a) "speak for themselves"
    (b) illustrate principles

24. Are visionaries
   (a) somewhat annoying
   (b) rather fascinating

25. Are you more often
   (a) a cool-headed person   (b) a warm-hearted person

26. Is it worse to be
   (a) unjust   (b) merciless

27. Should one usually let events occur
   (a) by careful selection and choice
   (b) randomly and by chance

28. Do you feel better about
   (a) having purchased   (b) having the option to buy

29. In company do you
   (a) initiate conversation   (b) wait to be approached

30. Common sense is
   (a) rarely questionable   (b) frequently questionable

31. Children often do not
   (a) make themselves useful enough
   (b) exercise their fantasy enough

32. In making decisions do you feel more comfortable with
   (a) standards   (b) feelings

33. Are you more
   (a) firm than gentle   (b) gentle than firm

34. Which is more admirable:
   (a) the ability to organize and be methodical
   (b) the ability to adapt and make do

35. Do you put more value on the
   (a) definite   (b) open-ended

36. **Does new and non-routine interaction with others**
    (a) stimulate and energize you
    (b) tax your reserves

37. **Are you more frequently**
    (a) a practical sort of person
    (b) a fanciful sort of person

38. **Are you more likely to**
    (a) see how others are useful
    (b) see how others see

39. **Which is more satisfying:**
    (a) to discuss an issue thoroughly
    (b) to arrive at agreement on an issue

40. **Which rules you more:**
    (a) your head   (b) your heart

41. **Are you more comfortable with work that is**
    (a) contracted   (b) done on a casual basis

42. **Do you tend to look for**
    (a) the orderly   (b) whatever turns up

43. **Do you prefer**
    (a) many friends with brief contact
    (b) a few friends with more lengthy contact

44. **Do you go more by**
    (a) facts   (b) principles

45. **Are you more interested in**
    (a) production and distribution
    (b) design and research

46. **Which is more of a compliment:**
    (a) "There is a very logical person."
    (b) "There is a very sentimental person."

47. Do you value in yourself more that you are
    (a) unwavering   (b) devoted

48. Do you more often prefer the
    (a) final and unalterable statement
    (b) tentative and preliminary statement

49. Are you more comfortable
    (a) after a decision   (b) before a decision

50. Do you
    (a) speak easily and at length with strangers
    (b) find little to say to strangers

51. Are you more likely to trust your
    (a) experience   (b) hunch

52. Do you feel
    (a) more practical than ingenious
    (b) more ingenious than practical

53. Which person is more to be complimented: one of
    (a) clear reason   (b) strong feeling

54. Are you inclined more to be
    (a) fair-minded   (b) sympathetic

55. Is it preferable mostly to
    (a) make sure things are arranged
    (b) just let things happen

56. In relationships should most things be
    (a) renegotiable
    (b) random and circumstantial

57. When the phone rings do you
    (a) hasten to get to it first
    (b) hope someone else will answer

58. Do you prize more in yourself
    (a) a strong sense of reality (b) a vivid imagination

59. Are you drawn more to
    (a) fundamentals   (b) overtones

60. Which seems the greater error:
    (a) to be too passionate   (b) to be too objective

61. Do you see yourself as basically
    (a) hard-headed   (b) soft-hearted

62. Which situation appeals to you more:
    (a) the structured and scheduled
    (b) the unstructured and unscheduled

63. Are you a person that is more
    (a) routinized than whimsical
    (b) whimsical than routinized

64. Are you more inclined to be
    (a) easy to approach   (b) somewhat reserved

65. In writings do you prefer
    (a) the more literal   (b) the more figurative

66. Is it harder for you to
    (a) identify with others   (b) utilize others

67. Which do you wish more for yourself:
    (a) clarity of reason   (b) strength of compassion

68. Which is the greater fault:
    (a) being indiscriminate   (b) being critical

69. Do you prefer the
    (a) planned event   (b) unplanned event

70. Do you tend to be more
    (a) deliberate than spontaneous
    (b) spontaneous than deliberate

Answer Sheet

Enter a check for each answer in the column for **a** or **b**

	a	b		a	b		a	b		a	b		a	b		a	b		a	b
1			2			3			4			5			6			7		
8			9			10			11			12			13			14		
15			16			17			18			19			20			21		
22			23			24			25			26			27			28		
29			30			31			32			33			34			35		
36			37			38			39			40			41			42		
43			44			45			46			47			48			49		
50			51			52			53			54			55			56		
57			58			59			60			61			62			63		
64			65			66			67			68			69			70		

```
  1      2  3      4  3      4  5      6  5      6  7      8  7      8

  1      2  3      4            5      6            7      8
   E  I      S  N                T  F                J  P
```

Directions for Scoring

1. Add down so that the total number of "a" answers is written in the box at the bottom of each column (see next page for illustration). Do the same for the "b" answers you have checked. Each of the 14 boxes should have a number in it.

2. Transfer the number in box No. 1 of the answer sheet to box No. 1 below the answer sheet. Do this for box No. 2 as well. Note, however, that you have two numbers for boxes 3 through 8. Bring down the first number for each box beneath the second, as indicated by the arrows. Now add all the pairs of numbers and enter the total in the boxes below the answer sheet, so each box has only one number.

3. Now you have four pairs of numbers. Circle the letter below the larger number of each pair (see answer sheet below for illustration). If the two numbers of any pair are equal, then circle neither, but put a large X below them and circle it.

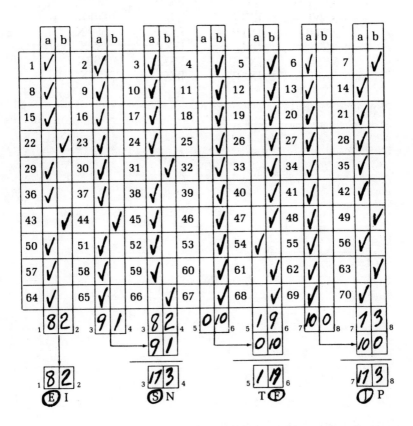

You have now identified your "type." It should be one of the following:

INFP	ISFP	INTP	ISTP
ENFP	ESFP	ENTP	ESTP
INFJ	ISFJ	INTJ	ISTJ
ENFJ	ESFJ	ENTJ	ESTJ

If you have an X in your type, yours is a mixed type. An X can show up in any of the four pairs: E or I, S or N, T or F, and

J or P. Hence there are 32 mixed types besides the 16 listed above:

XNTP	EXTP	ENXP	ENTX
XNTJ	EXTJ	INXP	INTX
XNFP	EXFP	ENXJ	ENFX
XNFJ	EXFJ	INXJ	INFX
XSTP	IXTP	ESXP	ESTX
XSTJ	IXTJ	ISXP	ISTX
XSFP	IXFP	ESXJ	ESFX
XSFJ	IXFJ	ISXJ	ISFX

Having identified type, the task now is to read the type description and to decide how well or how poorly the description fits. You will find a description or portrait of your type on the page indicated in the table of contents. If you have an X in your type, yours is a combination of two types. If, for example, the E and I scores are equal and the type is, say, XSFJ, then you would read both ESFJ and ISFJ portraits and decide for yourself which parts of each description are applicable.

One may also profit from reading the portrait of one's *opposite* to see how things are "on the other side." (How one proceeds after reading one's own type portrait depends largely upon temperament. Some of the types will read several other portraits before returning to the text, while others will return immediately to the text. Some may never read all sixteen of the type descriptions.) As will be shown, the typology is useful if an observer can distinguish between four types of temperament. It is not at all necessary to make these finer distinctions. However, such differences can become useful after long study.

The Four Pairs of Preferences

Having read a description of your type and perhaps a few other type descriptions, you may well wonder what the "temperament sorter" or "type indicator" was based on. What did Jung mean by extraversion (E), Introversion (I), sensation (S), intuition (N), thinking (T), feeling (F), perceiving (P), and judging (J)?

First, it should be noted that Jung did not say that a person is either one or the other of these four pairs. Rather, one can be extraverted in some *degree* as well as introverted in some degree, thinking in some degree and feeling in some degree, and so on.

Second, Jung did not say that one doesn't change in the extent of preference for one or another of the four differences. As time passes one's preference may strengthen or weaken. Of course, it is not at all clear what Jung meant by "preference" other than that, for one reason or another, a person chooses one way of doing or being over another.

Third, the question of whether these preferences are "inborn" or develop fortuitously in infancy and youth remains unsettled. Jung apparently believed the former, though his pronouncements are not very clear on this point.

Whether inborn or chosen later, the "functions" according to Jung develop and become stronger through use. If, for example, a person uses his intuition, the intuition becomes more powerful; if a person uses his feelings, they become stronger. Conversely, if one doesn't use one's thinking or judging, or whatever, these "functions" do not develop and become, so to speak, rusty with disuse. This is an interesting hypothesis, perhaps worthy of research.

At any rate, what is important about the Jungian typology are the descriptions of how people differ in their preferred actions, quite apart from Jung's accuracy or inaccuracy in choosing names for these preferences.

Extraversion vs Introversion

The person who chooses people as a source of energy probably prefers extraversion, while the person who prefers solitude to recover energy may tend toward introversion. In temperament shorthand, extraversion is abbreviated by the letter **E** and introversion by the letter **I**.

Sources of Misunderstanding: Extraverts, with their need for *sociability*, appear to be energized, or "tuned up," by people. Talking to people, playing with people, and working with people is what charges their batteries. Extraverts experience loneliness when they are not in contact with people. When an extreme extravert leaves a party at two o'clock in the morning, he may well be ready to go to another one. His batteries are almost overcharged, having received so much energy from the interaction.

While the extravert is sociable, the introvert is *territorial.* That is, he desires space: private places in the mind and private environmental places. Introverts seem to draw their energies from a different source than do extraverts. Pursuing solitary activities, working quietly alone, reading, meditating, participating in activities which involve few or no other people —these seem to charge the batteries of the introvert. Thus, if an extreme introvert goes to a party, after a "reasonable" period of time—say, half an hour—he is ready to go home. For him, the party is over. He is no party pooper; rather, he was pooped by the party.

Introverts, too, are likely to experience a sense of loneliness— when they are in a crowd! They are most "alone" when surrounded by people, especially strangers. When waiting in a crowded airport or trying to enjoy themselves at noisy cocktail parties, some introverts report experiencing a deep sense of isolation and disconnectedness. This is not to say that introverts do not like to be around people. Introverts enjoy interacting with others, but it drains their energy in a way not experienced by extraverts. Introverts need to find quiet places and solitary activities to recharge, while these activities exhaust the extravert. If the latter goes to a library to do research, for example, he may have to exercise strong will power to prevent himself, after fifteen minutes or so, from taking a "short brain break" and striking up a conversation with the librarian.

It is quite the opposite with an introvert, who can remain only so long in interaction with people before he depletes his reserves.

The question always arises, "Does not an extravert also have an introverted side and does not an introvert also have an extraverted side?" Yes, of course. But the preferred attitude, whether it be extraversion or introversion, will have the most potency and the other will be the "suppressed minority." The preferred attitude will be expressed in the conscious personality, and will reflect the aim, will, and achievement of the conscious personality. The suppressed minority is only partly in consciousness and reflects "what happens to one." This less-favored side of a person's temperament is less differentiated and is less energized, and is apt to be more primitive and undeveloped. Jung even claims that if, through pressure on the part of the mother, the child is coerced into living out of his inferior side, this falsification of type results in the individual's becoming disturbed in later life.

If a person prefers extraversion, his choice coincides with about 75 percent of the general population (Bradway, 1964). Only 25 percent reported introversion as their preference, according to Myers (Bradway, 1964). Indeed, Western culture seems to sanction the outgoing, sociable, and gregarious temperament. The notion of anyone wanting or needing much solitude is viewed rather often as reflecting an unfriendly attitude. Solitary activities frequently are seen as ways to structure time until something better comes along, and this something better by definition involves interacting with people. As a consequence, introverts are often the ugly ducklings in a society where the majority enjoy sociability. There is the story about a mother heard to protest loudly and defensively, "My daughter is *not* an introvert. She is a lovely girl!"

Introverts have reported that they have gone through much of their lives believing that they *ought* to want more sociability, and because they do not, are indeed ugly ducklings who can never be swans. As a result, the introvert seldom provides adequately for his very legitimate desire for territoriality, for breathing room, without experiencing a vague feeling of guilt.

Cue Words: The main word which differentiates an extravert from an introvert is *sociability* as opposed to *territoriality*, but the extravert also finds *breadth* appealing where the introvert finds the notion of *depth* more attractive. Other notions which give a cue to this preference are the idea of *external* as opposed to *internal;* the *extensive* as opposed to the *intensive; interaction* as opposed to *concentration; multiplicity of relationships* as opposed to *limited relationships; expenditure of energy* as opposed to *conservation of energy; interest in external happenings* as opposed to *interest in internal reactions.*

Intuition vs Sensation

The person who has a natural preference for sensation probably describes himself first as practical, while the person who had a natural preference for intuition probably chooses to describe himself as innovative. In temperament shorthand, the sensation preference is designated by **S**, the intuition preference by **N** (the first letter of intuition, I, cannot be used, since that letter denotes introversion). Seventy-five percent of the general population reports a preference for sensation while 25 percent indicates a preference for intuition (Bradway, 1964).

Sources of Misunderstanding: Although extraversion and introversion are important differences in understanding ourselves and others, especially others we live with, these preferences are minor compared with *sensation* and *intuitive* ways of thinking about things. The two preferences of sensation and intuition are, of any of the preferences, the source of the most miscommunication, misunderstanding, vilification, defamation, and denigration. *This difference places the widest gulf between people.* It is the difference, in fact, that Kretschmer saw so clearly as schizothymia vs cyclothymia. The schizothyms (intuitives) are understood in terms of sensitivity/insensitivity, awareness/unawareness, while the cyclothymes (sensibles) are understood in terms of happiness/sadness, optimism/pessimism. For Kretschmer this was the fundamental dimension of human difference, while for Jung it was merely one of four bases of difference.

The sensation-preferring or "sensible" person wants facts, trusts facts, and remembers facts. He believes in experience and knows through experience (history), both personal and global. He might be described as earth-bound, as grounded firmly in reality, anchored to earth—a terrestrial. When a sensible talks to people, he is interested in their experience, their past. For example, if a sensation-preferring employer interviews someone for placement, he wants to know what experience the applicant has had. This is important to this employer, because, if an applicant has had experience, the employer feels he has a sound basis for decision. The intuitive-preferring employer, on the other hand, is likely to have confidence not in what the applicant has done in the past but in what an applicant verbalizes about the future of the organization—what he would do in a hypothesized situation, what he might see as possibilities for growth for the organization, or how he would propose to handle a given problem.

The sensation types notice the actual and want to deal with that. They focus on what actually happened rather than worrying too much about what might have been or what will be in the future. These people remain in reality and, when work is the issue, tolerate no nonsense. They usually are accurate in observing details, perhaps because, when a sensible type approaches something, his eyes tend to pick up a specific element. This is quite different from the intuitive who, when entering a situation, seems to scan, glance, radiate at things and people, at times aware only of that which is related to his current preoccupation, missing details noted by the sensible.

The kind of language which inspires the intuitive has no ring to the sensible. The intuitive finds appeal in the metaphor and enjoys vivid imagery. He often daydreams, reads poetry, enjoys fantasy and fiction, and can find the study of dreams fascinating. The intuitive acts as if he is an extraterrestrial, a space traveler engaged in explorations beyond the realities of the present and the past. The possible is always in front of him, pulling on his imagination like a magnet. The future holds an attraction for the intuitive which the past and the actual do not. But, because his head is often in the clouds, the intuitive can be subject to greater error about facts than the sensible, who pays better attention to what is going on about him. For the intuitive, life is around the bend, on the other side of the mountain, just beyond the curve of the horizon. He can speculate for hours about possibilities. He operates in future time, sees "around corners," and knows "out of the unconscious." The intuitive sometimes finds complex ideas coming to him as a complete whole, unable to explain how he knew. These visions, intuitions, or hunches may show up in any realm—technology, sciences, mathematics, philosophy, the arts, or one's social life.

Of course, people who prefer sensation have hunches also, but they do not pay much attention to them, and after several years of ignoring their intuitions, not acting on them, and not trusting them, the intuition is heard as mere static. The penalty one pays for ignoring that inner voice is that it diminishes. The penalty paid by those who prefer imagination—the intuitives—is that if they ignore reality too long, they end up out of touch with the realities of their environment.

The intuitive lives in anticipation. Whatever is can be better, or different, and is seen as only a way station. Consequently, intuitives often experience a vague sense of dissatisfaction and restlessness. They seem somewhat bothered by reality, constantly looking toward possibilities of changing or improving the actual.

The intuitive can skip from one activity to the next, perhaps completing none. Jung (1923) described the intuitive as one who plants a field and then is off to something new before the crop is even beginning to break ground. Instead of staying around to see his vision come to fruition, he is off looking for new fields to plow. Others can be left to reap the benefit of the intuitive's past inspirations. Thus, to the sensible, the intuitive frequently appears to be flighty, impractical, and unrealistic. The intuitive, on his part, at times views the sensible as plodding and exasperatingly slow to see possibilities in tomorrow.

The difference between intuitives and sensibles is most noticeable in their attitude about child-rearing. The intuitive parent, especially if augmented by an intuitive spouse, is likely to worry if the child doesn't spend much time daydreaming and fantasizing and is not captured and intrigued by the more fanciful tales and myths. It is as if such parents want their offspring to develop their imaginations by utilizing them daily. Nothing is more valued by the extreme intuitive than a *vivid* imagination.

In contrast, the sensible parent becomes concerned should the child spend what seems an inordinate amount of time in fantasy. One must develop one's *usefulness*. The child should spend much of his time outdoors playing, practicing—and when older, working.

Cue Words: Careful listening to one's own choice of words may demonstrate how each person verbalizes his preferences. Through choice of vocabulary, and through intonation, one very often transmits one set of values over another. People who prefer sensation (S), for example, tend to value *experience* and the wisdom of the *past*, and want to be *realistic*, while the people who prefer intuition (N) tend to value *hunches* and a vision of the *future*, and are likely to be *speculative*. The S person depends on *perspiration* where the N person is more likely to depend on *inspiration*. Words such as *actual, down-to-earth, no-nonsense, fact, practical,* and *sensible* are music to S people; words such as *possible, fascinating, fantasy, fiction, ingenious,* and *imaginative* are apt to light the eyes of N people.

Thinking vs Feeling

Persons who choose the impersonal basis of choice are called the thinking (T) types by Jung. Persons who choose the personal basis are called the feeling (F) types. Both of these ways of selecting what to do or not to do are necessary and useful. It is a matter of comfort. Some people are more comfortable with impersonal, objective judgments and uncomfortable with personal judgments. Others are more comfortable with value judgments and less with being objective and logical. The more extreme feeling types are a bit put off by rule-governed choice, regarding the act of being impersonal as almost inhuman. The more dedicated thinking types, on the other hand, sometimes look upon the emotion-laden decisions and choices as muddle-headed. Each person is quite capable of both types of decision. It's rather a matter of preference.

Sources of Misunderstanding: More women than men (6 out of 10) report that they prefer deciding on the basis of personal impact (F), and certainly there is cultural sanction on this type of behavior on the part of females. More men than women (6 out of 10) report that they prefer to make decisions on the basis of principles, that is, logically and objectively. Thus more men prefer the thinking and more women feeling, although this sex difference is relatively minor and gives little edge in predicting behavior. The T–F dimension is the only pair of preferences which shows a sex trend (Myers, 1963), and is distributed equally in the general population (Bradway, 1964).

People who use the F preference as the basis for decisions claim, at times, that T-preference people are "heartless," "stony-hearted," "have ice in their veins," are "cold," "remote," and "intellectualizers who are without the milk of human kindness." On the other hand, the T-preference people who use the impersonal principles as the basis for decisions may claim, at times, that the F people are "too soft hearted," "unable to take a firm stand," "incapable of standing up in the face of opposition," "too emotional," "illogical," "fuzzy thinkers," "intellectual dilettantes," and people who "wear their hearts on their sleeves."

Misunderstandings can occur when F and T people are expected to make decisions in an unnatural way, that is, in the mode which is not preferred and therefore a way which is not the most comfortable. For example, an F wife may insist that her T husband "let his feelings show," while he might wish she "would be logical for once!"Yet, neither way of going about making decisions deserves denigration from those with an opposing preference.

People with the F preference may have an advantage over those with the T preference for developing the less-desired preference. Formal schooling addresses the T areas far more than the F. Thus, those with a natural preference for F also tend to develop their T, while those with a natural preference for T do not have an equal opportunity to develop their F side, which may remain relatively primitive.

Sometimes the feeling types are seen as more emotionally sensitive than the T people, but this is not the case in actuality. Both types can react emotionally with the same intensity; the F person, however, tends to make his emotional reactions more visible, and others may see him as warmer and capable of deeper feelings than a T person. When the F type does become emotional—when his hands become moist, when color flushes or drains from his face, when his body trembles, when his heart beats faster, and when conscious control of the body is lost—others are affected by this. Indeed, the emotional reactions of F people tend to be contagious and to generate heat. When the T person becomes emotional, however, the same body reactions are not as evident, and, therefore, not as much noticed by others. Thus T people are often described as cold and unemotional, while in reality they may be experiencing as intense emotion as is an F person. The T person, in fact, sometimes seems embarrassed by a show of intense emotions, while the F person sometimes seems to enjoy the excessive show of feelings.

The T versus F preference need not cause serious problems in interpersonal relations if the two different ways of going about making decisions are understood and appreciated. To be sure, this dimension can be complementary between two people in a way which the other preferences are not. (The E versus I dimensions and the N versus S dimensions are apt to be more oppositional than supplemental.) The F person needs a T person to present another point of view and vice versa. Once an F person understands that a T person *does* have deep, though not always visible, emotions, and once a

T person realizes that an F person *can* think logically, although he may not always verbalize his logic, misunderstandings between them are apt to dissipate.

Cue Words: Persons who prefer impersonal choice as a way of making decisions (T people) tend to respond positively to such words as *objective, principles, policy, laws, criteria,* and *firmness,* while persons who choose in the context of the effects of the choice on themselves and others (F people) tend to react positively to words such as *subjective, values, social values, extenuating circumstances, intimacy,* and *persuasion.* T people tend to use the *impersonal* approach, where F people choose to be more *personal* in dealing with people and projects. Ts like the sound of words such as *justice, categories, standards, critique, analysis, allocation,* while Fs like the sound of words such as *humane, harmony, good or bad, appreciate, sympathy, devotion.* The T person tends to give priority to objective criteria, and is apt to be good at argumentation, attempting to win people over to his point of view through logic rather than appeal to the emotions. The F person tends to be good at persuasion and makes choices in the context of the personal impact of the decision on the people around him.

Judging vs Perceiving

Question: Do I prefer closure and the settling of things or do I prefer to keep options open and fluid?

Persons who choose closure over open options are likely to be the judging types. Persons preferring to keep things open and fluid are probably the perceiving types. The J is apt to report a sense of urgency until he has made a pending decision, and then be at rest once the decision has been made. The P person, in contrast, is more apt to experience resistance to making a decision, wishing that more data could be accumulated as the basis for the decision. As a result, when a P person makes a decision, he may have a feeling of uneasiness and restlessness, while the J person, in the same situation, may have a feeling of ease and satisfaction.

Js tend to establish deadlines and to take them seriously, expecting others to do the same. Ps may tend more to look upon deadlines as mere alarm clocks which buzz at a given time, easily turned off or ignored while one catches an extra forty winks, almost as if the deadline were used more as a signal to start than to complete a project.

A curious phenomenon can sometimes be observed in P people who are responsible to their superiors for meeting deadlines. Apparently not trusting subordinates to take deadlines seriously, the P person is likely to become anxious and react by moving real deadlines ahead to artificial ones. The J person, in the same situation, is apt to communicate to his subordinates the actual deadlines set by his superiors and expect the deadlines to be met.

The difference between Js and Ps is easily observed, especially when the preference is extreme in either direction. Unfortunately, just what Jung meant by "judgment" and "perception" was not at all clear. Judgment was to mean "concluding" and perception was to mean "becoming aware." But this definition was merely a substitution of controversial constructs with equally controversial ones. Fortunately, Jung's identification of observable differences in actions is independent of his speculation, so that the detection and description of types need not suffer in the least from these excursions.

Sources of Misunderstanding: There appears to be about as many Js as Ps in the general population (Bradway, 1964). This preference can be a source of irritation in relationships, because Js push toward decisions, while Ps hold out until there can be additional search for data and perhaps more options. In addition, the meaning of the judging and perceiving concepts is vulnerable to misinterpretation. The term judging is often seen as "judgmental," and perceiving as meaning "perceptive." J people are no more judgmental than P people, and P people are no more perceptive than J people. A more useful distinction can be made by describing judging as a desire or valuing of closure, and perception likewise as a desire or valuing of the open-ended.

Apparently, all Js—whether intuitive or sensible, thinking or feeling, introverted or extraverted—share an attitude toward work and play quite different from that of the Ps. The judging types seem to have a work ethic such that work comes before all else. One's work must be done before one rests or plays. This outlook has marked effect on what Js are willing to do to get the job done. Js will do all sorts of preparation, maintenance, and cleaning up afterwards just because these are necessary. Not so with Ps.

Ps, on the other hand—whether intuitive or sensible, thinking or feeling, introverted or extraverted—seem to have a *play* ethic. Ps seem to be more playful and less serious than Js. The work doesn't have to be done before play or rest begins. And if the process of work is not directly instrumental (is mere preparation, maintenance or clean up), then the P may balk at doing it or find something else to do. Ps are much more insistent than Js that the work process is enjoyable. One might say that Ps are process-oriented while Js are outcome-oriented.

At work especially, Ps and Js can criticize each other.

J people can be heard to describe Ps as "indecisive," "procrastinating," "foot-dragging," "aimless," "purposeless," "resistive," "critical," "sophistic," and "blocking decisions." Ps may, at times, become impatient with Js because they feel pressured and hurried by what they view as the J's unnecessary urgency and unfortunate tendency to "jump to conclusions." Ps will occasionally claim that Js make hasty decisions and are "driven" and "driving," are "too task-oriented," are "pressured and pressuring," "rigid and inflexible," "arbitrary," and "premature in planning and deciding." Usually, irritation by another's preference will dissipate when J and P behaviors are studied. Most people become fascinated and entertained by these differences, and with continued understanding, find it easy to make allowances for the other's way.

Cue Words: Expressions which sound good to J people are words such as *settled, decided, fixed, plan ahead, run one's life, closure, decision-making, planned, completed, decisive, "wrap it up," urgency, deadlines, "get the show on the road."* What sound good to P people are expressions such as *pending, gather more data, flexible, adapt as you go, let life happen, keep options open, "treasure-hunting," open-ended, emergent, tentative, "something will turn up," there is plenty of time, what deadline?, let's wait and see.*

In summary, the four differences may be characterized by pairs of words and phrases:

E (75% of population) versus I (25% of population)

Sociability .... Territoriality
Interaction....................... Concentration
External .... Internal
Breadth.......................... Depth
Extensive .... Intensive
Multiplicity of relationships .... Limited relationships
Expenditure of energies .... Conservation of energies
Interest in external events........ Interest in internal
reaction

S (75% of population) versus N (25% of population)

Experience...................... Hunches
Past .... Future
Realistic .... Speculative
Perspiration..................... Inspiration
Actual.......................... Possible
Down-to-earth .... Head-in-clouds
Utility .... Fantasy
Fact .... Fiction
Practicality .... Ingenuity
Sensible .... Imaginative

T (50% of population) versus F (50% of population)

Objective .... Subjective
Principles....................... Values
Policy .... Social values
Laws .... Extenuating
circumstances
Criterion........................ Intimacy
Firmness........................ Persuasion
Impersonal...................... Personal
Justice.......................... Humane
Categories .... Harmony
Standards....................... Good or bad
Critique......................... Appreciate
Analysis .... Sympathy
Allocation....................... Devotion

J (50% of population) versus P (50% of population)

Settled.......................... Pending
Decided......................... Gather more data
Fixed .... Flexible

Plan ahead...................... Adapt as you go
Run one's life.................... Let life happen
Closure .... Open options
Decision-making .... Treasure hunting
Planned......................... Open ended
Completed .... Emergent
Decisive .... Tentative
Wrap it up .... Something will turn up
Urgency .... There's plenty of time
Deadline! .... What deadline?
Get show on the road............. Let's wait and see . . .

Thus far the concept of type of preferences on four dimensions of difference has been examined. Out of this Jungian theory have emerged sixteen types. In order to use the typology to understand others and predict what they will do, one would have to become familiar with all sixteen. That is a tall order.

The real usefulness of the types comes not in memorizing the sixteen portraits, but in understanding the temperamental base of the types. There seem to be four temperaments, as indicated by Hippocrates centuries ago and by Spranger more recently. The next chapter will examine this view.

II
THE
FOUR
TEMPERAMENTS

In our effort to describe the four temperaments of Hippocrates —the Sanguine, Choleric, Phlegmatic, and Melancholic—we can stitch together the useful theoretical contributions of Jung, Kretschmer, Freud, Adler, Sullivan, and Maslow, recognizing the insight of each at the same time that we keep them from canceling each other out.

In taking our cue from Kretschmer in the temperament hypothesis we must abandon Jung's idea of "functions." But in giving up Jung's "function" we must not abandon his behavior descriptions, for they have great predictive value. By knowing a person's type we can anticipate rather accurately what he will do most of the time. This is not something to give up lightly, so it is not so much that the "function type" is abandoned but rather subordinated to the concept of "temperament," the latter having a much wider range of convenience as an explainer of behavior.

What is meant, first of all, by temperament? This question is not as naïve as it sounds, for American psychology has rarely considered the idea and so is in no position to define it or pronounce its uses. Temperament can denote a moderation or unification of otherwise disparate forces, a tempering or concession of opposing influences, an overall coloration or tuning, a kind of thematization of the whole, a uniformity of the diverse. One's temperament is that which places a signature or thumbprint on each of one's actions, making it recognizably one's own.

This consistency in actions can be observed from a very early age—some features earlier than others—long before events have had time or occasion to imprint the person. It is tempting, therefore, to say that form is given, not acquired, and that temperament is the inborn form of the living being. Maslow (1954) said that motives displace each other as a person grows up. We start, he said, with *physiological* needs. We learn to take it for granted that these needs will be fulfilled and, once fulfilled, are no longer motivating for us. We graduate to *safety* needs. Soon these are taken for granted and are no longer motivating. So we ascend to *social* needs—to love and caring. Most people are able to arrange their lives to fulfill these needs as well and so ascend to the need for *esteem;* that is, the need to be well regarded by self and others. A few (not very many really, says Maslow) are able to accumulate enough esteem to take even *it* for granted, and so emerge finally at what he called the "self-actualizing personality," no longer motivated by the lower physical needs or by needs for safety, love, and self-esteem. But, Maslow implies, those people who don't make it to the top have a latent or potential need for self-actualization which would break forth as a full-blown motive once they overcome their fixations at lower levels.

This hierarchical view of motivation is reminiscent of the Freudian stages of psychosexual development, although desexualized. It also resembles a theory of motivation proposed by William Sheldon (1936) some fourteen years prior to Maslow's.

In the light of Harlow's work with monkeys it may be necessary to rearrange the order of needs a bit, such that the first need is social, the second is safety, and the third is physical. In any event, it makes sense to say that we do not continuously search for social ties, or safety, or food, when they are continuously supplied and can be taken for granted most of the time. We turn our interest to the achievement of esteem, as Maslow argues. But beyond this point we are wise to part company with Maslow. Not everybody is keen to actualize the the Self, once liberated from the need for self-esteem. Not even most. Most people want something else entirely. Only the *choleric* are concerned with making the Self real.

It is not, then, that self-actualization is a step beyond self-esteem; rather, it is a *means* to self-esteem. Those who are choleric, which is to say, who wish for self-actualization, *like* themselves better in the degree that they achieve their aim. Certainly all of us must have self-esteem. Maslow was right in this. But self-actualization, far from transcending self-esteem, must be relegated to the position of but one of many routes *to* self-esteem.

There are other courses. For instance, Freud (1920) was right when he said pleasure is the way. But not for everybody, as he supposed, and not as an end in itself, but for self-esteem. Only the *sanguine* like themselves better when they live freely and spontaneously. Sullivan was also right. The security of social status is important—for some, and in the service of self-regard. Those who are *melancholic* hold themselves in higher regard when they achieve position and belong to social units. Likewise, Adler was right in that the quest for powers moves us—some of us—so that *phlegmatics* look upon themselves with pride as their powers increase.

The Hippocratic names for the four temperaments, however, are misleading. They derive from the four body fluids—blood, phlegm, yellow bile and black bile—and so have arcane (and limited) reference. On the other hand, four Greek gods, all of whom Zeus commissioned to make man more like the gods, represent the temperaments quite accurately, albeit metaphorically. These are Apollo, Dionysus, Prometheus, and his brother Epimetheus. Myth has it that Apollo was commissioned to give man a sense of spirit, Dionysus to teach man joy, Prometheus to give man science, and Epimetheus to convey a sense of duty. It will clarify things to name the four temperaments after gods because each god—and each temperament—has its followers. Who worships Apollo (spirit) does not worship Prometheus (science) and who desires Dionysian joy (or release) is not content with Epimethean duty. We see that the four temperaments are different from each other in very fundamental ways.

Another corrective on Jungian typology is required. In the perspective of temperament theory, Jungian types emerge from temperaments by way of differentiation, instead of being built up by way of combination of "functions." Growth is by individuation, a separation or splitting, rather than integration, association, or concatenation. A person becomes an ENFJ, or INFP, or whatever, because of his given temperament rather than because, for example, extraversion "somehow" combined with intuition. Thus, temperament theory replaces the principles of integration (always found in reductionist theories) with the principle of differentiation.

Further, the Jungian typology must undergo some rearrangement to conform to these temperaments. What Jung called intuition (N) appears to be equivalent to Kretschmer's schizothymic temperament. The Ns, or schizothyms, opt either for the Apollonean spirituality (self-actualization) or Promethean science (powers). Sensation (S) seems equivalent to Kretschmer's cyclothymic temperament. The Ss, or cycloids, choose either the Dionysian joy (freedom to act) or the Epimethean duty (social status). Note that Jung's *feeling* (F) now distinguishes the Apollonean self-actualization motive from the *thinking* (T) Promethean power motive. Also, note that Jung's *judgment* (J) distinguishes the Epimethean duty motive from the Dionysian freedom motive (P).

Spranger's views on character or temperament, contemporary with Jung's, are very useful, for he spoke of *values* rather than functions. In his book *Types of Men* (1928) he named four values which distinguish one type from another: Aesthetic, Economic, Theoretical, and Religious. The other two values he named, Social and Political, pertained to all, and hence were not distinguishing. Careful reading of this extremely complicated work reveals a rather clear correspondence with the Jungian typology as follows: the NF values Religiosity (Ethics), the NT values the Theoretical (Science), the SP values the Aesthetic (Artistry), and the SJ values the Economic (Commerce). Temperament or character theory was in the air of Europe at century's turn. The other characterologists surely affected Jung, Kretschmer, and Spranger. The similarities of these many views on character are hard to overlook (Adickes, 1907; Apfelbach, 1924; Levy, 1896; Sternberg, 1907). Bulliot's (1901) eight types especially bear close resemblance to Jung's.

Very simply, temperament determines behavior because behavior is the instrument for getting us what we *must* have, satisfying our desire for that one thing we live for. The god (or temperament) we were born to has left each of us a hunger that must be fed daily. Sisiphus was punished by Zeus so that he had to push an enormous rock to the top of a mountain, only to have it roll to the bottom while he rested. In a sense we are all Sisiphus. Today we satisfy our hunger for powers, or status, or freedom, or meaning—whatever our temperament dictates—but find tomorrow we must do it over again. Yesterday's achievement will not do.

The Dionysian Temperament

The minute you climb into that truck, the adrenalin starts pumping. If you want a thrill, there's no comparison, not

even a jet plane, to climbing on a steel truck and going
out there on the expressway. You'll swear you'll never be
able to get out the other end of that thing without an accident. There's thousands of cars, and thousands of trucks
and you're shifting like a maniac and you're braking and
accelerating and the object is to try to move with the traf-
fic and try to keep from running over all those crazy fools
who are trying to get under your wheel.

[Studs Terkel, *Working*, p. 209.]

These are the SPs (ISTP, ESTP, ISFP, ESFP), differing from
each other in important ways, but resembling each other in
even more important ways.

At bottom, the Dionysian SP must be free; he will not be tied
or bound or confined or obligated. To do as he wishes *when*
he wishes, that's the ideal. To wait, to save, to store, to prepare, to live for tomorrow—that is not the way. For the SP,
Epicurus was right; today must be enjoyed, for tomorrow
never comes.

Duty, Power, and Spirit are of secondary, if any, importance
to the SP. Action's the thing, and to understand the SP it is
necessary to understand the kind of action he insists upon.
Action must be its own end—it cannot serve a purpose or be
instrumental in achieving a goal. Although the SP does not
object when his deeds contribute to ends held by others, that
cannot be his reason for doing what *he* does. He does things
because he has the urge, the whim.

SPs are, in essence, impulsive. They *want* to be impulsive. To
be impulsive is to be really alive. SPs covet their impulses,
enjoy feeling them well up within; and they love discharging
them, like setting off an explosion. SPs even feel guilty if they
don't have impulses! At one time or another we all feel these
sudden urges to *do* something, but most of us ignore them,
looking instead to more distant, more patient goals. We discipline this impulse to freedom in the name of Duty, Powers, or
Spirit, while the SP feels only bound and confined.

This is not to say the Dionysian SP does not acquire goals
and ties just like the rest of us. He does, of course, only they
are fewer and more tentatively held. If the ties become too
numerous or too binding, then the SP is likely to become restless and perhaps experience the urge to take off for "somewhere else."

The idea of action for itself can best be understood by comparing "practice" with "compulsion." Practice, first of all, is what we all do to improve our skill in preparation for performance or work. It is not for keeps, not for real, we know it doesn't count, that it is mere rehearsal. SPs, however, do not wish to practice, since it is only preparation for action later on. SPs do not practice; they *do*. Indeed, the SP *must* do what he feels the urge to do. Sometimes this action can be excessive, going for many hours without pause, such excessive action being mistaken for "discipline" by observers of other temperaments. But this is not discipline; rather, it is action by compulsion, as if the SP is caught in its traction, feeling a necessity, as it were, to do his thing. Like the man who climbs a mountain because it's there, the SP is only inarticulately aware of the sovereignty he gives his impulse. He must do whatever his impulse dictates and continue the action as long as the urge compels. When the urge lets up, he no longer "feels like" racing, climbing, or whatever.

More than other temperaments the SP is subject to what Karl Buhler calls "function lust": a hunger for action without fetter or constraint, an exploratory action without the necessity for rules or practice. The SP thrives on situations where the outcome is not known, where there is freedom to test the limits. Of all the styles, the SP works best in crises, and the deeper the crisis, the more apt he is to respond quickly and dramatically. If a situation with little variation occurs, the SP becomes disinterested; as the range of possibilities and emergencies increases, the vigor with which the SP takes on the task accelerates. In fact, when circumstances become too dull and routine, the SP has been known to *create* a crisis—just to liven things up a little.

Man has three things the animal doesn't: symbols, gods, and tools. The Dionysian is usually not captured by the gods and is largely indifferent to the symbolic. But tools are his master. The tool is to use and the SP cannot *not* put it to use. He must drive the bulldozer, fly the plane, fire the gun, toot the horn, wield the scalpel, brush, or chisel. There is something about tools which strikes a chord in the character of the SP, attracting him almost as if addictive. Somehow the tool becomes an extension of the self, augmenting, amplifying, and sharpening the effects of action—and *this* gives a greater kick to the discharge of impulse.

More than action, however, the SP wants others to see him as being free to act, a free spirit as it were. It is not so much that the SP takes pride in being capable, or in having the power to do something—these are the prides of another style. Rather, the SP prides himself precisely (and only) on his *freedom*. He is not *saving* knowledge or accumulating power; he is *spending* life as freely as he can. Action cannot be saved for tomorrow, and each new day brings a need for excitement, adventure, risk, testing one's luck. Resources are to be expended; machinery is to be operated; people are to be enjoyed. The SP has a hunger for operation threading through all his behaviors, and, beneath his activity, the need to be seen as free to operate.

Cultural approval provides the male SP with a far greater opportunity to express his preferences for action than the female SP. Perhaps the influence of the feminist movement will make this style of life acceptable for females also; nonetheless, current realities simply exclude the SP female from typical SP occupations, in spite of the fact that half of all SPs are women. True, a few women have entered the building trades, many have infiltrated the military, and some have succeeded as troubleshooters in business; but the action occupations, involving precision, endurance, strength, boldness, and timing, have mainly been the province of men and are seen as masculine occupations. The majority of women still enter the traditional three female occupations of nursing, teaching, and clerical work, none of which is likely to satisfy the SP's hunger for action.

Dionysians frequently are described by friends as "exciting, optimistic, cheerful, light-hearted, and full of fun." Socially, SPs tend to be charming and witty conversationalists, often having an inexhaustible repertoire of jokes and stories. Wherever they go, SPs (especially the extraverted SPs) lend an electricity to the environment and the people in that environment. The SP brings to work and to play a sense that something exciting is about to happen. The atmosphere takes on a glow, seems brighter, more colorful—charged with adventure.

In fact, SPs can easily become bored with the status quo. They like to vary their work patterns each day; they are usually ready to take time out for entertainment, trying out new foods, new places to eat, and vacation spots. An SP is likely to enjoy randomness, varying the dinner hour, wanting to eat whenever the impulse strikes. This tends to be disconcerting to the more orderly personalities (the SJ for example), and can lead to difficulty when an SP marries. Yet SPs do live life with a flourish, which others often envy and admire. Auntie Mame defies a disapproving world, urging her friend (at the end of Act II) to take some risks: "Yes! Life is a banquet, and most poor sons-of-bitches are *starving* to death! Live!" And her friend catches the spirit, responding, "Yes! Live, live, live!" (Lawrence and Lee, 1957).

An SP can be only temporarily defeated. He has the ability to survive setbacks which might leave other types permanently devastated. "Easy come, easy go," he says. Jennie Churchill, Winston Churchill's extraordinary mother, was such a type. She lived with an intensity which is rare, even in SPs. Ralph Martin caught her style when he wrote of a low point in Jennie's life:

> For Jennie, the year 1895 began bitter and bleak. After a lingering illness, her husband had died of syphilis, raving mad. Only weeks before, her lover, unwilling to wait any longer, had married. Her sons, Winston and Jack, both had problems which required her full attention. Physically and emotionally she felt drained . . . So here was Jennie, with the man who had loved her most now married to someone else, little money, not even a home of her own . . . And yet, such was the inner resource and resilience of this woman that her life soon took on an excitement and vitality such as she had never dreamed of. As her friend, Lady Curzon, said in a letter to her, "You are the only person who lives on the crest of a wave."
>
> [Ralph G. Martin, *Jennie*. Signet, Vol. II, p. 15 & 17.]

Life for an SP means having impulses and acting spontaneously on those impulses. Since an impulse, by definition, is short-lived, the SP *must* live in the immediate moment. For the SP, to wait is psychological death; delay effectively kills his impulse. To other types this may not make much sense, and others find it hard to understand why a person wants to live impatiently and impulsively; but to an SP, a life of action which repudiates long term goals, objectives or plans is life at its freest and most intense.

> "I have no desire to have children, so why get married? Ladies, for the most part, want to get married and have children. Most have been conditioned that way. I can't handle it. Inside of me I get a little crazy. I start feeling locked in if I have to be somewhere at a certain time and then I worry if I'm not there, she'll worry. Man, the biggest burden I ever had was love."

[Cheryl Bentsen, "This Man is Madly in Love." Los Angeles *Times*, Part III, Sunday, Feb. 15, 1976, p. 1, Story of Joe Namath, football professional.]

The SP does not punctuate his experience with goal-dominated syntax. His language is operational and functional. Hence, he does not have to "endure" or "put up with" anything. No matter how tired, hungry, and painful an adventure may be, it is an adventure, not a commission. The SP does not think with a goal frame of reference, and thus the notion of endurance is irrelevant. "Hardship" is "endured" *only* if the behavior is seen as instrumental toward some end, some goal. But the SP's behavior is not subordinated to an end because the behavior is its own end. A hole is to dig, a door is to open, a hall is to run in, a bell is to ring, a mountain is to climb. This urge to action can be expensive at times, as seen in the Los Angeles *Times* story about one of Elvis Presley's whims. Presley had parked his custom-made Cadillac near a car lot, and when he returned he found a total stranger with her head in his car, looking it over longingly. Elvis asked the woman if she liked it, and then offered, "This one is mine, but I'll buy you one." He caught the stranger by the arm, took her to the nearby car lot, and told her to pick one. After she had selected a gold and white model, which listed for $11,500, Presley learned that it was the woman's birthday, so he handed her the keys to the car, wished her happy birthday, and told his aide to write a check so that the woman could "buy some clothes to go with the car." (Los Angeles *Times*, 1975.)

Oddly, the SP seems to have endurance beyond that of other types; he seems able to put up with discomfort, deprivation, hunger, fatigue, pain, and show courage in a way other types do not. But this is because other types *are* goal oriented, reluctant to exert themselves unless there is a reason. Thus, other types suffer hardship, discomfort, and fatigue as they work and shortly begin to wonder how much more they can stand. This is a fatal question and is self-defeating, in a sense its own answer. But since the SP is not moving toward a goal, he does not experience his action as duration, as a distance to endure, never questioning his capacity to do so. He simply continues—often beyond reasonable limits for other types.

This penchant for acting on impulse contains a seeming paradox, for SPs, living only for immediate action, become the world's great performing artists: the virtuosos of art, entertainment, and adventure. The great painters, instrumentalists,

vocalists, dancers, sculptors, photographers, athletes, hunters, racers, gamblers—all need the skills which come only
from excited concentration on an activity for long periods. No
other type can mobilize what virtuosity takes: untold hours
of continuous action.

But how can this be, in a style which is driven by impulse and
which (as we have discussed) disdains rehearsal and commitment? Once caught up in his action-hunger, the SP can persevere in that action for hour after hour, continuing long after
other types would have abandoned the effort. And it is this
impulsive stamina that makes virtuosity possible. The SP
seems to be the sole possessor of *perfection in action*, and yet
he never practices in the sense that others do. The NT, for
example, seeks perfection; yet perfection evades him. The SP
is oblivious to the pursuit of perfection, does not practice in
order to achieve it, and yet achieves it. The NT knowingly
and deliberately practices—by the clock, by the book. The SP
simply and spontaneously acts, endlessly, tirelessly, caught up
and possessed by the act itself, having no end beyond the
doing. Somehow caring about perfection and working for it
only get in the way; the act-in-itself alone realizes perfection.

Performers in the arts (for example, Nijinsky, Rubinstein,
Heifetz, Casals, Callas) are apt to be SPs; but also the racer,
the surfer, the soldier of fortune, the magician, the card sharp,
even the gunslinger of the Old West. In fact, the gunslinger
was just as much a virtuoso as the great performing artists,
and he was similarly idealized. The gunslinger could draw his
long-barrelled Colt 45, cock it, aim it, and fire it, hitting un-
believably small moving targets, without even putting the gun
up in front of his eyes. He was able to perform this feat in less
than one-fifth of a second—so swiftly that the motion of his
hand could not be seen. The fast draw of the gunslinger is
just as incredible as the flying movements of the violinist's
fingers or the gravity-defying leaps of a prima ballerina.

In a sense, the SP does not work, for work implies production,
completion, and accomplishment. The SP has no such desire
for closure, completion, finishing. He is process-oriented. What
ensues from his action is *mere* product, *mere* outcome, *mere*
result, and is incidental. Thus, the SP's "work" is essentially
play. He is no Sysiphus, despairing when his rock rolls down
the mountainside each night after his day's toil of pushing it
up. The SP's joy is in the *act* of pushing the rock, not caring
that no permanent edifice remains as a monument to his efforts.

The SP gravitates toward jobs where action is involved. Not only the performing arts, but construction work, jobs where heavy machinery is employed; the building operations for dams and skyscrapers, for freeways and mines; for leveling forests in a wilderness; operations for putting human force against the forces of nature, such as working the oil fields and logging the giant redwoods; mercenary soldiering; loading freight at docks; promoting enterprises; driving ambulances and racing cars, motorcycles, aircraft. The statesman-negotiator, the entrepreneur who enjoys and succeeds in pulling businesses out of the red, the bellhop, the bartender, the porter, the hair stylist, the model, detective, police, rescue squads, magicians, professional athletes, ombudsmen, are all in occupations which demand action and freedom to respond to the demands of the moment. All work against pressures and all usually do their best in crisis situations. For example, Arthur Hailey describes the extraordinary skills (and the non-reflective, danger-courting behavior) of an SP in the following scene from *Airport:*

> ". . . Mister, there's spilled gasoline around here. You'd better get that cigar out."
>
> Patroni ignored the instruction, as he ignored almost all smoking regulations. He waved his cigar toward the over-turned tractor-trailer. "What's more, son, you'd be wasting everybody's time, including mine and yours, trying to get that hunk of junk right side up tonight. You'll have to drag it clear so traffic can move, and to do that you need two more tow trucks—one on this side to push, two over there to pull." He began moving around, using his electric lantern to inspect the big articulated vehicle from various angles. As always, when considering a problem he was totally absorbed. He waved the cigar once more, "The two trucks together'll hitch onto three points. They'll pull the cab first, and faster. That'll overcome the jackknifing. The other truck . . ."
>
> "Hold it," the state trooper said. He called across to one of the other officers. "Hank, there's a guy here sounds like he knows what he's talking about."
>
> [Arthur Hailey, *Airport*. Bantam Books, Inc., p. 43, 1968.]

The SP, of all the types, is most likely to answer the call to wander, and he can sever social ties more easily than can others even though he may be aware of the distress his behavior causes those close to him. The SP can abruptly abandon either an activity or a pattern of living, walking away without a backward glance. The paint brush lies where it is dropped; responsibilities are abandoned as if they never existed. Although the SP himself created these ties, now he sees them as binding and a burden. At midlife particularly, the SP's need for freedom may be so intense that he becomes unusually restless. Gauguin, in his early forties, turned away from his home and sailed off to Tahiti, where he produced unforgettable masterpieces; but, no doubt, he left broken trust behind.

Yet, in the SP's paradoxical way, he is also the most fiercely fraternal of all the styles. He lives esprit de corps, is loyal to his brothers, and defends his group against all attacks. This can be observed, for example, in the Marines, or in a fraternal order like the Elks.

The SP can miss romantic nuances which may be apparent and precious to other types. Although the SP is the master of the grand gesture—such as the dozens of yellow roses, the extravagant mink coat, the three-carat diamond ring—he can forget a promised telephone call or neglect a small word of affection.

The SP uses whatever resources may be available and is more than willing to share with others. He tends to live life at the level of a gourmet feast (if, that is, he is not short of funds, which *surely* is only temporary). Even in times of short supply, however, his egalitarianism may show. He is the most likely of the types to think in terms of "share and share alike" and to "make do with what we have." What is his is yours, and what is yours, his. To the SP, everything is negotiable in a crisis. An SP will go along with rules and regulations obediently for long periods; then a crisis occurs or an impulse strikes, and an apparently different personality surfaces. New situations demand new actions and earlier commitments may have to be jettisoned—with regret perhaps, but still abandoned. Today is today, and yesterday's arrangements must give way in the face of more urgent demands.

The SP's need to live more fully in the present than any other style sometimes irritates others who expect to maintain the same level of intensity. Although friends enjoy the SP's generosity and good cheer, they sometimes report that they felt they knew their SP friends very well at first meeting and never any better years later. Indeed, the style is often subject to denigration. People become fascinated and charmed by the

SP's way of life, then disappointed when the SP does not live up to the projections other types place on him.

SPs do not get very excited about complex problems of motivation. For them, whatever is, is. That is sufficient for the SP to know what to think, what to do, and what to believe. As super-realists, they do not require that their actions be governed by established policy, rules, or natural laws, as do other styles. Because the SP often leaps before looking, he is more subject to accidents than other temperaments; he injures himself through inattention to possible sources of defeat or accident, his optimism living on his abiding sense of luck.

The Epimethean Temperament

Like the SPs, the SJs comprise roughly 38 percent of the population, or about 80,000,000 people in the United States. There are four of these in the Jungian typology: ISFJ, ESFJ, ISTJ, and ESTJ. These four types are as much alike as they are different from each other, especially in their longing for duty. In this they are Epimethean—they exist primarily to be *useful* to the social units they belong to.

Epimetheus, brother to Prometheus and Atlas, captures the spirit of the SJ style as well as Dionysus typifies the style of the SP. The myth, embedded in the story of the more famous brother, Prometheus, recounts that Prometheus advised his brother Epimetheus not to accept any gifts from their father Zeus. Prometheus followed his own advice and refused to marry the beautiful women Zeus fashioned for him. Epimetheus, following his brother's lead, did likewise when Zeus then offered Pandora to him—at which point Zeus's wrath erupted in full fury.

Epimetheus, frightened by Zeus's terrible punishment of Prometheus, hastened to reconsider his decision and accepted Pandora, even though he was fully aware of the dangers presented by this gift, the most beautiful woman ever created! Soon Pandora gave in to curiosity and investigated the golden chest she had carried with her from Olympus, but which she had been forbidden by Zeus to open. But Epimetheus stood by his wife even after she raised the lid of the forbidden box, letting escape all manner of ills onto mankind: old age, labor, sickness, insanity, vice—and passion. Epimetheus suffered their stings as did Pandora, but never did he abandon her;

rather, he accepted his fate in good conscience, seeking out the *should's* and *ought's* which would guide him as a shield against these evils now abroad in the world.

When Epimetheus responded to the demands of Zeus to marry Pandora, he gained worldly wisdom. He gained the knowledge of how to use public opinion to control and harmonize with the world. Thus, through his obedience, Epimetheus gained the self-assurance of good conscience. He suffered all of mankind's ills, but he also received the treasure of hope (and forboding), the one good in Pandora's box of evils. (Grand, 1962; Graves, 1955; Hamilton, 1940; Jung, 1923.)

So the SJ must *belong*, and this belonging has to be earned. Here is no freeloader, urging his dependency upon the donor as if it were his god-given right. Dependency, for the SJ, is neither a legitimate condition nor desire. The SJ feels guilty for his dependency as if derelict in his duty and negligent of his obligations. Moreover, he must be the *giver*, not the receiver; the *caretaker*, not the cared for.

This is almost a parental attitude in the SJ, and it makes its appearance early in life. If we watch a newly convened kindergarten class, we can easily observe about a dozen five-year-olds earnestly and tensely seeking out the cues which tell them what they are "s'posed to do." The rest of the children (mostly SPs with a smattering of NFs and NTs) are more like puppies, tusseling, sniffing, and chewing the happy hours away. School is made for SJs and largely run by SJs and kept mainly to transform these frolicking puppies into serious, duty-oriented little parents who seek only to know what they are "supposed to do."

By the time the SJ shows up at school he has already shifted from the fraternal to the parental outlook. Of course, he will feel dependent for many years, all through childhood (until he gets a paper-route or other earning source), but the feeling is not enjoyed in the least. This is not a desire for independence (as with the SP); rather it is an unfulfilled desire to serve, as if the SJ is impatient to be useful.

Notice that the SP is compelled to be *free* and *independent*, while the SJ is, in effect, compelled to be *bound* and *obligated*. These might usefully be viewed as reciprocal needs. Indeed, it may well be that the character of the SJ can better be illuminated if seen in reciprocity with the SP character.

First, while the SJ lives a Stoical ethic, the SP lives an Epicurean ethic—a work ethic as against a play ethic. We must emphasize that these *both* are ethics. One is not bad and the other good; they are both differing views of the good. And, anticipating for a moment, we can examine still other perspectives of the good in the NF and NT ethics.

Second, while the SP supports his fraternal and libertarian outlook with a belief in and desire for equality, the SJ supports his parental and responsibility purposes which a belief in and desire for hierarchy. For the SJ the hierarchical structure of society is the essence of society. There should be subordinance and superordinance. There should be rules which govern the interactions of members, certainly in the city, school, church, and corporation, but also in the family. And one's status in such social units must be earned—one must do one's part. The SP has no such outlook. One is equal to others in whatever social unit one belongs to, and status of any level is a matter of luck, not earnings. And rules? Why, those are merely disguised means of maintaining the status one acquired by accident, or so it would seem to the SP.

Further, even the most cursory glance at a through-and-through SJ will detect a theme of pessimism coloring all his deeds, in reciprocity to the SP's optimism. The Boy Scouts' motto, Be Prepared, must have been made up by a strong SJ; surely SJs invented the Boy Scouts and preside over Boy Scout groups across the nation. Above all else, indeed, the SJ is prepared. Many of his actions are preparations for those setbacks and untoward events that are bound to occur. We must not conclude that the SJ is gloomily forecasting calamity and disaster —though Chicken Little was clearly an SJ; rather, we should see him as being realistic about error and shortages. Best to set aside something for rainy days.

Aesop's "The Ant and the Grasshopper" gives us a splendid analogy for viewing the reciprocal relationship of SJ to SP. In the fable, the Ant is industriously and dutifully transporting large crumbs of bread from site to storage while the Grasshopper reclines on a blade of grass near Ant's path, playing the fiddle, chewing tobacco, and singing "The World Owes Me a Living." Ant, without losing stride in his burdensome work, scolds Grasshopper for not preparing for the upcoming winter months. "Join me," urges Ant, "and we will together *fill* the storehouse, thus *ensuring* that none will suffer cold or hunger." Grasshopper replies, "And, if you keep up this feverish pace, you won't make it to winter, succumbing to ulcer, high blood pressure, or colitis. Join me on my blade of grass, and we will enjoy together the warm summer, the food that abounds, and celebrate the world's debt to us in song." Each, of course, ignores the other's request and goes his own merry or tedious way. When it turns out to be a long, cold, hungry winter, Grasshopper must knock at Ant's door and stand there frostbitten and starving; Ant, snug in his storehouse of goodies, can only let Grasshopper in. And so it is with SJs and SPs— they marry each other with high frequency and play out this eternal drama.

One further note concerning the Epimethean pessimism: Murphy's Law states that "whatever can go wrong will" or that "everything takes longer and costs more." Only an SJ could make up such a law.

The SJ's desire to be useful often comes in the guise of member-ship hunger. Here the SJ appears to have a larger appetite than others. To belong to social units is central to his style. The SJ recognizes by his actions the social nature of man. He, far more than others, creates and fosters the continuity of social units: the family, the church, the service club, the municipality, and the corporation. The social unit can become for the SJ an end in itself, just as action is its own end for the SP. The SP, on the other hand, may join the social unit, but he requires and expects that unit to serve and fulfill his needs in return for his membership.

Tradition becomes more and more important as the SJ gets older. Look for the SJ member of the family, club, church, or company to observe traditions. If traditional ceremonies and celebrations are nonexistent, the thorough-going SJ soon man-ages to establish some and thereafter maintain them. We might note in passing that others are happy to attend these festivities, rites, and ceremonies—"members of the wedding." And we might further note that, unlike the Little Red Hen (who planted the seed, grew the wheat, ground it, and baked the loaf all by herself), the SJ accepts all at the banquet despite the ingratitude of the feasters.

Still, the SJ has a keen sense for detecting ingratitude and lack of appreciation, dealing as he does in giving, service, and care. Strangely though, he cannot ask for gratitude or appre-ciation because it is his *duty* to give, serve, and care for. He feels obligated, responsible, and burdened, and wants to feel that way. To feel otherwise is to be useless and not belong. To receive, be served, and be taken care of are not legitimate desires and must be expunged and hidden from oneself whenever they appear. Witness the SJ who goes to a party, but in order to have a good time helps the host serve the refreshments and clean up afterwards! On the other hand, watch an SP throw a party and note that the SJ guests end up catering to *his* desires. True, he started it, but look who finished it!

There is no mystery surrounding the SJ's choice of work. The institutions call him and he comes to them to *establish* them, nurture them, and *maintain* their continuity and perpetuity. Teaching, preaching, accounting, banking, clerking, medicating, rehabilitating, securing, insuring, managing, selling (providing)—note in all of these a single strand of desire: to conserve. The SJ is the conservator no matter where he goes or who he's with or what he does. He *saves*, one way or another, sooner or later. His complement, the SP, *spends*, one way or another, sooner or later. The SJ is the foundation, cornerstone, flywheel, and stabilizer of society, and we might well rejoice at his presence.

Conservation can be so strong a desire in the SJ that it colors most of his actions and attitudes. For one thing, it can make him incapable of refusing added responsibility. We need only ask the SJ to take on an extra load and he cannot refuse. He wonders, "If I don't do it, who will?" and worries, "there'll be loss." Of course, the SJ may feel some bitterness over the lack of appreciation and even feel a sense of loss, ironically occasioned by the very act of trying to prevent loss. But this feeling of not being appreciated is not something the SJ can express freely, since he is after all indebted and obligated by his very nature. In a sense, just as he cannot store enough reserves for future contingencies, so he cannot take on enough duty and obligation to discharge his sense of indebtedness.

The desire to conserve can also kindle in the SJ a hankering to become an official of some kind. And once an officer in whatever enterprise or establishment, the SJ is likely to apply his authority with an eye on conservation and perpetuation of heritage.

Heritage and heritability loom large in the perspective of the true Epimethean. The transitory, temporary, and expedient seem almost an affront to the corporate, municipal, or family heritage. Though these may not be immoral or illegal, they at least are to be viewed with a measure of suspicion. For they are *change*, and change means *losing* the heritage. The SJ knows as well as others that change is inevitable, necessary, and even, on occasion, desirable; but it should be resisted when it is at the expense of the tried and true, the accepted and approved. Better that change occurs through slow evolution than by abrupt revolution. As conservator of the heritage, the SJ is the enemy of the revolutionary.

Title and entitlement are important to SJs, as is office, for title means approved and officially registered ownership. The SJ does not agree that possession is nine points of the law; rather, "law is nine points of possession." Illegal possession is high on the SJ's list of evils. Having and not-having are, for the SJ, just as deeply involved with their obligation-hunger as giving and receiving. In fact, we move much closer to an understanding of the SJ if we can see the strongly parental and parochial basis for his attitudes about having and giving, relinquishing and receiving.

The SJ is society's natural historian, and it is the historian who learns, for society, the lessons of history. Will Durant says that history's most important lesson is the reciprocity of freedom and equality. As freedom increases, equality decreases, and as equality increases, so then does freedom decrease. Unfortunately, this lesson of history is not learned by most—witness the Utopias promising freedom *and* equality at a maximum—but the SJ instinctively knows it, seeing in inequality (hierarchy) the only way to freedom. This same sanction for hierarchy is also expressed in the SJ's reverence for elders and in their belief that elders should be respected and deferred to.

Just as history should govern what we do in the future, so there are *fundamentals* which should serve as foundations for what and how we build and how we maintain our edifices and our institutions. The SJ is just as strong an advocate of fundamentals as he is of antecedents. Now there well may be considerable variation between SJs as to what they think the fundamentals are, but whatever the SJ considers to be a fundamental is strongly held to.

There is never an end to how much responsibility the SJ accepts. If there is a job to be done, a task to be executed, a duty to fulfill, the SJ feels that he somehow has an obligation to see that the end is accomplished, even if he already is overburdened to the point of unreason, and even if others are contributing far less than he. In truth, people do at times take advantage of the SJ's inability to refuse an extra load. "Jane will do it," they say, with little awareness or appreciation of the demands this may make on Jane, who only too often, as a result of insufficient appreciation for her zealous discharge of duty, is exhausted, worried, sad, and even ill. At times, this takes the form of depression, a condition to which the SJ is particularly vulnerable. Even such a brilliant SJ as Abraham Lincoln experienced this debilitating state:

> "I am now the most miserable man living. If what I feel were equally distributed to the whole human family, there would not be one cheerful face on earth. Whether I shall be better, I cannot tell. I awfully forbode I shall not . . ."
>
> [Gillette, *Mary*, Paul & Hornbeck.]

Ironically, the SJ's tendency to be responsible does not always gain him well-deserved appreciation. People who have benefited most from the SJ's contributions may turn away, even while taking advantage of his willingness to do more than his fair share. Recipients, at times, show little awareness that the SJ is receiving far less appreciation than is his due. And the reason for this may lie in a tendency of the SJ to assume a serious, even forbidding, mien—an appearance which little reflects his warm heart. Hawthorne's Hepzibah in *The House of the Seven Gables* personifies this seriousness:

> Her scowl had done Miss Hepzibah a very ill office in establishing her character as an ill-tempered old maid . . ." How miserably cross I look!" she must often have whispered to herself and ultimately have fancied herself so . . . But her heart never frowned. It was naturally tender, sensitive, and full of little tremors and palpitations; all of which weaknesses it retained, while her visage was growing so perversely stern, and even fierce.
>
> [Nathaniel Hawthorne, *The House of the Seven Gables*. Scholastic Magazine. New York, 1965, pp. 33–34.]

The care of others, especially the young and the old, and those in positions of authority, is the special concern of the SJ. SJs have a deep commitment to the standards of society and usually attempt to live up to those standards themselves and to transmit them to the young. It is important to the SJ that the framework in which he works reflects standards also; he

does not like to be associated with people or institutions which
are outside of the social pale.

> Pictures like that weren't decent. Mary focussed incredu-
> lous Catholic eyes on the contours of the rotund huzzy
> lolling in nudeness and lace. If a daughter of hers should
> frump around like that . . .
>
> The O'Neills were forever shocking Mary. She shocked
> as easily as she bruised and any little knock left a purple
> spot on her flesh for days. Poor Mary. She'd have left
> long ago if it hadn't been for Bobby. The way they were
> *raising* that child! Never a piece of meat to eat. A little
> *lamb* now and then. Nothing but calories and carbo-hyde-
> something or other. And precious little he'd know about
> his Saviour if she hadn't taught him.
>
> [Tiffany Thayer, *Thirteen Women*. New York: Claude
> Kendall, 1932, p. 1.]

As expected, given the SJ's dedication to established social
norms and institutions, there is a high frequency of SJs in
business, in service occupations, in secretarial work, in general medical practice, in banking, in middle management, in
accounting, in dentistry, in barbering, in traditional hair-
dressing salons, in civil service posts, in pharmacy; all of
which are occupations which involve serving others and
belonging to established, recognized institutions. A high percentage of educators—teachers, administrators, librarians—
are SJs. The percentage may vary between school districts,
depending upon size and employment procedure: the larger
the district and the more centralized the management practices, the greater the proportion of SJs. In any district, though,
over half of the teachers at elementary and secondary levels
pursue an SJ style of life. This occupational choice makes
sense for SJ teachers, since the school personifies the truly
stable and valued institution, committed to the transmission
of the values and mores of society to the next generation.

> You get into a classroom and you have all the power of
> the institution. You tell people what to do and they do it,
> what to read and they read it. You tell people what to
> think, how to interpret things . . . You can make them feel
> guilty because they haven't read certain things, because
> they're not familiar with them. Teachers are playing that
> kind of game all the time. And I was right in there, with
> both feet.
>
> [Studs Terkel, *Working*, p. 566.]

SJs also gravitate toward those occupations organized around nurture, such as in hospitals. The majority of members of the nursing profession are apparently SJs, particularly SFJs. Institutions which house the poor and the sick are the special responsibility of SJs.

The SJ is truly the stabilizer of the social and economic world. He gives a good day's work for a good day's pay and cannot understand anyone who does not. The SJ has a well-developed sense of tradition, takes the "rights and wrongs" of the culture seriously, and usually is disapproving of wrongdoers. The SJ gives short shrift to transgressors against social mores and institutions unless the transgressors are repentant. The person who strays from the accepted way of behaving is frowned upon unless he expresses his regrets and intent to reform.

SJs themselves tend to do the right thing at the right time. Each day they hunger for belonging and they hunger to contribute to the institutions they serve. Never do yesterday's contributions suffice for today's. Each and every day the SJ seeks to confirm that he does, indeed, belong, and each and every day he seeks to prove this by taking up the responsibility of his duties. Not to do one's duty is offensive; not to conform to the standards of society is in bad taste. Such terms as steadfastness, dependability, stability, reliability, "salt-of-the-earth," "backbone of society," "pillar of strength," describe the SJ, who indeed is the enculturator of society.

The Promethean Temperament

To make man more like the gods, Prometheus gave him fire, the symbol of light and energy. In harnassing light and energy mankind gains control and understanding of nature. To understand and control nature is to possess powers, and it is *that*—the desire for powers—that sets the Promethean apart from others.

These are the NTs: INTP, ENTP, INTJ, ENTJ. They are rather infrequent, only about 12 percent of the population or some 24 million people. In school, before there are selective factors operating, only four in a class of 32 would be NTs. Of these four, only one would be introverted—an INTP or INTJ. So an entirely different social environment surrounds the NTs. They must live with aliens, while the SPs and SJs are continuously surrounded by their own kind. The teachers and parents of

NTs are more likely than not to be SPs or SJs (about one family in 16 would have both parents as Ns and only one in a thousand families would have both NT parents).

Power fascinates the NT. Not power over people, but power over nature. To be able to understand, control, predict, and explain realities. Note that these are the four aims of science: control and understanding, prediction and explanation. Scratch an NT, find a scientist.

These forms of power, however, are but means to an end, the end best expressed by the word *competence*. So it is not exactly power that the NT wants but rather competencies, capabilities, abilities, capacities, skills, ingenuity—repertoire.

The Promethean NT loves intelligence, which means: doing things well under varying circumstances. The extreme NT can even be seen as addicted to acquiring intelligence, hooked on storing up wisdom, just as Aesop's Ant must store up goodies. Tell the NT that he is a fake, a liar, a cheater, lacking in responsibility and in spontaneity, and he will reflect on your criticism and reply that "you may have a point there." Not that he is not perturbed or offended, for he often wonders and doubts his sense of freedom, responsibility and authority. But tell him he is foolish, stupid, or incompetent and discover the exact value he places on your warrant to say so. Only he can judge his capability and he does so with ruthless self-criticism.

"Wanting to be competent" is not a strong enough expression of the force behind the NT's quest. He *must* be competent. There is urgency in his desire; he can be obsessed by it and feel a compulsion to improve, as if caught in a force field. The NT's compulsion is similar in its tractor base to the SP's compulsion to perform, though different in its object: The SP must act, but has no interest in improving (though his performance becomes superb); the NT must improve, but has no interest in action as such (though he *does* act, and with increasing precision and exactitude). In a sense the SP is the NT's mirror image. For the SP, ability is mere means which sets him free to perform, while for the NT, performance is only a means for enabling him to store up his beloved abilities:

	Means	**Ends**
NT	Performance	Abilities
SP	Abilities	Performance

(In passing, we might anticipate finding that neither the SJ nor the (as yet) mysterious NF has more than meager concern and interest in performances and abilities. And we perhaps can understand both NF and SJ temperaments better if we notice this relative disinterest. They would seem to have other fish to fry and may well be puzzled by the militance shown by extreme SPs and NTs; those militant about ability or performance are just as puzzled by others' indifference.)

The NT is the most self-critical of all the styles. He badgers himself about his errors, taxes himself with the resolve to improve, and ruthlessly monitors his own progress. He continually checks the pulse of his skills and takes his conceptual temperature every hour on the hour. He must master understanding of all objects and events whether human or extra-human, physical or metaphysical, in whatever domain he stakes out as his area of competency. And the more extreme the NT style, the more exacting and stringent the demand placed by the NT on himself in the acquisition of skill and knowledge. The NT must be competent in whatever domain of enterprise or inquiry he chooses; he will settle for nothing less.

In contrast to the *should's* and *ought's* of the SJ, the NT has many *should know's* and *should be-able-to*'s itemized in massive lists inside his head. He is inclined always to accumulate more items, never deleting any. He runs a kind of bureaucracy of excellence, and thus can be a perfectionist, becoming tense and compulsive in his behavior when he comes under too much stress. Constantly alert to his shortcomings, to his failures to reach perfect competency, he may greet with scorn and amusement the criticism of others concerning his powers. He may or may not express this reaction, although the extraverts are more likely to do so, but the NT is very conscious of the credentials of his critic and in what degree they license comment. Allied to this demand for competency in critics is a recalcitrance on the part of the NT—even from an early age—to accept without question in the domain of ideas even a widely accepted authority. The fact that a certain person proclaims something, whatever his or her title, reputation, or credentials, leaves the NT indifferent. The pronouncement must stand on its own merits, tried in the court of coherence, verification, and pragmatics. "I understand that Einstein said so," comments the NT, "but even the best of us can err." This recalcitrance to established authorities tends to make an NT, particularly those with extreme Promethean temperament, seem unusually individualist and even arrogant.

> Ever since I was twelve, I had been occupied with the
> question of the meaning of human existence . . . (No doubt
> this was intensified by the cowlike drifting of the people
> around me.) . . . I was obsessed by the idea that there must
> be a scientific method for investigating the question of
> human existence. At fourteen I discovered Shaw's *Man
> and Superman* and realized with a shock that I was not
> the first human being to ask the question.
>
> [Colin Wilson, *The Outsider*. New York: Dell Pub. Co.,
> 1956, pp. 289–90.]

NTs often report (to those they trust!) that they are haunted
by a sense of always being on the verge of failure. *This* time,
surely, the necessary degree of competency will not be produced and failure is at hand. *This* time acquired knowledge
will be inadequate for this issue. Constant self-doubting is the
lot of the NT. Because of these doubts, the NT, particularly
the NTP, may have difficulty in taking action. He can be so
immobilized by self-doubts that his resolution fades.

Somehow the Promethean never believes that he knows
enough, or that he does what he does well enough. And he
adds to this discomfort by escalating his standards of performance. What may be accepted by him as satisfactory today may tomorrow be judged only passable. And the more
extreme the NT, the more likely he is to increase his standards
of performance to coincide with unusually good performances
which occur now and then. His ordinary performances are
thus viewed as short of the mark, and the NT experiences a
pervasive sense of inadequacy. He intensifies his belief in his
inadequacy by making unyielding demands on himself, taxing
himself with constant improvement, holding a sort of mental
stopwatch over himself, recording his gains and losses. He
must be wholly competent in his work and in his play, and he
never gives himself respite from this self-imposed level of
excellence.

Watching an NT at "play" is apt to be touching and a little
sad when compared to the SPs abandon. The NT, knowing logically that recreation is necessary for health, *schedules* his
play, and during that "playtime" taxes himself with improving his recreational skills. For example, when engaging in a
card game, he must make no mistakes. At the bridge table,
others may make mistakes, but the NT does not allow himself
lapses of logic or strategic inaccuracies. In tennis, each set
must be the occasion for the improvement of certain strokes

or the elimination of previously-noted errors. The NT even demands of himself that he have a good time, since recreation is so defined.

The NT may find himself sending two contradictory messages to those he contacts. The first message is that he expects very little from others, since clearly they do not know much, nor can they do much well. One way the NT sends this message is to express subtle surprise when he *does* find competency or comprehension in others. The NT often assumes that people cannot completely comprehend the intricacies of the ideas he discusses and he somehow transmits this attitude. This is in contrast with the other three styles, all of whom assume to some degree that people are able to comprehend their communications.

The second, contradictory message the NT sends to those around him is that they are expected to at least attempt to achieve at the same exacting standard as the NT imposes on himself. And since neither the NT nor anyone else can live up to these standards, all are found wanting. The NT thus can be seen as unduly demanding on those around him—which, in truth, is often the case.

An unfortunate by-product of these two messages sent by the NT is that those around him come to feel intellectually inadequate. In time, they become defensive, withdraw, and make fewer and fewer attempts to communicate their ideas. The NT can thereby become isolated from the intellectual experiences of others, who withhold their reactions in the fear that they will be labeled "stupid" in the mind of the NT. The consequences of these transactions, is, of course, that the NT confirms his perceptions of the trivialities in the minds of others.

While this arrogance does not endear the NT to the hearts of others, it can produce documents which have had profound influence on the thinking of man. For example, Machiavelli demonstrates this stance as he "instructs" Lorenzo the Magnificent in the art of statesmanship, even though he, Machiavelli, is a "man of humble and obscure condition":

> It is customary for those who wish to gain the favour of a prince to endeavour to do so by offering him gifts of those things which they hold most precious, or which they know him to take especial delight. In this way, princes are often presented with horses, arms, cloth of gold, gems,

and such-like ornaments worthy of their grandeur. In my desire, however, to offer to Your Highness some humble testimony of my devotion, I have been unable to find among my possessions anything which I hold so dear or esteem so highly as that knowledge of the deeds of great men which I have acquired through a long experience of modern events and a constant study of the past.

With the utmost diligence I have long pondered and scrutinized the actions of the great, and now I offer the results to Your Highness within the compass of a small volume; and although I deem this work unworthy of Your Highnesses' acceptance, yet my confidence in your humanity assures me that you will receive it with favour, knowing that it is not in my power to offer you a greater gift than that of enabling you to understand in a very short time all those things which I have learnt at the cost of privation and danger in the course of many years.

[Niccolo Machiavelli, *The Prince*. Mentor Classic, New York: 1952, p. 31.]

In his communications the NT is likely to speak with little or no redundancy. His communications tend to be terse, compact, and logical. He has a deep reluctance to state the obvious, restricting his verbal communications because, he believes, "Of course, everyone knows that . . ." And, it follows, for the NT, that if he did state the obvious, his listeners surely would be bored. The NT tends to place little reliance on nonverbal qualifiers and, at times, is oblivious to emotional "meta-messages" in others' communications. The NT is inclined to be precise in his choice of language and hopes that others will be the same, though he soon learns that they will not. Henry the Eighth's daughter, Elizabeth the Great, who ruled England so competently for four and one-half decades, illustrated this characteristic as she replied to the pressures of her courtiers to declare her matrimonial intentions:

Elizabeth's reply was impressive: "What I shall do hereafter I know not, but I assure you, I am not at this time otherwise minded than I have declared unto you." Words could scarcely speak plainer.

[E. Jenkins, *Elizabeth the Great*. New York: Time Publication, 1958, p. 57.]

Elizabeth offers a fascinating contrast in personality with her antagonist of a lifetime, Mary Queen of Scots, who lived her life in an NF style. Elizabeth always was somewhat remote from those around her; Mary drew others close—even her "jailers" came to love and adore her. Mary's behaviors were conceived and carried out in emotionality. Mary willed the possibility of her becoming Queen of England and acted on that naïveté, never believing that her own son, James, might refuse to come to her rescue. Elizabeth's reaction was predictable: logical, ruthless, the necessary action taken with deep regret and sorrow, but with as little personal involvement as possible in condemning Mary to the executioner.

Because the NT is so serious about the knowledge he must have to be competent (and to be seen by others as competent), he does, in fact, frequently gain outstanding proficiency in his field. The dominance of his power hunger over his lesser hungers for action, duty, or self-actualization often exerts itself early in life, usually taking the form of a childish curiosity as to how things work, especially machines. The NT begins his search for explanations as soon as he has the language for questioning. He is puzzled by the world around him and is not satisfied with *non sequitur* answers from his elders. He wants the answers given to him to "hang together" and to make sense; he can be insistent in his efforts to gain these data, to the extent of annoying others. Learning for the NT is a 24-hour preoccupation, and this characteristic exerts itself early, particularly in the case of the extreme NT.

Because of the NT's passion for *knowing*, he can develop a large repertoire of competencies by the time he finishes his formal education. His early start and his persistence enable the NT to excel above the other styles in technology. And, as the intellectual ability of the NT increases, the tendency to seek the sciences, mathematics, philosophy, architecture, engineering—indeed, anything complicated and exacting— also increases. These occupations, therefore, are heavily populated by NTs.

Perhaps more than any other style, NTs live in their work. For the NT, work is work and play is work. Condemning an NT to idleness would be the worst sort of punishment. Work is done not so much to achieve a product or for the pleasure of action, but for the *improvement, perfection,* or *proof* of skill or knowledge required by the work. The NT does not have the function-lust of the SP; rather, he has, through his work, a *law* lust. He ever is searching for the *why's* of the universe. He ever attempts, in his Promethean way, to breathe a fire of understanding into whatever area he considers his domain.

NTs usually enjoy developing models, exploring ideas, and building systems. They, understandably, are drawn to occupations which have to do with the formation and application of scientific principles. Science, technology, philosophy, mathematics and logic, design and engineering, research and development, management, manufacture, criminology, cardiology, securities analysis—all appeal to NTs. Sales and customer relations work do not hold such attraction, nor do NTs tend to gravitate toward services such as clerical work, repair, maintenance, entertainment, or distribution. They can be found in high frequency in engineering and architecture, in the teaching of mathematics, sciences, and philosophy. Wherever they are and whatever they do, the NTs strive (and usually succeed) to perform competently.

And wherever they are and whatever they do, the NTs, especially the NTJs, are compelled to rearrange the environment, either through constructing physical edifices or building institutional systems. Ayn Rand, master of the NT character, again describes this characteristic in Howard Roark, her protagonist in *The Fountainhead:*

> He tried to consider it. But he forgot. He was looking at the granite.
>
> He did not laugh as his eyes stopped in awareness of the earth around him. His face was like a law of nature—a thing one could not question, alter or implore. It had high cheekbones over gaunt, hollow cheeks; gray eyes, cold and steady; a contemptuous mouth, shut tight, the mouth of an executioner or a saint.
>
> He looked at the granite. To be cut, he thought, and made into walls. He looked at a tree. To be split and made into rafters. He looked at a streak of rush on the stone and thought of iron ore under the ground. To be melted and to emerge as girders against the sky.
>
> These rocks, he thought, are here for me; waiting for the drill, the dynamite and my voice; waiting to be split, ripped, pounded, reborn, waiting for the shape my hands will give to them.
>
> [Ayn Rand, *The Fountainhead*. Signet Books, Bobbs-Merrill Co., New York, 1943, p. 15–16.]

The Promethean is likely to listen attentively to new ideas, to accept changes in procedures and policies without distress, as long as the changes make sense. He wants to learn about competing ideas and is usually able to give them consideration with an open mind. The NT has an inquiring attitude and values the development of will, self-control, and intelligence. He tends to be straightforward in his dealings with others, although others report often finding the NT cold, remote, and enigmatic. Yet if an NT is asked outright his position on any issue, he is more than likely to state his ideas on the subject without equivocation.

The NT is vulnerable to the all-work-and-no-play syndrome and can easily become isolated in an ivory tower of intellectualism, seemingly cut off from the world other types find as reality. The NT is, at times, the eccentric genius. Einstein shuffled in the streets of New York in his bedroom slippers and communicated intelligibly with only a few. Doubtless, Einstein had no regrets concerning this situation, and fortunately his work has not been lost. There always is, however, the danger that the work of NTs will be lost to others because of this tendency to communicate at levels of abstraction others find unintelligible.

NTs as a group tend to enjoy playing with words, finding pleasure in exploring verbal intricacies. Convoluted phrases and paradoxical statements fascinate them. Contemplating Einstein's comment, "The laws of mathematics, as far as they refer to reality, are not certain, and as far as they are certain, do not refer to reality," would give delight to the NT, as does the reading of satire and the savoring of such complicated word structures as those found in Lewis Carroll's *Alice in Wonderland*.

NTs tend to focus on the future, regarding the past as something dead and gone. What matters most is what might be and what might happen next. The past is useful only as means of giving direction to the future and for deciphering the lessons of history, taking heed to the warning that "He who remains ignorant of history is doomed to repeat it." The NT is never willing to repeat an error. He is impatient with his initial mistake; to repeat such a behavior is anathema. Clearly, *if* principles were sufficiently understood, a repetition of errors would be unnecessary! And it is quite humiliating for an NT to be in the position where others are witness to the errors he makes in his work, especially errors in logic.

Once an NT masters a technology or theoretical framework he is apt to move onto other challenges. Having isolated the rules which provide order and reason in his activity, and having mastered the necessary skills, whether it be work or play, the NT turns his eyes to other challenges; always, however, he expects to improve in his competency in *every* subject, new or old.

As the NT speculates about the possible motivations and thoughts of those he is with, trying to fit his experiences into some system he carries around in his head, he sometimes misses direct experience. He may be so occupied with trying to figure out what is happening as it is happening, that he misses *living* the event. At times, the NT seems to stand *beside* instead of *in* the stream of life, seeming to watch bemusedly as the river flows by—a little distanced, a little detached, a little uninvolved. This distancing sometimes causes the NT to make personal commitments which he later regrets. In particular, the NT whose "feeling" is not developed can become involved with members of the opposite sex who might be totally unsuitable as life companions. Forester catches this tragedy as he describes his famous hero at the altar:

> "Repeat after me," said the parson. "I, Horatio, take thee, Maria Ellen—"
>
> The thought came up in Hornblower's mind that these were the last few seconds in which he could withdraw from doing something which he knew to be ill-considered. Maria was not the right woman to be his wife, even admitting that he was suitable material for marriage in any case. If he had a grain of sense, he would break off this ceremony even at this last moment, he would announce that he had changed his mind, and he would turn away from the altar and the parson and from Maria, and he would leave the church a free man. "To have and to hold . . ." He was still, like an automaton, repeating the parson's words. And there was Maria beside him, in the white that so little became her. She was melting with happiness. She was consumed with love for him, however misplaced that might be. He could not, he simply could not, deal her a blow so cruel . . . "And thereto I plight thee my troth," repeated Hornblower. That settled it, he thought. Those must be the final deciding words that made the ceremony legally binding. He had made a promise and now there was no going back on it. There was comfort in the odd thought that he had really been committed from a week back, when Maria had come into his arms sobbing out her love for him, and he had been too softhearted to laugh at her and too—too weak? too honest?—to take advantage of her with the intention of betraying her. From the moment

that he had listened to her, from the moment he had returned her kisses, gently, all these later results, the bridal dress, this ceremony in the church of St. Thomas a Becket —and the vague future of cloying affection—had been inevitable.

[C. S. Forester, *Hornblower and the Hotspur*. Boston: Little Brown and Co., 1962, p. 3-4.]

At times, an NT can be quite oblivious to the emotional responses of others and may not always be sensitive to the complexities of interpersonal relations. People report that they sometimes feel that they do not exist when they are in the presence of an NT, and they may react to this by hostile, attacking comments, directed to the personality of the NT. NTs generally react to these comments with bewilderment and seldom strike back. If he chooses, however, the NT is capable of biting sarcasm that can be devastating to the person at whom it is directed.

The spirit of the NT is caught in the myth of Prometheus, the Greek God who created man from clay. Disappointed in his lifeless sculpture, Prometheus enlisted the help of Minerva. She carried him to heaven where he stole fire from the wheel of the sun. Prometheus applied the stolen fire to the breast of man, giving him life. Prometheus paid for his theft by being "nailed hard and fast in chains beneath the open sky" (Grant, p. 200). A greedy vulture tore at his blackened liver all day, year in and year out. And there was no end to the pain: every night, while Prometheus hung bound on the cliff, exposed to cruel frost and freezing winds, his liver grew whole again. Prometheus rescued man from ignorance, even though he had to rob heaven to do so. He proclaimed the doctrine of progress for man and secured the gifts of science and technology.

The Apollonian Temperament

We encounter a special difficulty in attempting to put into words the nature of the Apollonians, the intuitive-feeling (NF) types: INFJ, ENFJ, INFP and ENFP. Where the others—the Dionysian, Epimethean, and Promethean—pursue ordinary goals, the goal of the Apollonian cannot be seen as other than extraordinary. Indeed, so extraordinary is his goal that not even the Apollonian himself can talk about it in a straightforward way. It defies his description. Carl Rogers, certainly one of the more able exponents of the Apollonian way, presents an excellent illustration of the tortuous and convoluted rhetoric seemingly required:

> Becoming a Person means that the individual moves toward *being*, knowingly and acceptingly, the process which he inwardly and actually *is*. He moves away from being what he is not, from being a facade. He is not trying to be more than he is, with the attendant feelings of insecurity or bombastic defensiveness. He is not trying to be less than he is, with the attendant feelings of guilt or self-depreciation. He is increasingly listening to the deepest recesses of his psychological and emotional being, and finds himself increasingly willing to be, with greater accuracy and depth, that self which he most truly is.
>
> [Carl Rogers, *On Becoming a Person*. Boston: Houghton Mifflin, 1961, p. 176.]

Although this passage is seen by other styles as at best speaking in riddles, and at worst sheer nonsense, that same passage is revered by the NF as elegantly expressing the Apollonean way—the search for Self.

The purposes of SPs, SJs, and NTs are understood by SPs, SJs, and NTs alike, although they may not embrace them. The NT can understand the SP's desire to be free of responsibility just as he can understand the SJ's satisfaction in its possession. So can the SP see the NT's desire to store up capabilities and the SJ's desire to store up commodities. He would be the last to look a gift horse in the mouth, for that matter, since these stores tend to be given out to those who need them. The SJ even admires the NT his technical storehouse and envies the SP his generous and receiving nature. But here the mutual understanding of purposes ends. None of these understand the aim of the NF, and in turn, the NF cannot really grasp the others' commitment to what seems to the NF to be false goals. For the NF pursues a strange end, a self-reflective end which defies itself: *becoming*.

While the SPs, SJs, and NTs can go after their goals straightaway and at full throttle, the NF's search for self is circular and thus perpetual: How can one achieve a goal when that goal is to *have* a goal? The NF's "truest" self is the self in search of itself, or in other words, his purpose in life is to have a purpose in life. Always *becoming* himself, the NF can never truly *be* himself, since the very act of reaching for the self immediately puts it out of reach. Hamlet wrestled with this same dilemma:

> To be or not to be, that is the question. Whether it be nobler in the heart to suffer the slings and arrows of outrageous fortune or to take up arms against a sea of troubles and by opposing end them . . . and enterprise of great pith and moment with this regard their currents turn awry and lose the name of action.

The Apollonian's cross-purposes have never been expressed better. To act (to achieve, to become) is to destroy one's being, while "to be" without acting is sham and therefore nonbeing. *One becomes oneself if and only if one does not.* This paradox is the NFs burden throughout life, and his job, quite apart from his goal, is to resolve the paradox. Most do, some do not. The ones that do are happy and productive; the ones that do not suffer.

"How can I become the kind of person I *really* am?" asks the NF. He hungers for self-actualization, to be and to become real. To be what he is meant to be and to have an identity which is uniquely his. His endless search most often causes him guilt, believing that his real self is somehow less than it ought to be. And so he wanders, sometimes spiritually, sometimes psychologically, sometimes physically, seeking to satisfy his hunger for unity and uniqueness, to become *self-actualized* into a perfect whole and to have an identity which is perfectly unique, even though the paths in search of self are never clearly marked:

> But where was this Self, this innermost? It was not flesh and bone; it was not thought or consciousness. That was what the wise men taught. Where, then, was it? To press towards the Self—was there another way that was worth seeking? Nobody showed the way, nobody knew it—neither his father, nor the teachers and wise men, nor the holy songs . . . They knew a tremendous number of things—but was it worthwhile knowing all these things if they did not know the one important thing, the only important thing?
>
> [Herman Hesse, *Siddhartha*. New York: New Directions Publ. Corp., 1951.]

To be a grain of sand lost on a beach with millions of other grains is to be nothing. To be lost in the crowd, to have the same meaning as others, to share a faceless identity is not to

be at all. In order to make a difference and to maintain individuality, the unique contributions made by the NF in his roles
as worker, friend, lover, parent, leader, son, daughter, homemaker, wife, husband, creator must be recognized. No matter
how the NF structures his time and relationships, he needs
to have *meaning*. He wants their significance appreciated, or,
at the very least, recognized as existing. Only through this
kind of feedback does the NF know that he has unique identity.

Self-realization for the NF means to have *integrity*, that is,
unity. There must be no facade, no mask, no pretense, no
sham, no playing of roles. To have integrity is to be genuine,
to communicate authentically, to be in harmony with the inner
experiences of self. To be inauthentic, false, two-faced, phony,
to be less than real is to lose self and live a life of bad faith.

Living a life of significance, making a difference in the world,
does satisfy the NF's hunger for unique identity. It is no wonder that he experiences life as a drama, each encounter pregnant with significance. The NF can bring to each relationship
a heightened sense of meaning, lending drama to the events
in those relationships. NFs are extremely sensitive to subtleties in gestures and metaphoric behavior not always visible
to other types; he is also vulnerable to adding dimensions to
communications which are not always shared or perceived by
others.

The NF's relationships can fall into a pattern of enthusiastic
anticipation accompanied by a considerable investment of effort and emotion, ending in a disappointment that what could
have been was not. The NF is seldom miserly in the energy
and time he is willing to devote to a relationship, especially
as it is developing. A like return need not be the *quid pro quo*
for the NF to continue investing generously, as long as *some*
response is forthcoming.

Although these Apollonians make up only about 12 percent of
the general population (or about 24 million people), their influence on the minds of the populace is massive, for most writers
come from this group. Novelists, dramatists, television writers,
playwrights, journalists, poets, and biographers are almost
exclusively NFs. Technical and scientific writers tend to be
NTs, but writers who wish to inspire and persuade, who produce literature, most often are NFs. The questions which this
group asks about the meaning of life, of their own lives, and
what is significant for humankind, saturate fictional litera-

ture. The theme of people in restless search of self runs through novel after novel, is voiced by protagonist after protagonist, and is the source of agony in drama after drama.

The search for meaning as a necessary pilgrimage for *all* people is advanced by the NFs in their writings. Very often the other types, the SJs, NTs, and SPs, are troubled by the thought that they *ought* to be pursuing these values, even if, somehow, the search for meaning and integrity does not beckon to them. This reluctance of 88 percent of the world to join the search for self-actualization is a great source of mystification to the NFs.

As NFs well know, the pen is mightier than the sword. But the impact of the NF is not limited to the written word. NFs heavily populate the professions of psychiatry, clinical and counseling psychology, the ministry, and teaching. More than any other group NFs can speak and write fluently, often with poetic flair. As members of the communication media, NFs may exhibit a sense of mission, using their creative efforts to win followers for their cause, whatever it may be.

But though an NF can get caught up in a cause, he may not stay involved for long if the cause fails to have deep, lasting significance, with opportunity to better the conditions of people in the world. For example, when the Flower Children movement was centered on the west coast in San Francisco's Haight-Ashbury district, it was joined by NFs, particularly NFPs, but it was chiefly populated by SPs. The NFs watched the SPs living in the moment, free of the past and future, and they wanted to experience this immediacy. But it was inherent in them to need to pursue a larger significance, a more profound application. The movement only held them for a brief time and they left, disenchanted. As fast as the NFs moved into the communes, they moved out to search elsewhere for self-actualization and ways to express their unique identities.

More often than not, their search continued in the causes and movements which had gained popular recognition and, to some degree, acceptance. Robert Kirsch catches this characteristic in the founder, mentor, and guru of Gestalt therapy, Fritz Perls:

> He came into his own very late. At 32 he was still living with his mother. At 53 he had only begun to break with his own training . . . Not until his mid-60's, wandering through America, experimenting with LSD, denied the academic

respectibility he always sought, did he find that his life and the world were beginning to come into confluence. The time had come for his idea. In California young psychologists were impressed with his gifts as a therapist, his almost uncanny ability to read people.

He would continue to wander to Kyoto to study Zen, to Elath in Israel—until he came to Esalen. He was not entirely happy there to begin with, at first one of the many competing stars. He despised rivals, called Abraham Maslow a "sugar-coated Nazi" and Rollo May "an existentialist without an existence." It was as much his bent for mischief and excitement as it was any sound assessment.

Perls was psychoanalyzed, bioenergeticized, dianeticized, Alexanderized, Rolfed, psychedelicized—experienced many of the roads to salvation offered in our times. He didn't find it. Perhaps it didn't exist. No forever-after happiness for him: "Life is a rose garden. The petals wilt and the thorns remain."

[Robert Kirsch, "Fritz Perls: Mining the Gestalt of the Earth." L.A. *Times Calendar*, March 23, 1975, p. 74.]

Whether a guru of Esalen or a teacher in a more traditional setting, the profession of transmitting ideas and attitudes tends to attract NFs. Together the SJs and the NFs make up the bulk of public school teaching faculties. Very few SPs or NTs staff the schools of the nation. If the NTs do go into teaching, they gravitate toward higher education. The SPs, as a group, do not seem to find teaching at any level particularly attractive, although a small number may enjoy the excitement of elementary school teaching. SJs outnumber NFs in the teaching field, however, roughly three to two. As their subject matter the NFs tend to choose the humanities and the social sciences as areas of interest.

Just as teaching appeals to the NF as an occupation in which to find himself, so do other occupations which have this as their goal. Work directed toward midwifing people into becoming kinder, warmer, and more loving human beings appeals to NFs. They tend to see potential good in everyone and often devote their lives to the cultivation of this potential. Both the ministry and missionary work understandably attract NFs, as did the Peace Corps. Some NFs are willing to make great personal sacrifices to help others find their way. The NF can be ruthless in making this come about for himself and for others.

NFs, as a group, show little interest in buying and selling or any commercial occupations, nor do they find the physical sciences particularly attractive. They prefer to work with words, and need and want to be directly or indirectly in communication with people. One of the ways they work with people is through the interpretive arts. Where the SPs are drawn to the performing arts, the NFs are drawn to the arts which involve verbal and written communication. As actors and actresses, the NFs take on the character of the person being portrayed. Where the SP would be playing himself dressed up in a costume (for example, John Wayne playing himself dressed as a cowboy, soldier, businessman, or lawman), the NF's personality is submerged in his role. The SP actor remains himself and is never in danger of questioning his identity; the NF actor, on and off stage, can acquire a different identity with each role he plays.

The NF has an extraordinary capability to appear to his beholder to be whatever the beholder wants to see. And seldom does the NF find it necessary, with his powers of empathy, to relieve the beholder of his illusions. Rather, the NF withholds his self-knowledge, except with those he cares for deeply. That his general public sees him as other than he knows himself to be is a matter of internal amusement. The NF is willing to let be whatever appears to be, if this is what the insignificant other seems to need and want.

> Gillian turned from the mirror. The mirror, after all, couldn't reflect the most essential attribute of them all. Gillian walked to the bar, made herself a pitcher of martinis, sat drinking, naked in the Eames chair—cold leather against skin, nice. The major quality was something reactive, a chameleon quality that somehow enabled her to transform herself in the eyes of any man. She could become—and she had felt the process often enough to know its validity—pale of skin, full-breasted, intellectual, sexy, aloof. She could be whatever the man happened to be looking for at the moment. She could become any man's dream woman, and somehow accomplish it without relinquishing her own identity . . . It was a process of becoming. It existed not in mechanical tricks but in acute sensitivity; it took place not in her physical alterations but in the eye of the beholder.
>
> [Penelope Ashe, *Naked Came the Stranger*. New York: Dell Publishing Company, 1969, p. 13.]

That "religion" of the 60's, the encounter group movement, was largely motivated and populated by NFs seeking greater intensity in their relationships, seeking an elusive intimacy.

They searched in T-groups, sensitivity groups, Gestalt groups, marathons (nude and otherwise), Transcendental Meditation groups, Primal Scream groups—all in an effort to find a way to give deeper meaning to their lives, to develop the ability to live more openly and honestly. They explored verbal and nonverbal dimensions of communication to become more fully aware of their emotions, hoping to reduce to a split-second the delay between the occurrence of an emotion and its awareness in consciousness. In many, many groups they found, for a time, the sense of intimacy they sought, describing the experience as an almost spiritual peak or rush:

> At the exact moment when I encounter someone I feel as if I am some place I have never been before. It's hard to describe. Like you and this other person are out in space with each other and looking down on the earth.
>
> [Terry O'Bannion and April O'Connell, *The Shared Journey*. Englewood Cliffs, New Jersey, Prentice-Hall, Inc., 1970, p. 23.]

Often, though, after the group experience was over, the intimacy faded in the dulling routine of daily living.

Some of the disenchantment which has been reported with the group experience may stem from an unrealistic expectation of what that experience could deliver, especially on the part of the NF, who may not have come to terms with his characteristic of sensing himself as divided. Indeed, NFs report over and over that they are subject to an inner voice which urges them to "Be real, authentic, meaningful." Always in the NF is that voice *dialoguing* about being whole, significant, and oneself. At once audience and actor, the NF is caught in a split in awareness; he is always on stage, and, at the same time, is watching himself being on stage. The irony of this consuming hunger for a sense of being oneself is that it condemns the NF to be ever split, standing to one side and watching himself be himself.

> "I think you're too conscious of yourself all the time, with everybody," she said to her sister.
>
> "I hope at least I haven't a slave nature," said Hilda.
>
> "But perhaps you have! Perhaps you are a slave to your own idea of yourself."
>
> Hilda drove in silence for some time after this piece of unheard-of insolence from that chit Connie.
>
> "At least I'm not a slave to somebody else's idea of me:

and the somebody else a servant of my husband's," she
retorted at last, in crude anger.

[D. H. Lawrence, *Lady Chatterley's Lover.* New York: Ban-
tam Books, 1928; 1968, p. 274.]

Perhaps because the work of the NF needs to give significance
as well as provide service which would content an SJ—and
because he needs work which matters to him and to others, often
the NF has difficulty placing limits on the amount of time and
energy he devotes to his work. Unlike the SP who can work on
impulse, the NF works toward a vision of perfection: the perfect
work of art, the perfect play, novel, film, the perfect relationship. And, of course, once the work is done, once the creation
is created, it never seems to live up to the magnificence of its
conception. Nonetheless, NFs tend to be unwilling or unable to
limit a commitment they make to a production, once they become involved. At that point, they can be unreasonably demanding on both themselves and others around them.

> As for Kubrick, he is still working 18 hours a day, over-
> seeing the final fine tuning of the sound track . . . "There
> is such a total sense of demoralization if you say you don't
> care. From start to finish on a film, the only limitations
> I observe are those imposed on me by the amount of money
> I have to spend and the amount of sleep I need. You either
> care or you don't, and I simply don't know where to draw
> the line between those two points."
>
> ["Kubrick's Grandest Gamble." *Time.* New York, Dec.
> 15, 1975, p. 78.]

Although he is apt to be passionate in his pursuit of a creative effort, the NF can be an intellectual butterfly, flitting
from idea to idea, a dilettante in his pursuit of knowledge
when compared to an NT. The NF wants to taste all the abundance of life, as does the SP, but always wants his experiences to have meaning beyond the mere event. NFs tend to
romanticize their experiences, their lives, and the experiences
and lives of others, and they are apt to be far more interested
in people-watching than in abstractions. As with the NT, the
NF is future-oriented and focused on what *might* be. But,
rather than thinking about the possibilities of principles as
does the NT, the NF thinks about the possibilities in people.
He enjoys bringing out the best in others and speaks often of
"actualizing the potential" of others and of himself. As with
his perception of himself, so it is with the NF's perception of
others: Whatever is, is never quite sufficient. The thought that
the visible is all there is is untenable for an NF.

The Greeks, of course, caught the spirit of the NF in their mythology in one of the most fascinating and complex of all the gods. SP Dionysus reveled in the pleasures of the vine and body, living fully in the here and now, responding to reality as he found it. He gave to man an understanding of enjoyment of the sensual. Epimetheus suffered all the evils of Pandora's box, but, in his loyal SJ way, he stood by her as his *should's* and *ought's* dictated, taking comfort in the one good thing in the box: hope. Man developed a social conscience, hoping always that tomorrow *must* be better! Sorrowing that man was mere clay, NT Prometheus stole fire from the sun, brought it to man and paid a terrible price. But he gave man technology. Apollo, in Greek mythology, stands as a direct link between the gods and man, giving man a sense of mission, showing man how to continue in his search for the sacred even though he has known the evil of the profane.

Apollo was the self-appointed bearer of Truth, and he undertook the task of interpreting for men the will of his father, Zeus. Apollo symbolizes the duality of the Hellenic spirit: the urge to ideals, to truth, to beauty, to spirituality and sacredness, and the accompanying desire to plumb the profane, the ugly, the corrupt, and the fleshly. He stood for the Grecian ideal of purity of spirit, of dedication to helping others, of the bringer of therapeutic music and song. He represented the healer of mind and body. He was the giver of prophecy, spokesman for the gods, the inspirer and the inspirational, the divine and the incorruptible. The primitive and violent side of Apollo only erupted when his supremacy was challenged or when he was frustrated in his efforts to bring peace and happiness to man. Within Apollo the sense of mission, the cult of the individual, the search for identity existed side by side with untamed lust, the willingness to murder for a cause, the willingness to use priestesses in his rites even at the expense of their sanity and, ultimately, the betrayal of his father, Zeus. In Apollo, side by side, existed the sacred and the profane.

In Apollo the NFs find their prototype. Their hunger is not centered on *things* but *people*. They are not content with *abstractions;* they seek *relationships*. Their need does not ground to *action;* it vibrates with *interaction*. As the NF seeks self-actualization in identity and unity, he is aware that this is a life-long process, an ideal toward being and becoming a final, finished self.

III
MATING
AND
TEMPERAMENT

All sorts of variables enter into the pairing activities of mates: parental prescription, economics, social stratum, educational level, national origin, racial origin, physique, and physiognomy. But a more powerful force, one that is more powerful than all of these, is the force of temperament. Other things equal—parental prescription, economics, social stratum, and so forth—the mates will pair according to temperament. It will be profitable, then, to look at how the types pair off and how the four temperament groups act as mates.

First — and this is said cautiously — two decades of type-watching (Keirsey began type-watching in 1956) reveal the astonishing fact that people are attracted to, and marry, *their opposites* with high frequency. Furthermore, if they have botched up the mating somehow, after 10 to 20 years the spouses just as often as not are *again* attracted to, and marry, their opposite.

Of course, the notion that one is attracted to one's opposite is a well-known cliché, but it is a cliché that few seem to believe. Witness the advent of mating bureaus and especially the entry of computer scanning for compatibility. They reveal a much more believed cliché: like is attracted to like. But it is the bureau and the computer that pairs like with like. People don't very often do it on their own. Now this is not to say that spouses that are alike don't get along with each other and don't stay together. Perhaps they do both. It means rather

that they don't *attract* each other. Opposites do. We might
wonder why.

Carl Jung said that opposites not only attract but even *fascinate* each other. He had a sort of spooky conception of the
opposite which he called the "shadow." One casts a shadow,
as it were, of all that one is not, or rather, of all that one has
not developed, expressed, or "lived out" in oneself. It's as if,
in being attracted to our opposite, we grope around for that
rejected, abandoned, or unlived half of ourselves, like a worm
cut in two that goes wiggling around trying to join up with the
other end. So the search for our other side is built-in, im-
printed, a priori, and quite imperative, just like sexuality and
territoriality.

(Now we don't have to buy Jung's reductionist localization
theory along with the imperative or a priori. It's okay to posit
a priori behavior as long as one doesn't localize it and thereby commit the homunculus or ghost-in-the-machine fallacy.)

So people instinctively seek out their opposites or, if Jung has
his way, their complements. The question is, *should* they? Do
such matings pay off? The answer is yes, *but* . . . Yes, if there
is no attempt to change the spouse. No, if there *is* an attempt
to change the spouse. This ambiguous answer—yes, *but*—
ushers forth the *Grand Hypothesis* regarding the primary
source of ruptured marriages: The Pygmalion Project.

In our Pygmalion Project we go to all the bother of finding and
promising to care for and take care of, a person quite unlike
ourself, in some cases exactly opposite in all respects—and
then pull all the stops in our attempt to transform our spouse
into our own image. It is as if the marriage license is construed
as a sculptor's license, giving each spouse the warrant to
chisel away until the other becomes the spit and image of the
sculptor. Consider the supreme irony were each spouse successful! Both Ovid and Shaw would turn over in their graves.

Of course, there is no way to change our spouse into ourself.
But the *attempt* to change the other is what does the damage.
By chipping away on our spouse we say, "You are not what I
want. I want you other than you are." Clearly what the spouse
is is not appreciated, even though it is precisely what the
spouse *is* that was the attraction in the first place! (Here it is
tempting to see us all as having a strong desire to *recast* ourselves, to be reborn, so we find what is in effect raw material,

a shapeless stone, that which is most distant from us; our sense of achievement, then, all the greater, the greater the transformation of our spouse. Are we not all Pygmalion?)

Suppose this seemingly ubiquitous desire to change our spouse is resisted? *Then*, and in *that* degree, can opposites live happily ever afterward, *maybe* . . . If we can recognize our (natural) impulse to instruct our spouse on the kinds and degrees of change he or she should make, pause each time the impulse strikes, and *button our lip*—then some interesting phenomena may begin to take place. For example, if we suspend our activities toward trying to force our spouse to change in our direction—to become more logical, or more responsible, or more spontaneous, or more meaningful—then we might, just might, come to *appreciate* that which attracted us in the first place.

Notice that it isn't that we want our spouse to *abandon* spontaneity or whatever he or she has in abundance. Rather, we want him or her to *take up* our task—the achievement of competence, for instance. What we may fail to realize is that in taking up our aim, our spouse must abandon his or her own. We cannot have our cake and eat it too.

We might ask for some clarification of what is meant by "opposite" in the context of temperament theory. In a very broad sense, Thinkers (Schizoid Aesthetes) are opposites of Sensibles (Cycloid Economicals). In the Jungian framework Thinkers are opposites of Feelers, Judicials are opposites of Perceptives, and Extraverts are opposites of Introverts. Of course, there is no such thing as an extraverted *type*, per se; there are eight extraverted types, as there are eight introverted types. Extraverts can be radically different from each other, just as are Thinkers and Judicials. Opposite *types* are as follows:

INTP	—	ESFJ	INFP	—	ESTJ
ENTP	—	ISFJ	ENFP	—	ISTJ
INTJ	—	ESFP	INFJ	—	ESTP
ENTJ	—	ISFP	ENFJ	—	ISTP

Opposite *temperaments* are:

NF	vs	NT
SP	vs	SJ

Now it appears that opposite *types* are more attractive to each other than opposite *temperaments*. The ENFP, for instance, seems to be more drawn to the ISTJ than he or she is drawn to the INTJ. Another example: the ENTJ seems to select the ISFP more frequently than the INFP. And it may be the case that he will go for the ISFP's sister type, the ESFP, more readily than for the INFP.

Now another rather important consideration ought to be surfaced regarding quality of "fit" in mating. Not everybody wants the same thing in a marriage. The NFs may want (or *say* they want) "a deep and meaningful relationship," but the NTs, SPs, and SJs are not very interested in either the "depth" or the "meaningfulness" of the relationships, and added to that, would be hard put to say just what "deep" or "meaningful" *means* in the marriage context.

The question is, then, just what do the types *want* when they mate?

Our cue must come from the nature of the person that is attractive. Perhaps a glance at the most fitting activity or occupation of each of the types would cast some light on the attraction. Now, it may seem excessively fortuitous that the hundreds of work categories can be neatly summed up by a mere 16 "vocations"—magically to conform to the motive base of each type. Well, yes. The "work of best fit" is a metaphor, of course; but it may give us an image of the sort of work in which each type would get his jollies. The types are paired as opposites:

> INTP (Architect) . . . . ESFJ (Seller)
> ENTP (Inventor). . . . . ISFJ (Conservator)
> INTJ (Scientist) . . . . ESFP (Entertainer)
> ENTJ (Fieldmarshal). . . . ISFP (Artist)
> INFP (Questor). . . . . ESTJ (Administrator)
> ENFP (Journalist). . . . . . . ISTJ (Trustee)
> INFJ (Author) . . . . ESTP (Promotor)
> ENFJ (Pedagogue) . . . . . . ISTP (Artisan)

Following with our thesis that opposites attract, then, the architect is attracted to the seller and the seller to the architect, the inventor to the conservator, and so on. Again, we must think broadly of these categories, else we lose sight of the intent.

The INTP "Architect"

Our "architect" is not merely a designer of buildings. There is the architect of ideas (the philosopher), the architect of number systems (the mathematician), the architect of computer languages (the programmer), and on and on. In short, abstract design is the forté of the architect and coherence is the primary issue.

Why would this abstractionist find the ESFJ "seller" attractive? Think broadly of selling. This amounts to persuading another to *receive* something of value *to the receiver*. The seller is essentially *caring for* the receiver (quite apart from the fact that the receiver pays). This is the essential attitude of the ESFJ seller, and this attitude is perceptible to the receiver (buyer); he *feels* this nourishing approach. *That* is what is attractive to the INTP architect-philosopher—the nourishment which anchors him to the real world.

What attracts the ESFJ "seller"? Here is a person who, like a balloon filled with hydrogen, is likely to escape the earth (in his abstract attitude). He needs to have a string attached so that he can be hauled down to earth now and then. In a sense, he needs to be "sold on reality," so indifferent is he to it.

Now the ESFJ (at *least* 15 percent of the population) "seller" has another likely target for mating which may be just as attractive. This is his or her opposite on the *sensible* (S) side: the ISTP "artisan." The artisan or craftsman is up to his eyeballs in the real world, but ironically couldn't care less about the product of his efforts. It's the *process* that counts. Moreover, he is likely to have some rather speedy machines around to satisfy his hunger for adventure and excitement. So, in a sense, he is just as far out of the real world as the INTP in his indifference to outcomes. Here is someone for the ESFJ to *anchor* to reality, to *give* to.

The INTP also has a second likely target to attract him: the ENFJ "pedagogue." What is a pedagogue? A catalyst of the growth process, someone who has that uncanny ability to "bring out" the other, to activate the differentiation or "unfolding" process in the learner. All NFs seem to have this capability in some degree and the accompanying desire to exercise it, but the ENFJ seems to have it in abundance.[1] This relationship—the ENFJ–INTP—can be "deep and meaningful"

---

[1] A study of teachers in which *all* types of teachers and administrators were asked to pick the most outstanding teacher they knew revealed that the teachers consistently chose ENFJs, who had no other close contenders. From J. Wright, Unpublished Dissertation, Claremont Graduate School.

for the former and anchoring in a charismatic way for the latter.

The ENTP "Inventor"

The inventive ENTP finds in the ISFJ a neat complementarity for his enterprise, for in the ISFJ he finds the supreme conservator. The conservator, broadly conceived, is morally bound to ensure the material and legal welfare of his or her charge. The inventor, also broadly conceived, is bent on replacing whatever tool, operation, or enterprise now exists with a *better* one. Out to exercise his *ingenuity* in bettering things, the ENTP is of necessity iconoclastic and tends to be so seen. So he can get into a bit of trouble with the elders, who usually are not all that pleased to see their tried-and-true tools, operations, and enterprises blithely set aside for the ENTP's better mousetrap. The ISFJ, mated to this inventive rascal, takes on the task of squaring things with the establishment.

The ENTP also may be attracted to his opposite on the N side: he approaches the INFJ. But the INFJ is humorously and preposterously different from the seemingly similar ISFJ. In the INFJ lies the soul of the "author"—the meaning-giver, the mystic, the oracle. Perhaps the INFJ is a conservator of the soul, a sort of messiah. At any rate, there is something about the "author" (*very* broadly conceived) which the ENTP covets. Prometheus had to pay dearly for giving fire to man. The Promethian ENTP may figure that, though his INFJ mate may not rescue his body from the vultures, at least the INFJ might rescue his soul from Hell.

The INTJ "Scientist"

Wishing to control nature, the INTJ "scientist" probably has more difficulty than all other types in making up his or her mind in mate selection. Even mate selection must be done in a scientific way. It may well be that the narratives, plays, and films impugning the "rational and objective" approach to mating have as their target our thorough-going scientist INTJ. Nevertheless, when young, the INTJ is attracted to the free-wheeling, spontaneous, fun-loving "entertainer" ESFP. But the INTJ requires that mating meet certain criteria, else it is not undertaken. So the INTJ doesn't often go through with what is begun by natural attraction. Since he or she proceeds in a rational and methodical way, the selection of a similar temperament is more likely than selection of opposite, following the assumption that those who are similar ought to do well together. The INTJ "scientist" is also attracted to the ENFP "journalist," probably because of the enthusiastic, effervescent, and apparently spontaneous enjoyment and wonderment this type exudes—the very antithesis of the careful, thoughtful exactitude of the INTJ.

The ENTJ "Fieldmarshal"

The ENTJ is a natural "fieldmarshal," that is, he's itching to get his hands on several "armies" so that he can marshal his forces and conduct the "war" as it should be conducted. If our ENTJ is in charge of any kind of enterprise, however small, his temperament dictates that he run it as he would his armies— with an eye to long-term *strategies* and their *derivative tactics, logistics, and consequences.* In startling contrast to this, the fieldmarshal is enamored by the "flower child," the bucolic artist ISFP, tranquilly ensconced next to Walden pond! Perhaps the ENTJ wishes a spouse who will share with him or her the quiet of the forest and field far from the madding crowd, thus separating home from work by a great, insulating distance.

The ENTJ is attracted also to his opposite in the Appolonian camp: the monastic and questing INFP. What in the saintly or knightly (St. Joan of Arc, Sir Galahad) INFP calls the ENTJ fieldmarshal? First note the outward similarity of the INFP and the ISFP. Perhaps it is this, the underlying missionary outlook of the INFP. In a sense, both INFP and ISFP have missionary zeal, the former enlisting the spouse in the quest, the latter in the tranquil respite of nature.

The INFP "Questor"

The INFP questor probably has more problems in mating than any other type. Let us be mindful of their relative infrequency: about 1¼ percent, say two and a half million people in the USA. Their problem lies in their primary outlook on life. "Life," says the INFP, "is a very serious matter." Now when a person makes his life a kind of crusade or a series of crusades, then there's bound to be some taxing of the spouse. If the INFP takes the other tack, the "monastic" (and the same person can tack back and forth—now a crusader, now a monastic), the spouse will find himself again taxed, trying to draw the monastic out of his dark meditative cave.

The opposites of our crusading monastic seem well equipped for this alternating-phase taxation: ENTJ and ESTJ. Both are anchored in the real world with a vengeance. The ENTJ marshalling his or her forces toward distant objectives, the ESTJ administrating in a solid, dependable, and traditional way whatever is his or hers to administer. Both provide anchorage to a person who might otherwise get lost in meditation or in crusade. Selection of a mate of irrelevant form (e.g., an ISTP artisan or an ESTP promoter) would not be the wisest of tactics in so serious a business as life.

The ENFP "Journalist"

Here is the herald, the spirited bearer of tidings. But underneath this effervescent enthusiasm is a person fiercely dedicated to "meaning" in life and reminiscent of the INFP crusader. Only the ENFP neither crusades nor meditates, not for long anyway. The ENFP is into everything, frisky, not unlike a puppy, sniffing around to see what's new. ENFP has to be in on everything, can't bear to be left out of anything. That's why they make such splendid reporters, newscasters, and journalists. Mercury. Now who would enjoy this frisky, bubbly—yet serious—person? The Rock of Gibralter, of course—ISTJ, the "trustee." ISTJ, who revels in "keeping the books in order," "balancing the budget," "securing and ensuring," "stabilizing and steadying," "honoring contracts," "keeping the ship on a steady course" and "shipshape," delights also in providing anchorage and safe harbor for the heraldic ENFP.

Who else is attractive and attracted to our curious journalist? Strangely, the abstract scientist: INTJ. Lost in his abstract world of hypotheses, he finds anchorage in the person who knows what's going on in the real world! So ENFP can *be* an anchor or *have* an anchor, and who can tell which will be chosen?

The INFJ "Author"

The oracular INFJ may opt for the inventive ENTP, but also may go for a different kind of contrary, namely the ESTP. The

ESTP and ENTP, to the casual observer, look pretty much alike. Charming, suave, urbane, humorous, witty, fantastically easy to approach, venturesome, even reckless. But one is out to invent, the other to promote; this is no small difference. It takes an inventor to make a mousetrap, it takes a promoter to make an enterprise. To succeed, the promoter has to be, in the best sense of the word, a con artist. He must be able to get people's *confidence.* Now why would a meaning-giver INFJ be intrigued by an entrepreneur ESTP? Because he wants to help the entrepreneur find his soul and his significance in the scheme of things. Similarly, why is INFJ attracted to ENTP? Because he wishes to rescue this iconoclast from his seeming folly (and let's face it, most inventions are abortive, or still-born).

The ENFJ "Pedagogue"

Who can complement this growth-catalyst? The opposite on the S side is ISTP, the "artisan." It is not difficult to see how the teacher[2] inherent in the ENFJ would want to "bring out" the craftsman in the ISTP. The artisan, however, has another side to his nature that pops up occasionally and in some cases is a life theme: adventure and exploration. The ISTP can, so to speak, be wayward, take off for parts unknown. It is difficult to imagine a similar desire on the part of the ENFJ to bring out adventuresomeness.

The ENFJ, as already pointed out, finds the INTP attractive. Now here is a splendid target for our catalyst, for beneath the cool, collected, detached, and doubting exterior lies an architect of buildings, machines, tools, operations, tactics, languages, mathematics, or whatever can be designed. If, that is, this latently capable designer can be "activated" or "brought out."

The ESFJ "Vendor"

We have seen the mutual attraction of ESFJ and INTP. The ESFJ, wanting to serve as an anchorage for the INTP's flights to the higher levels of abstraction, finds in the ISTP an even

---

[2]If the ENFJ actually becomes a professional teacher, at any level, then the desire for complementarity may be attenuated so that the ENFJ *may* not be as strongly attracted to his opposite as he would otherwise. But, of course, most ENFJs don't become teachers, there being around 10,000,000 of them.

more likely target for anchorage. The ISTP's flights are often *literal*, not figurative: He really does fly. Look in the cockpit of almost any aircraft and you'll find an ISTP. Of course, most ISTPs do not fly in the literal sense; but the hankering for adventure and exploration symbolized by flight is there, and it is *this*, the hankering, that draws the ESFJ like a moth to a flame. How does this serve the giving, caring, comforting nature of ESFJ? Why, when the adventurer *returns*, of course; the giver of comfort is there to provide rest and recreation.

The ISFJ "Conservator"

We saw how the conserving nature of the ISFJ nicely comple-mented the iconoclasm of the ENTP "inventor." There would seem to be an even greater affinity in the mating of ISFJ with the ESTP "promoter." The dashing, glittering, wheel-and-deal capers of the ESTP calls for anchorage. The ESTP tends to have "high" periods during which there is a whirlwind of euphoric activity. The ISFJ provides, and likes to provide, a place to "crash" for our high-rolling entrepreneur. Usually, the ISFJ finds employment that requires this ministering, nurs-ing, helping sort of activity. Even so, he or she doesn't seem to mind doing the same thing at home, and so tends to get bur-dened with a bit more duty than others. If the spouse does not show appreciation now and then for this overtime work, he may be in for an increase in physical complaints and "wor-ries" on the part of the unappreciated ISFJ.

The ESFP "Entertainer"

The affinity of the INTJ "scientist" for the ESFP has been examined. This type of mating, however, is so infrequent as to be of mere academic interest (the INTJ is a mere 1 percent of the population and, furthermore, rarely comes in contact with ESFP). More frequently the ESFP is drawn to the ISTJ "trustor." Here is the entertaining ESFP, bursting with energy and hankering to put on a show of some kind. More than others the ESFP yearns for the bright lights, the party, the excite-ment of gatherings. In a sense, the ESFP is the life of the party. How many times have novelist and screenwriter told the story of "the showgirl and the banker" or "the playboy and the owner"? The ESFP wants to *liven up* this Rock of Gibralter at the same time he or she wants to be *settled down* by this very stable and responsible person.

The ISFP "Artist"

Pursuit of two themes—closeness to nature and artistic activity—places the ISFP quite a distance from the utilitarian outlook. Yet it is precisely that outlook that seems to attract the bucolic spirit. The opposite on the N side is the ENTJ "fieldmarshal," the most militant of all the types in his desire to run things. ISFP is most likely to become a pacifist or environmentalist, and yet also is likely to seek out the person who is temperamentally suited to tactical leadership, military or otherwise. ISFP is likewise attracted to the ESTJ "administrator," the person temperamentally suited to be "in charge" of establishments. Note that the person most likely to deprecate *the* establishment is attracted to the head of *an* establishment. It is rather doubtful, should an ISFP actually marry an ENTJ or ESTJ, that there is any intent or desire to change the spouse into a pastoral. Of all the types, ISFP is most likely to "let be" whoever and whatever. It seems more likely that the latter provides a kind of anchorage to enterprise and to civilization.

The ESTJ "Administrator"

To preserve the establishment, to keep it healthy, steady, balanced, well insured, that's what is enjoyable and satisfying to the ESTJ. Yet the ESTJ is attracted to the disestablishmentarian, the ISFP! Does he hope to redo this bucolic spirit in his own image? Seemingly not. Perhaps he sees in this person's extreme laissez-faire a respite from the great responsibilities he manages to accumulate.

He can and sometimes does find another sort of complementary opposite, the INFP "monastic." This is very infrequent, there being 15 ESTJs for every one INFP. It is doubtful if the ESTJ finds any rest in the INFP, because underneath the monastic is a fierce crusader—hardly what he bargained for. He may soon find himself asked to increase the "depth" and the "meaningfulness" of the relationship without being given even the slightest clue on how to proceed. His renewed efforts to "stabilize" and "solidify" the relationship will only be taken as signs of superficiality and/or meaninglessness.

The ISTJ "Trustee"

Here is the paragon of insurance, preparation, and consolidation—a person with a strong desire to be trusted. Small wonder that he looks upon accounting, banking, and securities with a benevolent eye. Try to imagine him married to one of his own kind: Two Rocks of Gibralter, each steadfastly tempering the other's steadfast tempering! We can safely guess that this sort of relationship wouldn't work very well.

The attraction, rather, is for the "entertainer," for the vivacity and sparkle of ESFP, the opposite of ISTJ. ISTJ is the ultimate *saver* who is fascinated by, and frequently marries, the ultimate *spender!* Here is complementarity to the nth degree! Just as often,[3] ISTJ finds his or her opposite on the intuitive side: the ENFP. Perhaps he senses in the ENFP's desire to spread the word something similar to the ESFP's desire to put on a show. Certainly the vivacity and sparkle is apparent in both, an attribute which must be quite enchanting to the sober and careful ISTJ.

The ESTP "Promoter"

The relative rarity of the ESTP's opposite on the intuitive side, INFJ (about 1 percent compared to the ESTP's 15 percent), means that such matings will be quite infrequent, as they should be. Imagine an oracle married to a wheeler-dealer! We should, however, be mindful that, whatever our own political beliefs, our more spectacular Presidents (J. F. Kennedy, L. B. Johnson, T. Roosevelt, F. D. Roosevelt) were ESTP "promoters" without peer. It would be a fascinating study to check on the temperament of their wives to see if any married their oracular INFJ opposites.

The seemingly correct—and, we can assume, attractive—choice is the ISFJ "conservator." Such complementarity should work out rather nicely, especially if the promoter is male and the conservator is female.[4]

The ISTP "Artisan"

The adventuresome artisan may seek out his opposite in the ENFJ "teacher." As noted previously, in the ENFJ he finds a catalyst to growth, certainly a complementary quality to his

---

[3] ISTJ and ENFP occur just as frequently in the population: about 5 percent.
[4] Cultural stereotyping may inhibit and even interdict the complementary pairing of male ISFJ with female ESTP. With a bit of work, however, such mates could set aside the stereotype and serve their completing function.

artisanship. There is nothing, however, in the nature of the ENFJ that is catalytic to the adventurer side of the ISTP's temperament. If this theme is dominant in the ISTP, then the ENFJ–ISTP mating is headed for trouble.

The ISTP is at least as attracted to the soothing, hosting, giving ESFJ. It takes the ESFJ "master of ceremonies" to get the ISTP off his motorcycle (surfboard, airplane, hang-glider) long enough to relate to others in more productive and facilitative ways. The ISTP needs this anchorage, else he wanders off into the frontier (when Horace Greeley said, "Go west, young man," the ISTP took him seriously and went!).

The Dionysian (SP) Mate

Whether Extraverted or Introverted, Thinking or Feeling, male or female, an SP may present the image of a bedroom virtuoso, a sexual superman or superwoman who voices an avid interest in experimentation. The details of the experimentation, however, are usually left for others to provide. SPs seem to enjoy talking about sex, may have an extensive repertoire of ribald sexual stories, and love to hear details of sexual activities of all types. Modern novels which focus on sex tend to describe the SP more than any other type. SPs are more responsive than others to tactile, auditory, and visual sexual stimuli which are concrete, real, and graphic. Symbolic stimuli (e.g., poetry) do not have the same power to excite the SP as they might other types.

The attitude that living is to be enjoyed applies to sex as well as work, play, or sleep. Variety in all things, including sex, is likely to appeal to an SP. An SP can become sexually excited by expressions of conflict as well as of lust and love, and perhaps will find quarreling, tears, and anger—whether these emanate from themselves or their mates—sources of stimulation. Horror movies, disaster and war films, pictorial presentations of the cruel, the terrifying, the graphically erotic may excite an SP. The slow-moving love story is less likely to have appeal, eliciting impatience in the SP to get on with it. The larger-than-life love goddess or sexual superhero performing on the screen can titilate an SP, who in the hedonic style, is ever seeking excitement and adventure. Romeo and Juliet, Heloise and Abelard were clearly *not* SPs; in fact, the two pairs of lovers and their styles of loving may appear to an SP to be rather pitiful.

An SP is likely to be compliant and agreeable with whatever is happening in the sexual sphere. They may seem quite decisive in sexual choices, but this is apt to be the result of impulse rather than the carefully thought through decisions that would characterize an NT. SPs can find themselves quickly involved with another, only to find this liaison a burden; then, they might be puzzled as to how to go about getting uninvolved. Confrontation is not likely to seem to be the way to solve this problem; rather, absence and silence are more likely to be the solution of choice. Long, drawn-out courtships are not apt to hold the attention of SPs, oriented as they are by their need for freedom, which includes being able to express emotions as they occur. Expressions of deep emotional commitment directed toward an SP are apt to cause the SP to become restive and to feel trapped. Under pressure, an SP is capable of tactlessness and even brutality, but once the scene is over, may be quite oblivious to any scars marring the relationship. If an SP does not meet another's expectations, he or she is readily willing to "reform," although it usually turns out that the promised new behavior doesn't last long. Generally, SPs tend to have uncritical, happy dispositions. They live so thoroughly in the present that they are not always reliable in meeting the obligations of daily life, but the intention to displease is seldom present. An SP may be as quick to anger as to act, but the anger is likely to pass as quickly as it arises. They can accept positive or negative comments about their behavior or character with perfect ease, not long bothered by either. In and out of the mating relationship, an SP may not bother to sort out priorities, responding to each successive demand with equal energy. A small crisis may be given as much attention as a crisis of great magnitude; a claim for attention from a stranger can be given as much attention as a claim from an intimate. This can lead to some dissatisfaction on the part of a mate. At times the delightfully generous nature of the SP (what is his is yours and what is yours is his to give away if the impulse strikes) troubles mates of differing perspectives.

SPs love to receive and give gifts. Not only is the SP temperament likely to give the extravagant gift, but the SP will especially appreciate having an audience to witness the effects of this exuberant generosity. A mink coat could well appear under the Christmas tree even though there might be only minimum necessities in the closet. SPs often express sexual attraction through bringing gifts to those they want to please. The transaction involved is what is stimulating to the SP; the pleasure of playing Santa Claus in and out of season is what delights him. The receiver's reaction of pleasure and surprise and the reactions of other witnesses are what count for an SP.

Although SPs give an impression of being extremely alert, their realism in accepting whatever exists at the moment can lead them into being oblivious to differences between quality and quantity of relationships. Whoever and whatever happens to be there is likely to be accepted, and in this process the SP may not differentiate between a person, for example, who is capable of great loyalty and a person who is only "passing through." An SP also is, at times, not alert to potential dangers in relationships. This can lead female SPs particularly into involvements which might be unwise. SPs truly do often rush in where angels fear to tread—sexually, socially, and, at times, economically. For an SP, living may be feast or famine. They may be good providers today, but spendthrifts tomorrow. Money, like sex, is to be used and enjoyed. SPs do not tend to attach much priority to saving for a rainy day, sexually or financially, as might an SJ; rather, time, money, and energy might be used to explore the newest restaurant, the newest fashion, the newest companion, the newest car. Buying new gadgets or acquiring new acquaintances to tinker with might well fascinate an SP for hours, until interest is turned elsewhere.

As a homemaker, the SP female tends to find outlets for her hunger for action through arts and crafts. Her home tends to be filled with various projects in various stages of completion. Clutter is acceptable to the SP. She may get heavily involved in gourmet cooking for a time, and then move on to an avid interest in weaving or pottery. Color is likely to be abundant and strong. Plants are apt to be set about the rooms in profusion. Drop-in guests are sure to be welcome almost any time and the SP female is not apt, as would the SJ, to be put off-balance by a less-than-guest-ready home. She is more likely to share cheerfully and freely whatever is there, pushing aside current projects to make seating or eating room. The SP mother is likely to be very much in charge of her children. She is not subject to the notion that she ought to be of service to her children; nor does this mean she is subject to guilt, wondering whether she is doing the "right thing" or whether she did the same thing as other types. She does what seems right at the moment and that is that. More often than not, she expects and gets obedience, although she also allows her children a great deal of autonomy. She cannot be conned by her children and does not allow them to rule her. It is, perhaps, easier for the SP mother to allow others to participate in the raising of her children than it is for other temperments. When her firstborn goes to kindergarten, for example, the SP mother is apt to take it in her stride in a way other types may not.

SPs are usually energetic propagandists for their own personalities, and sexually they promote themselves well, whether extraverts or introverts. They are very likely to obtain the mate of their choice in a whirlwind courtship. If the SP's mate does not project onto the SP unrealistic expectations, the relationship can develop into a satisfactory, active way of life. If the SP is expected to be someone he or she is not, disappointment may be in store for both. Given a reasonable degree of compatibility in sexual rhythm, SPs are not apt to dissolve their relationships with selected mates. Unlike the NF, who is haunted by his lifelong romantic quest for the perfect love, the SP is not inclined to fantasize that another choice would have been all that much different.

The Epimethean (SJ) Mate

Epimethean temperaments (SJs), males and females alike, tend to be more solemn about their sexual activities than do the SPs. Sex is a more serious business. While an SP could use sex to forget his or her troubles, an SJ, particularly a male SJ, would be more likely to use sex to ease fatigue, wanting to be comforted both emotionally and physically. After sexual release has been obtained, the SJ is apt to be most solicitous of the physical comfort and welfare of the other.

While other types might see sex as a mutually pleasing activity, from which both males and females benefit equally, the SJ male is apt to express gratitude to his partner for the sexual experience, communicating the message that something has been done *for* him, that *his* needs have been served, that a favor has been done. The possibility of a mate enjoying the experience equally, or needing the experience equally, is not often conceptualized by him. A female SJ is likely to go along with this position, placing the sexual needs of her mate over any she might have, perhaps seeing sex as a wifely chore rather than a pleasure.

SJs are apt to be faithful to their marriage vows. Males may have sown their wild oats before marrying, but after mating become more interested in establishing a home and a family and devoting their main energies to their jobs. Female SJs probably have had only limited sexual experience before marriage, even in an age of sexual freedom. If such is not the case, it is likely that peer pressures led the female into sexual explorations because it was the "thing to do," because it was "embarrassing to be a 20-year-old virgin."

SJ males and females both may view sex as a service which is to be delivered by the female, performed dutifully and on request, presumably in return for social and economic security. They are not likely to experiment in sexual approaches. The tried-and-true time and place is usually the sexual mode for the SJ mate. The SJ male is likely to express concern for his partner, but neither male nor female SJ may believe that female orgasm is a requisite. Always there is that unexpressed attitude that "nice girls don't." At the same time, when SJ males are in social contact with other males (and selected females)—for example at conventions, hunting trips, and smokers—the SJ male can equal the SP in his command of vivid language and his repertoire of sexual jokes. Female SJs are not, whether with males or females, apt to discuss their sexual experiences.

Sex is clearly understood as a means of reproduction rather than mainly a form of recreation, and both male and female SJs may reflect the attitude that having children, who will bring joy and comfort and who will continue the family line, is expected and desirable. Sex generally is something one does at night, in the bedroom, as quietly as possible, and, after some years of marriage, perhaps as seldom as possible. Although this is less true in our so-called sexually liberated age, the view of sex as recreation is not a perception ordinarily held by most SJs.

The SJ tends to express affection in standard ways, verbalizing expressions of love in ritualistic language, and bringing gifts on appropriate occasions. These gifts have usually intrinsic value as objects and are to be kept and treasured. The transactional ritual is important, not the surprise or audience impression as with an SP. The notion of discussing philosophy, religion, aesthetics, or ethics as a precursor to erotic activities does not make much sense to either the SJ male or female. Sex is sex and philosophy is philosophy. The notion of the "grand passion" is likely to mystify an SJ mate, who may enjoy the fantasy, but who soon wants to get on with the business of living. For an SJ, courting is something one does before vows are taken. Once the bargain is sealed, they are prepared to give priority to getting ahead in business, establishing a home and family, making a circle of friends and establishing social connections. Sexual routines are apt to be established early in marriage and observed throughout life. The unexpected and unusual are probably not a part of the basic sexual repertoire of the SJ. A male SJ may, perhaps, explore other relationships outside the framework of his marriage, but only if particularly dissatisfied at home.

SJ mates may have some difficulty understanding the emotional needs of other types, particularly the NFs and NTs, where transactions outside the bedroom loom vital as a precursor to sexual response. An SJ could give way to a temper tantrum, to biting sarcasm, scolding, criticizing, the works—and then expect a mate to separate these behaviors from the sexual relationship. He or she may not understand the possible impact on sex which is clear to other types. This mate believes that, as long as he or she cares for the spouse and takes the proper responsibility for the spouse's health and welfare, the constructive "lessons" which he or she offers to correct the mate should not inhibit the other's affection.

SJs may be possessive about their family—often referring to "their wife," "their children," "their car," —and possessions can assume large proportions, claiming much interest and attention. These possessions are to be dutifully serviced and cared for, to be held and cherished, and never wasted in frivolity. SJs tend to be careful with money and are likely to budget carefully, planning well for the future, at times at the expense of much sacrifice in the present. Insurance policies, savings accounts, bonds, and the like make sense to the SJ, who understands their value. Also understood is the utilitarian value of property, tools, cars, clothes, and the like. Possessions should be functional and without undue ostentation. Goods should be used up, worn out, and then not thrown away, but donated to a charitable agency. "Waste not, want not" is understood and honored as a motto by the SJs. Property is likely to be well tended and the expectation of SJs is that those around them will do likewise, including their neighbors and colleagues at work.

For a female SJ, especially one who is introverted, home may be a focal point, to the exclusion of all else. Devotion to husband and children, the preparation of meals, keeping a clean and orderly house may take all her time and become her reason for living. At midlife, when the children have left home, this can occasion a major crisis. For the male SJ, retirement can bring about the same trauma; his job is often to the male SJ what the home and family are to the female SJ. Both may worry about loved ones when they are away from home and will tend to make frequent contact by telephone. SJs sometimes catastrophize and suffer with worry about unlikely calamities.

Frequent or rapid changes in home environment or rituals or frequent changes in work procedures or personnel are not welcomed by the SJ. Individual deviations from the traditional, accepted ways of behaving on the part of family members are not encouraged by an SJ parent. They have a sure sense of what is Good and Right and they do not hesitate to impose this on their mates and children. In truth, the SJ sees this imposition of standards as his duty. He requires things and people, procedures and products, to be consistent and stable, appropriately in harmony with traditional ways.

The past has a strong press for SJs. They have a sense of family history, and value stories and information about their families. They tend to entertain relatives, to keep in touch with the extended family circle, to honor the traditional rituals such as the Thanksgiving turkey and the Easter dinner. Church-related activities may often occupy the SJ's free time, as might community-based, organized activities, both charitable and social. An SJ mate is likely to belong to the organized civic groups of the community, and probably will be knowledgeable of the status hierarchy and pecking orders in those groups.

Time is apt to be structured by the SJ around productive activities, which have a clearly-defined task as the focal point. Wasting time in frivolity tends to be difficult for the SJ. For example, reading a newspaper is apt to have more appeal than would reading novels. SJs value time as a thing to be used, not to be wasted. They tend to be punctual and expect their mates to be also; they like to make and keep schedules for themselves and sometimes even their mates and children. The SJ mate wants social events to proceed in a preplanned, orderly manner, with pleasant but not uproarious hilarity. Generally, SJ mates do not mind members of their family (and others) making demands on their time, as long as the demand is for sensible reasons.

As mates, SJs seldom complain of boredom. They are content to live on an even keel, and are happy keeping within established routines. They may enjoy eating out at the same restaurant, say, every Friday evening. They may be willing to visit the same vacation spot year after year, performing the same recreational activities with the same people in the same place.

The SJ mate is apt to communicate an attitude of nurturance as well as an attitude of being critical. In the language of Transactional Analysis, they come from both the Critical and the Nurturing Parent ego states. For the SJ mate, caring for mate or children means having the responsibility to see to it that the other knows the Right Thing to do and the Right Way to do it, which means the ways learned from parents and tradition. Spontaneity in the SJ tends to be suppressed, although when fatigued or under stress, the SJ can erupt into a temper tantrum, use biting sarcasm, or even, in rare instances, attempt to make the point through violence.

SJs' need to be of service and to belong to established institutions make them faithful, steady, responsible, reliable mates who are predictable, loyal, dependable, and usually faithful. They are not likely to abandon their families at midlife or to squander lifelong savings in impulsive spending sprees. They make excellent homemakers, and belong in outstanding supportive ways in the institutions of the community—the home, the church, the government, and civic institutions—truly the pillars who hold up society.

The Promethean (NT) Mate

The mate of Promethean NT may well believe that the NT is quite oblivious to his welfare, and may see him as unaware of daily events which make up the stream of homely family life. The mate of an NT may long for more frequently verbalized expressions of affection and concern on the part of the NT. The NT, on the other hand, would probably be amazed that his or her way of relating and loving is experienced by the mate as aloof or uncaring.

NTs do seem rather cold and unemotional to other temperaments. They tend to control and hide their emotions behind an immobile facial stance, with only the eyes transmitting depth of reaction. A public display of emotion or affection is particularly repugnant to an NT.

Because of the NT's distaste for stating the obvious or being redundant, the NT is apt to verbalize expressions of affection rather infrequently. To other types this seems cold and miserly, and they often are hurt by the withholding. To the NT, stating what is already established is raising doubt where there is none. The commitment has been made, the position has been taken. And this commitment stands until notified. Therefore, clearly, it is unnecessary and inappropriate to restate the established and obvious.

In establishing sexual relationships NTs are not likely to give in to impulse, getting involved on a spur-of-the-moment basis. Rather they are likely to think through relationships carefully, giving prolonged consideration to projections. Once the matter is thought through, the NT is ready to proceed with investing in the relationship. If it does not work out, the NT is likely to shrug his or her shoulders and turn away, perhaps with only mild regrets. Once an NT has made a decision, however, a change of heart is not likely to occur on his or her part, provided, of course, that a response has been forthcoming from the recipient. And, in all likelihood, the NT will develop the relationship as he or she has conceived it. If the situation calls for a long-term commitment, a long-term commitment is made. If the situation calls for a short-term involvement, a short-term investment is made. A peculiar dynamic is here likely to occur: When the NT's intent is a long-term commitment, this fact is not likely to be verbalized, since for the NT, this intent is obvious. But if the relationship is to be short-term, this fact is likely to be verbalized, just in case it is not obvious. NTs are likely to honor a personal commitment once made, even though the relationship was not consummated as satisfactorily as anticipated. Nor is the NT likely to verbalize any disappointment or dissatisfaction if such is the case.

The NT mate is not apt to hold mates responsible for discord; usually the burden of doing whatever needs to be done will be seen by NTs as their own responsibility. The NTs, as a group, do not thrive on conflict at a personal level. They do enjoy intellectual dispute, but quarreling on an emotional level is something NTs find destructive; generally an NT will walk away from this kind of interaction.

NTs often have a curious amorality related to the generally-accepted standards of sexual behaviors. The rules of society have little pressure for NTs, but their own idiosyncratic standards of conduct do. These usually have been carefully considered, and are followed with or without society's approval.

The sexual ethics of an NT are generally his own; they may or may not conform to the general mores of sexual behavior current in any given time.

Establishing a sexual or social relationship with an NT, especially introverted NTs, usually requires more investment of time and energy than with other types. This is especially in contrast with SPs, who are more ready to establish relationships. Often, types who are not NTs are unwilling to invest the time and energy required to relate to an NT. Even the extraverted NTs, although apparently easy to get to know, are actually fairly difficult to understand, for the personality structure of an NT is characteristically complex and, at times, even convoluted. Friends and mates of NTs repeatedly express surprise at a facet of character they find in the NT, one that had not been apparent previously.

Female NTs, in particular, are apt to have their sexuality overlaid with intellectualism. Their preference for the logical can obscure expressions of their feelings, which may or may not be well developed. If not, the NT female may have difficulty with orgasmic responses unless her partner takes the time, makes the effort, and understands the necessity of making a sexual approach through mutual exploration of intellectual concepts. It is unlikely that an NT female will be sexually stimulated by a partner who is not her intellectual equal. Male NTs have a somewhat different expectation concerning intellectual equality. The preference here is for equality at most and some—but not too much—inferiority at best. Obviously, this places the intellectually-gifted female in a position of limited appropriate NT choices.

In any event, both female and male NTs can bring to a sexual relationship a willingness to explore possibilities of erotic arousal. If they have so marked it out as one of their areas of competency, NTs can be quite expert in sexual technology. They are very apt to possess skill in both the physical and psychological logistics involved in sexual intercourse, and to understand well the necessity for this relationship to be based on a wide variety of common interests outside the bedroom. Unlike the NF, who might consider it unromantic to study carefully scientific treatises on sexuality (e.g., Masters and Johnson, 1966), NTs would be likely to do so, finding it relatively easy to translate these objective findings into creative sexual, sensual behavior.

Outside the bedroom, NTs seem to have more difficulty than other types in engaging in play. They are, on the whole, apt to be rather serious, finding it amusing to dialogue at what they might call "the seventh plane of irreality," a pastime which other types are apt to find rather dull. For the NT, the amusing and humorous is usually subtle and, more often than not, based on a play on words. They especially enjoy humor which contains an unexpected double meaning, but—unlike the SPs and, at times, the SJs—they do not enjoy ribald sexual stories or practical jokes and find the recounting of both somewhat offensive, especially in mixed company.

A few deep relationships are the usual pattern of an NT's emotional history; promiscuity is typically regarded with distaste. The experience of partner swapping is apt to repel an NT, who would, in all probability, find this experience psychologically scarring. The NT mate is not likely to discuss past personal involvements with a mate or with others and almost never discusses a mate with friends.

Sensuality begins for an NT in the imagination, as it does for an NF; both types are capable of nuances of appreciation of the erotic which those with S preferences might find irrelevant or even unfathomable. As a sexual partner, an NT can be highly creative, imaginative, and exciting. The degree of satisfaction for an NT in a relationship will be correlated with the depth of the relationship. Still, mere sexual release is sometimes seen as necessary, particularly if sexual tensions are getting in the way of important work. In that event, the tension is cared for with dispatch and as conveniently as possible.

NTs tend to be relatively uninterested in acquiring wealth and as mates, therefore, tend to be satisfied with modest comfort. Possession as an end in itself seems not to motivate NTs; rather, enjoyment in the beauty of an object, pleasures of design and building, pleasure in elegant functioning in possessions all motivate an NT. A vintage car, a classic airplane, an elegant art object, owned or not, give pleasure to an NT. This characteristic NT trait—enjoying without needing to possess —often causes mates who do not share this detachment some impatience. The NT's usual disinterest in acquiring material wealth beyond that necessary for reasonable security and comfort can also provide some dissonance in the mating relationship. Although an NT periodically is inspired to acquire wealth, this urge seldom lasts long enough to acquire that fortune. The NT's attention quickly turns once again to the theoretical, and the momentary interest in becoming wealthy dissipates—only to return from time to time with the same result.

NTs seldom, however, lose interest in owning books and knowledge; these hold their interest year after year, and an NT's home is likely to be well-lined with books. In fact, the non-NT mate of an NT often perceives the NT as directing exclusive attention to the world of theory and techniques, at the expense of giving sufficient attention to the mate. Although NTs may seem oblivious to the home life going about them, they usually show interest when these events are brought to attention. NTs are somewhat vague about social time, especially the introverted NTs, and may be unaware, unless reminded, what hour, day, date, or season it is. This can lead to difficulty in the mating relationship when the mate is a type to whom anniversaries, birthdays, and the like are important.

Both NTs and introverted NFs tend to develop intimate relationships rather slowly; intellectual development seems to proceed at a faster rate than does social development. For both NTs and NFs, communications sent through the physical relationship are apt to become more and more complex over time, with their approaches to the sexual encounter threaded with subtleties and symbolism. The sexual act is usually given meaning beyond mere release from sexual tension. Sexual contact for the introverted NT may be less frequent than for the extraverted NT. Routines of daily living, such as working—especially if these daily routines are fraught with conflict—can be quite repressive to the emotional and sexual readiness of the NT, especially the introverted NT (as well as the introverted NF). NTs may engage in the sex act as a profound expression of love, or, at the opposite extreme, as an act of self-humiliation and self-denigration, resulting in disgust for self.

NTs usually take family responsibilities seriously, particularly their own responsibility to members of their family, including their parents. They are, however, often perceived by members of the family as having more psychological distance between themselves and others than do other types. The NT tends not to "own" the behaviors (or body) of his mate as might other types. The errors of others, whether family members or not, are not the NT's errors, and are handled objectively. The NT's own errors are those which are inexcusable, and unforgivable. Parenting is usually a pleasure, therefore, for an NT,

Introducing the new book by
Dr. David Keirsey

Portraits of
Temperament

Portraits of Temperament

By Dr. David Keirsey

In this, his most recent book, Dr. Keirsey has produced a scholarly work, yet one that glows with the warmth of his years of observing and helping people. It includes:

- An historic overview of the ancient quadratic theory of temperament, examining and synthesizing the contributions of Hippocrates, Paracelsus, Adickes, Spränger, Kretschmer, Fromm, Cassirer, Goldstein, and Myers to the understanding of human behavior.

- Comprehensive portraits of eight temperament types, examining intellectual, volitional, emotional, and situational traits, as well as four negative tactics employed in times of deep stress.

- The "Person Classifier," a quick test of temperament.

- Original drawings by Gary Palmatier, whimsically portraying the foibles and virtues of the various character types.

To order your copy, complete and return this form:

☐ I would like to order _____ copies of *Portraits of Temperament* at $9.95 each, plus applicable charges for shipping and sales tax.

NAME _____

COMPANY OR AFFILIATION _____

MAILING ADDRESS _____

CITY _____

STATE _____ ZIP _____

AREA CODE _____ TELEPHONE _____

NUMBER OF COPIES _____ **X $9.95** _____

6% SALES TAX (Calif. residents only) _____

$2.00 SHIPPING (Up to 5 copies) _____

Enclose this order form   **TOTAL** _____
with your check or
money order, and mail to: **Prometheus Nemesis Book Company**
                     Post Office Box 2748
                     Del Mar, CA 92014

who seems to watch the growth of children (and a mate!) with joy but as somewhat of a bystander.

The Apollonian (NF) Mate

If ever a person died for love, it was sure to have been an Apollonian (NF). Romeo and Juliet, both NFs, could not face the prospect of life without each other and so chose to die in a way which was symbolic of their single-minded and eternal commitment to each other. Other famous lovers, such as Heloise and Abelard, the Brownings, Antony and Cleopatra, Beth the landlord's daughter and her highwayman, all created a work of art in their courtships. This is not surprising, since one of the arts at which the NF is skilled is that of creating the romantic relationship. In fact, the term *sex* would seem somehow crude when used in discussing the NF; *love* better captures their appreciation of the physical relationship. Both the NF female and male respond to their mates with sympathy, tenderness, and frequent, passionate expressions of love, both verbal and nonverbal. Possessing facility with language, NFs are able to express nuances of emotions that may escape other types. NFs are not afraid of using poetry, music, and quotations to enhance their courting relationships; the romantic developments in the lives of NFs thrive on receiving these tokens of affection and dedication. NFs have a flair for dramatizing their courtships, making each the perfect love. A storybook flavor permeates their courtship behavior. The NF suitor is certain he will live happily ever after, and transmits this certainty to the object of romantic pursuit. The ideal of the perfect love that will never die motivates the NFs in their search for a partner who can relate *spiritually* as well as physically. They strive to be authentic lovers, capable of sustaining deep intimacy. Seeing their identity as mate is a major part of their personality.

Just as the possible rather than the actual lures NFs in other parts of their lives, so do the possibilities in relationships inspire them. When a relationship is being established, the recipient of the NF's attention is apt to be the center of his world. The pursuit is given almost single-minded attention and no effort is spared in the wooing. An undying love is in the offing, and once the physical relationship is consummated (for a male NF) or the words of love spoken (for a female NF) the relationship will be blessed with romantic bliss. Both NF males and females are likely to be blind to any flaws in their beloved in the early stages of a romance. Life will be happy ever after (although the details of this happy ever after are usually not explored in depth). The romantic gesture and the idealization of the relationship are characteristic of the courting behaviors of the NF. The dream is sometimes preferred to reality. At times, the fantasy of the sexual encounter cannot survive the reality of consummation, especially for the male NF.

It appears female NFs are more able to sustain the depth of romanticism involved with a relationship longer than male NFs. Once the physical side of the relationship is acted out, the male NF can lose interest and turn to another fantasy. In a Quixotic way, he seems to be compelled to pursue the impossible dream of a larger-than-life, giant-screen goddess who will be madonna, mistress, lover, whore, mother, daughter, and wife. His real-life mate is not always able to measure up. The NF male, in hot pursuit, is likely to express a love which is undying but which can vanish all too soon in the harsh light of the morning after. The female NF does not demonstrate this characteristic; rather, she is likely to increase her dedication after the physical relationship is consummated. She becomes more and more devoted, continuing to romanticize the relationship and believe in its perfection, to give small transactions profound significance, to dramatize the interactions with her mate, to be willing to die for love. She seems seldom disappointed in the sexual act; orgasmic response on her part is seen as inconsequential compared to the pleasure of giving pleasure to her mate. What matters is that *he* is fulfilled and satisfied. For the male NF, ennui can set in as a result of familiarity; for the female NF, this is not as likely to happen. The SP can say, and mean, with Dorothy Parker, "I'll be true as long as you, and not a moment after . . ."; the female NF is more likely to have as a part of her mating identity the image of falling in love once and for a lifetime. The fact that this does not always work out does not negate the possibility of the dream coming true. Fortunately, both male and female NFs have a capacity for deep affection and caring over and above sexual expression, and out of this capacity can grow a lasting, satisfactory relationship.

In the last decade or so a curious phenomenon has occurred, perhaps arising from the female NFs characteristic of maintaining her romantic dream even in the face of a contradictory reality. The group that spearheaded the sexual revolution were the female NFs. It has been the female NFs who have said **NO** to the double sexual (and other) standards. It has been the female NFs who have been most militant in demanding equal orgasmic rights. It has been the female NFs who have decided that they are not sure they will be true, even as long as their male partners. Somehow female NFs have decided that their vision of a better, more satisfactory mating relationship *can* be actualized. They seem willing, in ever growing numbers, to take whatever risks are necessary to find that relationship, either in or out of a legal contract. In fact, more and more the NF females seem reluctant to tie themselves down to a legal arrangement, putting off the urgings of their housemates, asking that both wait until she is sure she is doing the right thing. More and more NF females seem to be willing to bear their children outside a legal arrangement and to raise them alone. This is not to say that other types are not also involved in this movement, but it is the NFs, along with a limited number of NT females, who provide the vanguard of the revolution. Instead of being ready and willing to die for love, the current NF female seems to be willing to live for the possibility of a better way of relating to males.

Both male and female NFs are likely to be charming mates, and a source of continuing warmth, support, and understanding. They are usually ready to lend sympathy to a mate when the outside world turns hostile and are not apt to use that moment to point out the errors of a mate's ways, something which other types might be tempted to do. The NFs are generally skilled socially, and people usually feel wanted and well-hosted in their homes. They often are experts in the arts of appreciation, especially in the area of personal characteristics, and they are apt to be generous in expressing these appreciations to their mate. It is probably the NF who is the most loving, dedicated, affectionate, appreciative mate, and is unstinting in the expression of these emotions, both to mate and to children. Their conversations, particularly those of extraverted NFs, are apt to be sprinkled with terms of endearment, especially in private. The NF can be as extravagant as an SP when expressing love through the media of gifts, but the NF is more than likely to present the gift in private, and select with extraordinary care something with special or even symbolic meaning. NFs, both male and female, usually remember birthdays, anniversaries, and the like without being prompted, or at most needing only a hint, If, in turn, the NFs' milestones are not heeded, they are deeply hurt, as deeply as they are appreciative when theirs are noticed.

Although NFs, especially the male NF, become restless if

others (including mates, children, or parents) are dependent, NFs have in their own personalities characteristics that promote this dependency. They pride themselves on being sensitive to others and caring about them. It is almost impossible for NFs to be unaware of others' psychological needs. Yet the NF becomes restless when these ties begin to bind, as they do when the amount of emotional input becomes a psychological overload for the NF. At this point the NF can seem cruel, insisting unexpectedly that the other "stand on his own two feet." This shift in attitude is usually abrupt and the person who heretofore believed that he was very special in the eyes of the NF now finds himself apparently rejected. The NF does not mean to be unkind; he or she is simply disconnecting a relationship which can no longer be handled—in spite of the reality that the NF created this dependent relationship through expressions of empathy and unique understanding. Building empathic relationships is second nature to this temperament, a master of the art of intimacy. But as those around the NF want more and more attention, more and more expressions of this unusual appreciation, more and more signals of deep affection, the NF mate becomes restless and resentful of pressures to deliver what had seemed promised: the ideal love, the perfect friendship, complete understanding, and total acceptance.

The NF is vulnerable to this kind of misunderstanding because of his extraordinary capabilities to introject. He can take into himself the point of view, the emotions, and the psychological state of another so completely that the other feels totally received. The other person may not realize that the NF does this in most relationships, and may be hurt on discovering that he is not valued as uniquely as he first thought. When the NF leaves each person, the NF no longer resonates to that person, but relates to the person now present. Understandably, this can cause some difficulty in the mating relationship for mates who want this characteristic to be exercised more exclusively; the NF may not know how not to respond to the emotional demands of others.

After the honeymoon is over, the mate of an NF can feel let down when the reality of living with the NF may be in some contrast with what was anticipated. The discovery by the mate that the NF is, after all, less than perfect often results in feelings of resentment ill-deserved by the NF, but nonetheless real. NF mates themselves are in a dilemma. They are caught up in the romanticized expectations of the psychological and sexual experience generated in their own perceptions and encouraged by others. The fantasy is more than likely to be exaggerated by both the NF and the mate, and it is a common experience for NFs to express that anticipation was more delightful than consummation. The actual sexual act, in particular, can be less than anticipated, for, more often than not, the NF's romantic nature will not allow him or her to acquire sexual expertise through study. Rather they see themselves as somehow supposed to know the appropriate loving and tender approach intuitively. Consulting scientific studies is seen as cold and objective and somehow destructive. Thus, the actual sexual relationship may be a letdown initially and a disappointment to both partners until both acquire the necessary competency.

Although NFs are almost hypersensitive to the moods of their mates, especially if they are also introverts, they may not always be willing to deal positively with the other's emotional reactions. NFs report that they find their own emotional circuits often so overloaded with their own concerns that they cannot deal with the emotional experiences of others who are especially close to them, particularly when experiences involve conflict and hurt. Thus, the mates of NFs can see their mates responding to relative strangers with a degree of warmth and acceptance that may not be available to them.

As parents, NFs are sensitive to the viewpoint of their children, sometimes to the point of siding with them in a way which reinforces the youngsters' antisocial, self-defeating behaviors. An NF parent, for example, can rush to rescue a child from consequences of his wrongdoing and, in the process, not permit the child to develop necessary skills which he needs to deal with the realities of a less protective world.

NF mates may have difficulty detaching themselves from their jobs or social demands in order to preserve time for family. In this the NF is like the SP. They have some difficulty saying *no* to attractive offers and thus may neglect priorities. Whoever is there and demanding time gets it, even though others may be waiting elsewhere.

A danger an NF faces in his intimate relationships is that he will move from relationship to relationship rather than making the necessary effort to develop those already existing. The NF's tendency to experience anticipation as more attractive than consummation can cause him to use his energies pursuing the dream at the expense of what is actually available. Once an NF believes that he or she knows all there is to know about another, disinterest sets in; restlessness and a sense of boredom develop. NFs, as do other types, want a certain amount of variety and change in their lives. Other types, however, may seek this through intellectual pursuits, adjustment of living routines, vacations, new activities. The NF is most vulnerable to seeking this through searching out new relationships, more often than not at the expense of deepening those already existing.

A quality an NF can bring to intimate relationships is an extraordinary sensitivity and ability to communicate emotionally. In the affective areas the NF is without equal. No other type is as empathic to others as is the NF. As mates they can be a source of warmth, appreciation, and support which other types have difficulty emulating.

IV
TEMPERAMENT
IN
CHILDREN

The Pygmalion Project, so visible in mating, goes underground in parenting. A child, after all, is *supposed* to be different from an adult. It is only *later* that our offspring must end up a chip off the old block. But throughout childhood this is quite unconsciously reinforced. The parental focus is on what the child does, not on how he experiences what he does, and on how he is experienced by others, not on how he experiences himself. The unwitting assumption is that everybody who does the same thing experiences the same thing. So the issue is action, not experience.

If they are of radically different temperaments, two children doing precisely the same thing will have radically different experiences. And the adult who presides over these two experiences, whether parent or teacher, who remembers "what it was like when I was a child," is usually dead wrong in attributing a like experience to his two charges. *Acting* on the unwitting assumption of likeness, this well meaning adult is very likely to disconfirm and remain impervious to the children's perspectives. On occasion, the ever-benevolent adult will, based upon attribution and imperviousness, even intrude into the private space of the child as if the child were robotic. So there we have the four horsemen (of the Apocalypse of childhood): not pestilence, famine, etc., but attribution, intrusion, imperviousness, and disconfirmation, loosed by the benevolence of the parental other on the unconscious assumption of likeness.

Nature will no more allow a child to come into this world temperamentally formless than she would allow a snowflake to be
asymmetrical. Children are different from each other from the
beginning, and no amount of preachment or "conditioning,"
or trauma for that matter, will diminish that difference.

So let us consider the problem posed by this ubiquitous difference. Here is a parental other, an ISTJ, "trustee" father,
an ESFP, "entertainer" mother, with one INFP "monastic,"
one ISTP "artisan" and two ESFJ "vendors" as offspring:

	Male	Female
Parent	ISTJ	ESFP
		INFP
Offspring	ISTP	ESFJ
		ESFJ

Compound the problem, if you will, by making ISTJ father a
person of great physical strength, endurance, and athletic
prowess—which he never used, being a CPA. His ISTP son is
small-boned, like mother, slender, poorly muscled, average in
intellectual ability. Mother was once a chorus girl. Pretty, effervescent, sparkling.

Both parents "understand" the two ESFJ girls "perfectly," or
so they would have it. The INFP girl is not pretty, is the young-
est, is "understood" as "having trouble becoming one of the
family." Her brightness is completely missed. The ISTP boy
"just hasn't buckled down yet." (But he doesn't dig the
"buckle.") The problem would seem to be somewhat complex.
For the moment at least we ought to admit to being at a loss
for solutions.

Now, let us look at the teacher's dilemma. Here is a fourth
grade ISFJ "conservator," female teacher with a class of 32
splendidly different boys and girls—12 SJs, 12 SPs, 4 NTs, and
4 NFs. For convenience, let us assume that our conserving
teacher seats the children in rows and columns (SJ teachers
typically find appeal in the traditional seating arrangement).
For further convenience, let like be seated with like:

ESFJ	ESFJ	ESFP	ESFP	ENTP	INTP
ESFJ	ESFJ	ESFP	ESFP	ENTJ	
ESFJ	ESTJ	ESFP	ESTP	ENTJ	
ESTJ	ISFJ	ESTP	ISFP	ENFP	
ESTJ	ISTJ	ESTP	ISFP	ENFP	
ESTJ	ISTJ	ESTP	ISTP	ENFJ	INFJ

Now if this particular teacher sees her job as seeing to it that all of the children do their work neatly, diligently, and on time so that they will "develop good study habits" and eventually become "dependable, helpful, honest, and responsible citizens, ready, willing, and able to do their part," then she has an SJ version of what school is for; she will set out to *get the children to want* those things coveted by SJs. The children are regarded as all the same in this. True, some of them may not yet *realize* that they want obligation and belonging, but then that is the teacher's job to *bring them* to this increasing realization. Any messages to the contrary from the 20 children who don't get their jollies from the SJ corner are instantly (albeit unconsciously) *disqualified*, i.e., are met with attribution, or imperviousness, or disconfirmation, or even intrusion.

That's if she doesn't realize that many of the children are incredibly different from her and from each other. But suppose she has come to realize this ubiquitous and unchanging difference? What then? Is she to approach these children differently? Is she to give up her otherwise unquestioned perspectives on the very purpose of school? Must instructional *tactics* differ for different temperaments? Must instructional *content* differ for different temperaments? Is she, for instance, wise or foolish if she poses the same assignments, explanations, and questions for those five ESFJs in the front rows as she does for that lonely INTP in the back row?

These questions arise with the temperament hypothesis. If the hypothesis is abandoned or ignored, then we might suppose the teacher to be free to continue treating everybody as if they were destined to emulate her. But once she has embraced the hypothesis, she finds it a fatal embrace; fatal, that is, to all beliefs about the process and product of instruction. These now must be abandoned and then retrieved, one by one, only if they can be used in the service of fostering the emergence and development of each child's unique style of living. We sure as hell don't need 32 ISFJs even if it were possible to metamorphize them out of the 32 children that aren't that way. That, of course, could be said for any type. The teacher plainly has a very difficult problem. Solutions, if any, will be hard to come by. But *facing* the problem, even without solutions, is infinitely better than, for lack of solution, pretending the problem doesn't exist and consequently disqualifying almost all the children's messages, to their detriment.

The teacher is said to act *in loco parentis*—in place of the parent—and surely has the same job as parent. So nothing is lost and there may be some gain in thinking of the teacher as the parental other along with the father, mother, grandmother, and so on.

What is the parental other to do in the face of the complexity ushered in by the notion of basic differences in children? First, of course, the parenting individual must acquaint himself or herself with the nature of those temperamental variations. Then and only then can the question be asked upon each encounter, "What *kind* of person am I encountering, and on that basis what sort of messages from me will define the relationship in a facilitative and productive way?" True, the necessity of posing this question to ourselves makes all of our relationships with children problematic and, at first glance, lacking in spontaneity. But a closer look shows us that this question makes for spontaneity rather than limits it, and it is the previous, and hopefully abandoned, perspective—"my children are (underneath) just like me"—which precludes spontaneity in the relationship.

So to the familiarization.

First, let us look at the four differences posited by Jung—Introversion vs Extraversion, Sensation vs Intuition, Thinking vs Feeling, and Judgment vs Perception—as these differences show up in children's behavior. Even though the pattern of behavior probably comes from temperament, rather than Jung's "preferences," there is some utility in making observations having these in mind. Following this we can look at the four temperaments as they manifest themselves in childhood. Finally, we can examine the four temperaments as they affect teaching.

"Extraversion" vs "Introversion"

Observation: *Does the child show hesitation in approaching unfamiliar visitor, teacher, or game or does the child approach a visitor, teacher, or game quickly and actively without apparent reserve?*

The introverted child is likely to hold back when faced with something or someone unfamiliar, while the extraverted child is more likely to approach the situation without hesitation. The introverted child tends to be shy, quiet, and less intrusive than is the extraverted child. The introverted child is apt to be slower in responsiveness, musing over an idea or object, seeming to absorb its qualities before communicating a reaction. Thus, at times, the introverted child may seem less intellectually capable than he actually is. The introverted child is inclined to develop his habits more slowly than does the extraverted child, the introvert reserves from "public view" those aspects of his temperament which are in process of development. What is presented to the "public" are those qualities already developed—the feelings and beliefs of the introvert's yesterday. His "growing edge" is not available to his teachers, parents, or friends. Thus, as with the adult introvert, the introverted child can be a puzzle to those around him. Only too often he is judged "stubborn" by well-meaning adults, because the introverted child insists on holding back his responses until he has rehearsed internally.

Wickes (1968), a Jungian disciple, cautioned that the introverted child is particularly vulnerable to damage if asked to behave as an extravert. Unfortunately, it is the introverted child which *is* most often misunderstood and pressured to change. His reticence in dealing with others, his tendency to be retiring and shy, his slow development of social skills, his tendency to drop his head and put his fingers in his mouth before strangers, his fright when "swooped down upon" by an adult, his slowness to volunteer in the classroom, his hesitation in sharing the products of his mind and hands with others, his need for privacy, are all behaviors which parents and teachers may attempt to correct, and in the process, communicate to the introverted child that his natural, retiring, introverted ways are wrong.

The extraverted child, by way of contrast, is usually better understood and relates well and easily to others. He is at home in the social environment and tends to be responsive, expressive, and enthusiastic. The extraverted child is usually ready to enter into group activities, to accept the ideas of others, without having to "warm up." The extraverted child can adjust well if a family moves, quickly finds new friends in the neighborhood and in school, and moves quickly into play. Seldom is the extravert the isolate which the introvert may be. The extraverted child can tolerate negative contacts better than can the introvert, if necessary provoking ridicule and criticism rather than suffer neglect from significant adults. The extraverted child usually is in line with public opinion and is on the side of the majority on almost any issue which arises. The extraverted child tends to approach new situations quickly, to verbalize quickly, and to act quickly. He tends to have a number of relationships, while the introverted child may develop relatively few relationships. The extraverted child often appears eager where the introverted child appears reluctant. The extravert exhibits a certainty in approaching the new or the unfamiliar where the introvert seems to have a more cautious, reluctant approach—reacting as if the new or unfamiliar presented some sort of danger. Since extraverts exceed introverts roughly 3 to 1, the extraverted child gets considerably more confirmation of his behavior and attitude, both from adults and children, than does the introvert. In consequence, the extravert grows up with fewer doubts about himself than does the introvert.

"Sensation" vs "Intuition"

Observation: *Does the child daydream frequently and seem hungry for fantastic tales, even wanting them repeated over and over, or is the child more bent on action, getting involved in games and liking more factual stories?*

The intuitive or N child is apt to ask for a repetition of stories, whether read from a book or told over and over, and he is apt to want to hear stories of fantasy and metaphor. The sensation or S child is likely to enjoy the sequential adventure story about the familiar and factual, wanting the story to have action and to make sense. The S child likes stories with a large amount of detail and usually prefers a new to an oft-repeated tale. The S child is likely to be found engaged in playing games, or some type of other activity, abandoning storytime for action.

Only the extreme intuitives (Ns) can be spotted in their early years. The moderately intuitive tend to be concrete in their behavior and outlook and appear very similar to the moderately sensory children (Ss). This results in there seeming to be deceptively few N children in the elementary school classroom. In the adult population, as pointed out in Chapter 1, Ss outnumber Ns three to one; thus, even if every N were identified, the ratio is unbalanced. Compounding this imbalance, the slow surfacing of the N characteristic in children makes there seem to be very, very few with this preference, and so the extreme intuitive, especially the introverted feeling intuitive, is subject to feeling like an ugly duckling.

The N child is apt to anticipate future events more than does the S child. Also, if a promise is made to an N child, breaking that promise can be a tragic occurrence, where the S child might take the change of plans in stride. The child with the N preference may be difficult to handle. He always seems to have a core of "being his own person" which adults sometimes find objectionable and offensive. Because the N child is pulled toward the future and the possible, he may seem uninvolved and inattentive to the present. When the present is a classroom lesson or parental instruction, the N child can find himself in difficulty. He may seem opinionated to others, the NT in particular, and he often is very certain that he *knows*; at the same time, he cannot justify his convictions to others' satisfaction when questioned. The N child, therefore, can find himself accused of willful guessing and attempting to have knowledge which is not his.

In his friendships, the N child may display passionate devotion, even develop "crushes" that may be inappropriate and yet which may provoke the N child's deepest trust and emotional investment. If the N child's trust is violated, he is apt to suffer deeply. And if the N child is motivated by negative feelings, such as a thirst for revenge, he can put his finger on his victim's most vulnerable spot. Thus a hated teacher (and the N child can hate passionately!) can find himself embarrassed and humiliated by an N child, yet confused and helpless to deal with the situation—or with the N child—in any rational way. The N child can also place his teacher on an impossible pedestal which allows for no human frailty, and the object of this adoration can only endure the discomfort, hoping that the admiration will evolve into a more reasonable relationship. Both teachers and parents of N children, particularly the introverted N children, have in their care an extremely vulnerable self-conception; consequently, these adults are often uneasy in their dealings with this type of child. For example, the N child may produce imaginative creations of extraordinary quality and may be, in good faith, accused of copying by the well-meaning adult. If this misfortune occurs, the N child may suffer a stoppage in his creative processes, and can suffer considerable damage to his self-esteem. When the N child is engaged in chores or lessons, he may lapse into trances, causing his mentors to correct or even nag at him for dawdling.

S types of teachers, as well as S parents, may be bewildered by the N child and may find the S child far easier to understand and to work with. Where the N child might be daydreaming away the hours, the S child is apt to be relating to the world about him. He shines in the world of action. When a visitor comes to the home, for example, the S child is likely to choose just the right moment to give a small attention to mother—a caress or some other delightful performance. In the classroom, the S child tends to be in tune with the realities of the environment. He approaches his world mainly through relating to what and who is about him, and, generally, gives great power to those things and people. The S child responds to details, noting vividness and variety of details. He is apt to enjoy coloring books, for example, and to pay attention to the details of workbooks. Occasionally the N child is lucky enough to be assigned to a teacher who understands his particular characteristics; he can then do quite well in school. When an S child is assigned to a schoolroom, he usually finds a teacher who can relate to his ways. The S child frequently "connects" to others through an object, often a toy or a lesson produced in class. An S child may manipulate objects actively and contentedly for a period of time, but seldom does he get that far away look in his eyes as does the N child. Toys, for an S child, are more likely to retain their character. A truck remains a truck, to be used to move dirt, or run up and down a road. For the N child the truck might well be turned into a submarine or a deep sea monster, animated with the capacity to fly.

Teachers, as well as parents, may be bewildered by differences they do not understand. Comprehending the peculiarities of both the N child and the S child by significant adults can be vital to the welfare of both N and S children. It is, however, the N child who is most likely to be the one who seems "different" in an unacceptable way.

"Thinking" vs "Feeling"

Observation: *When asked to obey in a situation he does not quite understand, does the child tend to ask for reasons or does the child tend to seek to please?*

The child who prefers the "thinking" way is likely to want *reasons* for being asked to do something, while the child who prefers the "feeling" way is apt to want to know that he is pleasing the other person by his obedience. The F child is more likely to perceive the feelings of others and often can take unusual responsibilities in the home and classroom. He tends to be more aware of the physical and social comfort or discomfort of others. The F child is apt to perform small services for his parents or teachers and needs to know that these services are recognized and appreciated. The F child is most sensitive to the emotional climate of his home, perhaps becoming physically ill if subjected to constant conflict and insecurity. The T child seems more capable of detaching himself from unfavorable emotional climate, even being blithely unaware of the distress of those around him. The F child is apt to enjoy listening to adults discuss family and neighborhood happenings, while the T child may soon turn to other activities. The T child is likely to ask for objective explanations for everything and to be dismayed and impatient with such answers as, "Because I said so!" The F child is more likely to accept a "because" answer, and, although not content, apt to go on about his business as if his questions had been answered. The child who prefers "thinking" is likely to block off facial expressions of emotion in a crisis, while the F child is apt to show facial mobility and to verbalize reactions. The T child may not want to be touched and may have difficulty in approaching a parent with affection, while the F child usually responds easily to expressions of physical affection. The F child is likely to cry more easily than is the T child, and it is the T child who is apt to be the one who will *not* display a reaction when scolded or punished. Although the F child seems more vulnerable then does the T child to the approval or disapproval of a parent or teacher, this is usually mere appearance. The T child only seems indifferent and unresponsive. Inside he may be hurting just as much as the more expressive F child.

"Perceiving" vs "Judging"

Observation: *Does the child seem to want things settled, de-*

*cided, chosen or does he want to be surprised
and have choices at all times?*

The child who seems to want things established and in order
probably has a natural judicial preference. The child who
seems indifferent to the established, especially if imposed by
others, is more apt to have a natural perceptive preference.
It is the J child who is likely to be ready for school on time,
to worry about being late, and tends to have his closets and
drawers neat and orderly. The P child, on the other hand, may
seem unconcerned about whether he is on time for class or
not. He may have a jumble in his closets and make a rat's nest
of his dresser drawers—and has difficulty understanding why
this causes his mother discomfort.

The J child is apt to run the activities of his neighborhood,
especially if he is an extravert. The P child may have to be
reminded to get dressed, to come to dinner, to take out the
trash, to do his homework, and so on. The J child is more likely
to initiate carrying out these daily routines. The J child usually
seems more sure of himself than does the P child and more inclined to make "for sure" statements. The P child may be
more tentative in his speech patterns and may qualify his statements more often.

The Four Temperaments in Children

Just as the four-letter type can be generated for adults from
the questionnaire presented in Chapter 1, so can type be generated in a very tentative way for children from material presented in this chapter. The identification of preferences must
be especially tentative, for observation of children cannot be
as accurate as the self-report of adults when what is at issue
is a person's own preferences.

The following sections describe ways the four temperaments
grow up. The growing-up styles of the SP, SJ, NT, and NF are
described in that order. A profile of each completes the chapter under the subtitle, "Learning Styles."

The Dionysian (Sensible Playful) Temperament in Childhood:
The SP child is likely to be active. Although he may have the
same physiological response to food as some other type, his
psychological response shows a greater enjoyment of food

than that of his physical counterpart. He generally enjoys his food and is called "a good eater." He also tends to get into messes rather quickly, much to his mother's distress. Leave an SP in the yard even for a moment and he somehow manages to get dirtied. This often leads to a scolding; only too often an SP learns early to be indifferent to such remonstrances, for reprimands have come too many too soon. SPs are less likely than other types to understand demands for clean rooms or neat and orderly closets. Their rooms are rather likely to be a jumble of toys, clothes, and valued objects, collected from here and there, all in an apparent disarray; but, to the SP child, just as he wants it. He is too busy doing something to want to take time to hang and fold his clothes just so, and, anyway, he would say, "What difference does it make?" Such nonsense is a waste of time when a person could be off doing something that is fun.

And yet, if an SP is so inclined, he can get involved in an activity which captures his attention for hours on end. He can spend day after day manipulating the lids on and off pots and pans, he can spend hours on a musical instrument of *his* choosing, he can manipulate his toys over and over—only to lose interest completely in those toys or that instrument tomorrow. Those who do not lose interest, of course, go on to become the outstanding performing artists, the outstanding graphic and plastic artists, the outstanding artisans of all kinds. The SP needs movement and excitement, and he hungers for contest.

Given frequent change, and some excitement, the SP is cheerful in the classroom. He brings fun and laughter, whether or not this reaction is appropriate. The SP enjoys activities and throws himself wholeheartedly into instrumental play, musical performance, art activities, and games. He may enjoy the activity of working with tools more than caring about the product he makes. The SP appears to be flighty, jumping from one thing to another, disinterested in completion. He must do something if he is to learn. The more game-like the task, the better. The less an activity seems a mere preparation for something later, the better. The SP usually does well in kindergarten, where the action of playing with various objects may constitute the main curriculum. But as he moves through the grades and the work becomes more and more a matter of preparation, acquiring rules and facts through reading and writing, he becomes disinterested. The SP does not wish to "prepare" or "get ready" for anything. As the curriculum becomes less active, the SP does not find the activity and excitement he wants. As the demand is for concentration, he becomes restless and turns to activities of his own initiation. These often take the form of a disruption of class routines or increased absenteeism.

The extreme SP can easily become restless, jittery, bored, and engaged in random action to such an extent as to be labeled "hyperactive" by foolish school and medical personnel naïvely applying the current physicalism. On the other hand, he can be over-stimulated, get too excited and roused up and not be able to calm down very easily. It is important that the SP be provided periods of quiet activities and training in relaxation. He needs space in which he can move actively, but he also needs his own quiet place. The proxemics classroom, where each student has his carrel around the perimeter of the room, is ideally suited to the needs of the SP learner.

An SP is apt to be an active baby, although the introverted SP will be less so than the extraverted SP. Attempting to change an SP in any fundamental way leads only to malad-justment. He is not an SJ, nor an NT, nor an NF. His desire to perform supersedes his desire for responsibility, competency, and self-realization. He is not likely ever to be content to be confined in a play pen, but will want to be free to roam where his impulse takes him. He is likely to enjoy animals, although also likely to be somewhat rough with them. The SP child is apt to be rather hard on his toys and clothes and should be given sturdy, well-made objects. Simple games and objects are likely to hold his attention more than complicated ones.

Since the SP relates to others in a fraternal way rather than a parental way, he can be an excellent team player. He thrives on competition and contest. Equality is very important to have, as is liberty. He likes to talk with others, but he has a need to control his own activities. Unless he has full control over whatever project he undertakes, he is likely to lose interest as others "interfere." He prefers to discover his own order of doing his activities, although he usually enjoys interactions with others concerning his progress. To engage him one must entertain him. He does not learn well as a passive audience to explanations. He must be actively manipulating, operating, or making something. Whenever possible it is well to get him excited and let him risk himself.

When an SP child is given feedback, this should be in terms of the SP's *performance*. Praise for the *product* of the activity would have more appeal to the SJ child. The SP child is likely to feel good about himself and about those who have control over him if he is provided a great deal of room to move about and given many opportunities for action. Lecture-type presentations should be short, as should his reading activities. Quiet, solitary learning activities are best interspersed with opportunities for the child to be active in some area of personal interest. Frequent change from individual to small-group to large-group activities also may help overcome the SP's natural resistance. Dramatization is especially appealing to the SP. He gets to be seen performing, and that's exciting. Sociodramas designed around issues relevant to the classroom and school, role playing opportunities—these meet the SP's need for actions.

This is not to imply that an SP child should not be given practice in concentration, delay, or in dealing with complexity. He must develop these capabilities, and the first step to this development is to legitimatize his natural preferences and recognize that this type of child tends by nature to avoid complexities, owing to his impulsivity and his low tolerance for delay.

The SP can be a "control problem" in the classroom that demands that he learn exclusively in an SJ style. Such "teaching" techniques as tying an SP to a desk, placing him facing forward in a row of desks, asking him to interact only student-to-teacher, asking him to do his lessons because "he will need this when he grows up," or asking him to work all day with abstractions on paper, seem little more than exercises in futility. Such a situation so ill suits the SP that he turns away from school, enduring it only as long as he must and leaving it as soon as he can. Yet about 40 percent of the students in the ordinary classroom are of the SP style, which means 12 in a class of 32. It is quite understandable why this group tend to terminate their formal education with high school, to frequent the continuation high schools, and to be conspicuous by their absence in graduate levels in institutions of higher education.

The SP learning style does not well accommodate the precept, "Learn today so that, in some distant future, college doors will open." The SP wants to be free to discharge the impulse of the moment, to be free to get involved in physical activity, to learn in an atmosphere of excitement where risk, adventure, and competition are part of the curriculum, where sound, color, motion abound. In fact, very often the one thing an SP finds holding him in school is opportunity to play a musical instrument. SPs frequent the instrumental music classes, probably because this involves both action and audience, and on these the SP thrives.

The SP style of learning seems out of step with the usual teaching style of most classrooms. The majority of classroom teachers tend to be SJs, and, understandably, the SJ teaches in the SJ style. Thus the young SP is told to have distant goals, to study because this is the way to prepare oneself for work or for further education, to save their pennies because that is the way to guarantee the future, to make plans because that is the way to get ahead, to develop many social ties, because that is the way to have a place. These injunctions, however, do not make sense to the SP. To prepare is to set aside one's urges and impulses, and this will not do. Today is to be lived for the excitement it brings; tomorrow can be left to take care of itself.

Thus, here is the SP student, surrounded by mentors who are saying, "Sit still in class." "Face the front of the room." "Do your homework assignments." "Develop good study habits." "Observe the rules." "Work first; then play—if there happens to be any time left for such frivolity." "Wait." "Get in line." And so the SP finds himself standing in line, waiting, conforming to routine, working for tomorrow, restlessly waiting for recess. None of this has appeal for the SP, and as he moves through school he finds that it has less and less appeal for him. Consequently, the SP tends to be little represented at advanced levels of education. The SP does far less in school than he could do, were he given sufficient incentive. "Learning is its own reward," says the educator. Unfortunately the SP doesn't get the message. This is the student who is apt to be a source of mystification and frustration to his administrator, teacher, counselor, and parents, all of whom are likely to be projecting their desires onto the SP. And the SP will have none of it! The Dionysian way asserts itself in early childhood and never lets go.

The Epimethian (Sensible Judicious) Temperament in Childhood: The Epimethian (SJ) child is more vulnerable to family instability than the other temperaments. He seeks the security of parental firmness and agreement. To be caught between one parent who is strict and one who is lenient can be devastating. He needs to know, more than others, that what is so today will be so tomorrow. For example, frequent residential changes can be unsettling to an SJ child, whereas an SP, NT, or NF child might adjust more rapidly, albeit in different ways. The SJ child needs to be raised with friends who grow up with him; he needs the same neighborhood, school system, community as he grows up. He will thrive on relating to his extended family, his aunts, uncles, grandmothers, grandfathers, cousins, and so on. He will enjoy stories of family history and remember these histories when he has grown up. The SJ child does well in a large family, and having brothers and sisters usually will be a source of gratification to him, where this might not be as important to children from other groups.

The SJ child is apt to enjoy having routines and usually responds to the assignment of specific responsibilities, e.g., emptying the wastebaskets, taking out the trash, sweeping away the snow, tending a small garden, cleaning his room. He needs, of course, tasks within his ability to perform and perform well, but he tends to enjoy routine maintenance chores at home and school. His source of pleasure is the approval he is given by adults as he performs these activities. This feedback is vital to the SJ. The task as an end in itself soon loses appeal if adult approval is not forthcoming. The SJ also responds to scolding and negative criticism, under which he tends to try all the more. Probably more than the other three groups, the SJs respond to physical punishment as a means of correction.

The SJ child, as he moves into his school years, tends to adjust well to the school environment and school routine, although the introverted SJ child may demonstrate initial shyness. The SJ children tend to thrive on the clerical methods of teaching, such as workbook completion, repetition, drill, recitation, and answering rhetorical questions by teacher. The SJ child is likely to try rather earnestly to please the teacher and not to question the reasons for a lesson (as might an NT child). The fact that the teacher gives the direction is usually sufficient reason. Of course, the SJ child thrives as little on failure as do others; but he probably has more tolerance for self-evaluated failure than for teacher-evaluated failure, if this evaluation from the teacher is negative and if the child rarely succeeds in pleasing. The SJ child is apt to treasure his gold-starred papers, his trophies, ribbons, and badges. He enjoys the honor of being chalk monitor, line monitor, student body president, club manager. These all signify both peer and adult approval and so are valued.

SJ children seem to enjoy clerical skill practice, such as arithmetic, reading aloud, and spelling. The factual aspects of science, geography, and history appeal to them. When the SJ student reaches middle and high school he is apt to choose business-oriented instruction. Language increasingly becomes a work tool. Interest in literature or creative writing wanes and he tends to avoid the sciences and advanced mathematics. He is not wildly enthusiastic about drama or debate. In college the SJ tends to be strongly represented in business administration, accounting, teaching, nursing, and other services.

SJ children are likely to enjoy going with their parents to visit relatives and get tremendous enjoyment from the traditional holidays, such as Christmas and Thanksgiving. They respond happily to a well-established, clearly-defined routine, whereas constant changes, confusion, and crises cause them pain. Changing teachers at midyear can be unsettling to an SJ child, while an SP child might thrive under the same circumstances. The SJ child is likely to value orderly closets and his bureau drawers are apt to contain neatly folded clothes. Toys are arranged in order on the shelves.

As a learner an SJ child will respond better by being shown the new skill in a step-by-step order, being asked to demonstrate each new learning in small increments. Asking the SJ child to invent his own procedures or giving him vague directions will not inspire him as it might an NT child. The SJ child needs to know what is expected and needs to be certain as to the procedures to accomplish the task. He thrives on consistency.

Home crafts appeal to an SJ. He likes to make objects from wood, cloth, yarn, just as does the SP; but for the SJ interest is focused on the product. The process used to produce the product, however, must be done correctly. A gift of handwork from an SJ is from the heart and is to be appreciated, treasured, and prominently displayed.

The SJ learner needs constant feedback from the adults around him on how he is doing. Being right or wrong is important to an SJ child, and he wants to do things in the right way, that is, the way which will please the adult in charge. SJs pay attention to details. They hold high standards of achievement for themselves and for others. They gain satisfaction from, for example, placing the heading correctly on a paper. Good study habits are important, and study is best done on schedule. The SJ child needs his work carefully planned, clearly scheduled, and meticulously executed. The SJ child responds to verbal encouragement and needs to know that he is doing well.

SJ children generally have a relatively comfortable time growing. Statistical probability suggests that they are likely to have at least one SJ parent, and an SJ child is likely to get along well with an NF or NT parent. He might have some difficulty adjusting if he happens to have two SP parents, who might be rather unpredictable. An SJ child seems to need and enjoy pleasing others, and thus he tends to be responsive to the demands of his mentors, if they are clear. These demands need not be perfectly consistent or logical—only very clear in expectations. And the SJ child responds well to praise, such as, "You are a good boy/girl," "You did that just the way I wanted," "Your work is very neat," "You have very good handwriting."

The natural teaching style of an SJ teacher meets the learning needs of the SJ student. Focus on responsibilities, on the development of good study habits, on the development of proper social attitudes, on the completion of well-structured tasks executed in an approved fashion—all these appeal to both SJ students and SJ teachers. The SJ child acquires knowledge through diligent searching for facts, through frequent review, lectures, and traditional teaching materials, the textbook and workbook. Commercially-prepared learning materials are helpful to the SJ learner who seems to enjoy and responds to the carefully sequenced, step-by-step presentations. Programmed learning materials seem more likely to be attractive to an SJ child than to an SP, NF, or even NT. The SP learner wants more action; the NF child wants more human interaction; and the NT learner wants less redundancy. The SJ child thrives in a classroom where clearly-defined, routinized procedures vary little day to day. The SJ child thrives in a well-ordered, quiet, organized classroom and does not seem uncomfortable when interaction is predominantly teacher to student. Drills, rote recitations, Socratic questioning, and lectures laced with frequent illustrations of application are helpful to the SJ learner. He can even respond to rejection, sarcasm, and ridicule, although these aversive maneuvers are not recommended. The SJ child is apt to worry about his school-work and be conscientious and dedicated to pleasing his teacher.

The Promethean (Intuitive Thinking) Temperament in Child-hood: The NT baby is probably rather solemn and likely to be a puzzle to those around him if they are not also NTs. He may be precocious, talk early, and learn to read long before he goes to school. The chances of an NT having even one NT parent is rather low, since this group is represented by only 12 percent of the general population. The NT child often experiences the same rejection accorded to the SP, but for the SP this occurs when he enters schools and moves through the grades. For the NT this begins earlier. Over and over, NTs have reported their childhood experiences saying, "I thought I was the only person in the whole world who was like me. When I was growing up no one seemed to see things the way I did. Then I got to col-lege and, suddenly, there were lots of others like me. I was no longer so alone."

The NT child is apt to keep at a parent with *why* questions: "Why does the sun come up there and not there?" "Why can't I fly like a bird?" "Why can't I have dessert before my vege-tables if I eat both?" Usually rather independent, the NT child can often be also a nonconformist, although he also tends to be obedient and compliant in matters to which he is indiffer-ent. Just as the SP pursues his function-lust, so does the NT pursue his curiosity-lust, wondering, "What would happen if . . .?" And proceeds to attempt to find the answer, whether his mentors approve or not. "What would happen if I put my finger in the electric socket?" "What would happen if I put my bread in the water pitcher?" None of these exploring be-haviors are designed to annoy adults; their purpose is to satis-fy the NT's need to *find out*. He tends not to be the least bit interested in coming into conflict with those about him; al-though, if this happens as a result of his investigations, he is apt to accept these consequences impersonally. He is often a source of annoyance to his mentors for he tends to be some-what detached in his reactions to their reprimands. The NT child will quickly lose respect for those who are not logical in their reprimands or who issue edicts which are not plainly warranted by the circumstances.

Physical punishment is deeply violating to the NT. Although his body, as his world, is a source of curiosity—not *him* in the same way the body is for other types—he reacts to physical abuse of that body with what seems to be an exaggerated response, somehow seeing this abuse as a violation of his nature. Dignity usually is important to NT children, and they are often described as "prideful." Somehow, others often find this offensive and seem to take the NT's pride as a personal affront, which often presents a challenge to those around the NT to bring the NT off his high horse.

Parenting the NT mainly means hands off. The NT child needs an abundance of opportunities to experiment, find out, get answers. Shutting off this experimental behavior is likely to cause the NT child to engage in disobedience and disruptive behaviors, overt or covert. The parent of an NT should provide the child with a variety of toys, but only a few at any one time as opposed to giving an abundance. The NT child, as with all children, can easily become over-stimulated; the NT in particular can be seen as intellectually precocious and so parents might be tempted to supply toys appropriate for other children which are inappropriate for the child's age and social maturity. He usually will enjoy books and being read stories long after other children of other types have turned their attention elsewhere. He is likely to be deeply involved with a new toy, playing with it for hours, contemplating its properties—and then abandon it and seldom again show interest. Once the NT child understands the toy he is no longer interested. His enjoyment in being read to is probably a function of his curiosity, and through stories he encounters complexities which he cannot gain through his own reading, but which excite his mind. He may become impatient with the content of his primers and fail to learn to read because of disinterest, much to the surprise of his teachers. This circumstance, however, is the exception with the NT child.

The NT child is devastated by ridicule and sarcasm concerning ability. He more than others is self-doubting, and he badly needs an abundance of success. He is particularly vulnerable here. Owing to his early interest in technology, well-meaning parents and teachers may ask of him that which is beyond him. He then experiences failure and is likely to retreat into himself. Seldom does an NT child respond well to negative criticism. Helping him when he asks for help, providing him with patient answers to his almost endless questions, giving him appropriate play materials in appropriate number, and giving him room to develop his own answers in his own world permits an NT to grow up with his need for competency and his thirst for knowledge encouraged and nurtured.

Socially the INT child can be somewhat retarded, although intellectually he may seem precocious. Awareness of social interactions, which is so natural for an NF, is somewhat of a mystery to an NT. It seldom occurs to him to think about manners, and he usually is quite oblivious to the reactions of others. Often, therefore, the NT does not develop the winning ways which often the NF, SJ, and SP display, each in his own style: the SP with his bubbling, happy-go-lucky cheerfulness, the SJ with his thoughtful gestures of service, often quite unexpected, and the NF with an appreciation of adult and child personality. The NT usually displays none of these if he is introverted. The INT especially seems, at times, unable or at least reluctant to express affection, drawing back from expressions of physical affection from others and seeming to have a shell around him—an expression of his self doubt.

Ensuring an abundance of success, providing sufficient intellectual stimulation, giving frequent encouragement, and coaching in social skills—these help the NT child. Showing him off, allowing him to become an intellectual snob, allowing him to look down on others who are perhaps less intellectually gifted and therefore judged to be "inferior" will not do much for him. NTs usually do well in school. They usually do not skip the difficult subjects, such as the hard sciences and advanced mathematics. As the NT moves through his schooling, he can become over-involved in these studies and, as a consequence, fail to participate in school recreational and social activities. The INT, in particular, may be somewhat of a loner in the classroom, being highly independent, and preferring to go his own way in pursuit of his own interests. The ENT may be an outstanding leader, sometimes in opposition to the direction taken by a teacher; thus the two find themselves engaged in a power struggle. The stubborn aggression of the ENT over correctness of procedure is duplicated in the INT over the correctness of wording of ideologies.

The NT child's capability-hunger is soon attached to inner standards of improvement. He must meet these standards, however overdrawn they may be. One of his tasks in life is to come to terms with the fact that he cannot know everything, and that he must, therefore, set priorities. Both parent and teacher can and need to be of assistance to the NT in setting these priorities.

NTs tend to be high achievers in academic work and generally approach their learning through seeking out and understanding principles. A logical presentation of learning materials is apt to appeal to an NT. He usually enjoys the lecture method of instruction, if well done, and may not always find discussion methods useful. In fact, at times, he can be somewhat impatient and rude in rejecting the ideas and opinions of others, especially those he views as being beneath him intellectually.

Because it is important to the NT that others see him as competent, he can be affected negatively by report cards. Once he has achieved high grades, he may come to believe himself incompetent if ever after he does not continue to receive straight As. Pursuit of this kind of reward is, obviously, unreasonable and may be unwise, for the NT may never find time for activities other than study.

An NT can be, intellectually, a big fish in a little high school pond. When he enrolls in college he finds competition of a different sort. At this point, the NT may react by giving up his scholastic efforts altogether or by giving only erratic attention to a few studies, perhaps succeeding brilliantly in some and ignominiously failing others. If parents and teachers have provided for a sufficient number and variety of experiences for the NT, some of which are not his forte, this is not as likely to happen, for the NT has the background to place what may be threatening competition in an accepting perspective.

Family rituals and ceremonials are usually not appealing to the INT child since he requires reasons for doing things and, perhaps, needs help in understanding that rituals and ceremonies are important events for other people. The NT may be erratic about the way he maintains his room and clothes. He may at one time be very organized and at another let dust and chaos escape his notice. Probably the frequent condition of his room is one of apparent disorder, but the NT child will be likely to know where each and every treasure is placed. He is apt to have extensive collections: rocks, animal artifacts, coins, stamps, butterflies, and the like. Anything which can be collected and which requires technical documentation and classification is apt to have appeal for the NT child.

The NT likes to be given content or directions only once and becomes impatient with repetition, unlike the SJ learner who enjoys being given detailed directions and usually does not object to repeated content. The SP, on the other hand, is not apt to pay much attention to directions whether clear or not.

At the very least he redefines the task before complying. The NF tends to erase distinctions in directions and probably should be given both oral and written directions.

The NT learner needs to receive feedback on the *quality* of his work, and he usually defines quality as coherence and efficiency. He can be directed toward independent study and usually counted on to pursue these efforts with little or no encouragement or additional direction from the teacher or parent. He is very likely to enjoy developing his vocabulary and may, at times, use this expanded vocabulary as a debate weapon with others. Intolerance of others' difficulty with complexity is often a characteristic of the NT, both child and adult, and helping the NT child understand the impact of this attitude can be a contribution which a parent or teacher should make.

The Appollonian (Intuitive Feeling) Style in Childhood: Even at an early age the NF child is apt to display a gift for language. He is likely to begin to talk early, and extraverted NFs may seem to their parents to never stop talking. NFs tend also to have a charm which draws people to them. They seem to have a natural talent for relating socially, both to peers and to adults, although the introverted NF child will have some difficulty communicating, especially outside the home. The NF needs and seeks recognition that he is valued by those around him, and he needs that reassurance each and every day.

The NF child can be the one who makes up stories and recounts them with vivid imagery. At times, then, he may be accused of lying when in fact he is only exercising his imagination. NFs, especially introverted ones, are likely to daydream a lot. The NF is hypersensitive emotionally to rejection and to conflict; if he is reared in a home where the parents quarrel very much, the NF child is apt to become withdrawn and insecure. He needs the assurance that those around him are in harmony if he is to develop his own tenuous identity.

As the NF seeks a sense of self, he engages in often deep identification with characters in stories, especially fairy tales. The Princess and the Prince are apt to be very real to the NF child, and his daydreams often take him off on royal quests. Often stories of the medieval era, of knights and their ladies, of dragons and grails appeal to the NF child. Some caution should be exercised in monitoring the reading material of the NF child, who can easily be over-stimulated by the vivid imagery he is likely to experience when reading stories of dragons, witches, ogres, slayings, and so on.

NF children, as do NT children, usually enjoy being read stories which are beyond their own reading capabilities, but which spark their imaginative powers. And, like NTs, they may want the same story read over and over. They also are apt to enjoy complicated, detailed illustrations, rich with subtle colorations. NF children are apt to enjoy "people" toys, dolls or animals to which they can attach a personality, and these treasured toys become very much a part of the NF's life. A lost toy friend is indeed a real tragedy to the NF child. Winnie the Pooh, Piglet, Mr. Toad, Alice in Wonderland, Dorothy and her Oz friends are all real for the NF child to a degree not shared by other types. The NF child is apt to play with all his toys as fantasy objects, just as does the NT, but the NF is more likely to weave stories around them rather than try to understand them. It is interesting to conjecture whether the common invisible companion which some children have in their childhood is not more characteristic of the NF than the other types. One could certainly predict that the rejection or ridiculing of this imaginary friend by others would crush an NF child, who would himself feel rejected.

Competition for an NF child does not have the appeal it might have for other styles. The NF child is apt to be almost hypersensitive to another's feelings. He tends to suffer with the loser; even if he is the winner, he feels bad about the loser. Cooperative games and competition against himself are more likely to be something which appeals to and is healthy for an NF child.

Although all children are subject to sibling rivalry and to problems of rejection when a new member is added to a family, this transition needs to be very carefully handled with the NF child, who always is seeking for his sense of self, always looking for his meaning in the world. The NF child is apt to have the same experience as the NT child when he goes to school, in that he may find himself out of step with the other children. Somehow he feels different, and indeed he is in the small minority until he, too, reaches college.

The INF child, in particular, may be painfully shy and hypersensitive to even the slightest gesture or word of rejection from his teacher—NF children are apt to idolize their teachers. They also, however, can hate them with equal fervor if rejected or ridiculed. NF children thrive on an abundance of personalized attention and do not respond to physical punishment. They need the security of well-established routines, but those which permit frequent interaction between adults and other children. Interactions with peers do have impact on the NF child, who can be deeply hurt by apparent cruelties received from others. This type of child, especially the introverted NFs, lacks defenses against behaviors which other types would handle easily.

In the classroom, NF children are apt to be most nourished when they are in an interactional arrangement, rather than stationed in desks arranged in rows and columns, all facing forward. NF children need and like to discuss the content of their lessons. They learn and are sensitive to materials in the affective domain, usually respond well to poetic language, and, as stated earlier, tend to be talented verbally. They are not impatient with discussions which, to the NT, may seem needlessly redundant and wandering.

NF children are likely to experience distress if they work with a teacher who uses ridicule or who seems to reject them personally. In fact, the NF is troubled by any rejection of any student and tends to empathize with the hurts and embarrassments of others, at times beyond the discomfort felt by the actual recipient of the rejection. Promises are important to an NF child; if these commitments are not honored, the neglect is felt very deeply and taken very personally. If this happens too often, an NF child may develop physical symptoms, for example, eating problems. Conflict, in the home or in school, is a source of discomfort; he flourishes in an atmosphere of love and harmony.

NF children tend to do well academically, as many have outstanding linguistic fluency. Languages are their forte, and they usually learn to read easily, are good at written and spoken communications, and enjoy the process of communicating. They like to work in small groups and thrive in a democratically-run classroom. They tend to conform to adult expectations, if they believe that the adult likes them. The NF child is usually pleasant and agreeable, and wants to please. He or she needs feedback from others that they themselves are valued by others. When an NF child tenders a creative product, he gives from the heart; the slightest rejection is apt to devastate him out of proportion to the degree of rejection. The NF child is not really comfortable in large groups where instruction is not individualized, or in situations when the teacher is too harried to be sensitive to the needs of this type of student. The NF needs to be loved by his teachers as well as his parents.

An NF student usually enjoys social studies as well as languages, since both deal with people in a transactional way. People's attitudes and values, what they prefer, how they respond, what they wish for, what they say, all fascinate the NF child who sees the world from a personal focus. He likes the world of ideas and values, but always tends to process these ideas with himself as the center.

An NF may have difficulty handling anger in himself and in others, and this is particularly true for an introverted NF. He is repelled by ugliness, and turns away in disgust.

Cognition for the NF child may be impressionistic. He tends to be satisfied with a global, diffuse grasp of learning. If he gains a general impression, glossing over details, he still believes that he has sufficient mastery of the subject. An NT child, by way of contrast, would want to master details in all their precision and is almost compulsive in his over-learning.

The NF wants and hungers for a sense of identity, and one of the way he gains this is through personalized acknowledgment. Physical touch, or at least physical closeness, usually transmits a projection of love and warmth to the NF child. The messages they value most are those which say, "I value *you;* you are important to me."

Learning Styles

Four profiles follow which summarize the ways the four types learn; their preferred instructional technology, their preferred curriculum content, and their response to appropriate feedback from their mentors is discussed.

SP Learning Style: The child who has the SP combination hungers for action and for being seen as having the freedom to act. *Performer, player, adventurer, active, fun-loving, uninhibited* are all words which portray the SP student. *Immediate,* *the good life, the here and now, spontaneity,* and *pleasure* describe attitudes which have appeal to the SP.

Of all children in school, the SP style is the most misunderstood and most subject to denigration. Yet 38 percent of the children of an ordinary classroom (where attendance is compulsory) are SPs. This group is the least represented in institutions of higher learning and tends to have the lowest correlation between academic ability and grade point average. The truth is, unfortunately, that the usual classroom does not fit the unique learning style of the SP child.

The SP student needs physical involvement in his learning. He needs a hands-on experience; he needs activity; he thrives on competition; he loves to take risks; he enjoys performing; he learns from media presentations; he loves to be entertained and to entertain.

The SP can be an excellent team member if there is a *contest.* His outlook is basically fraternal, and he may develop extreme loyalty to his team mates, club mates, group mates, and he has very little of the parental outlook. He can be fiercely egalitarian. Consequently, seeing no need for "bosses," he tends to rebel against close supervision and sees instructions as something to outwit. He enjoys dialoguing with others to report progress, but he does not particularly want to use the democratic group process to make decisions as does the NF. He wants a constant change of pace and constant variety. Holding an SP to the same routine day after day, week after week is deadly and leads him to absenteeism or acting-up in the classroom.

The SP gravitates toward music, drama, art, crafts, mechanics, construction, or anything active, while SJs tend to enroll in clerical or business classes, the NTs in math and science, and the NFs in the humanities and social sciences. The SP has a function-lust, and manipulating objects satisfies this longing if such opportunities are provided. Thus placing in his hands materials which he can *move* attracts him. If this kind of activity is not provided legitimately, the SP is most likely to find outlets which may be disruptive, such as banging furniture, poking classmates, and loudly shuffling feet.

Continuation schools tend to be heavily represented by the SPs, for they often find the usual traditional instructional technology something with little appeal. And, as soon as they legally can, they may drop out of school to go where the action is. The SP usually brings fun and excitement to a classroom, although at times this fun and excitement is initiated inappropriately, often to annoy the teacher. If, however, the SP believes that he is genuinely liked, he can be most cooperative. He can be popular with other students; they seem to admire his boldness and devil-may-care ways. If an SP becomes involved in a musical group, this alone, at times, can cause him to remain in school to complete his formal schooling. He may be somewhat flighty and jump from project to project, beginning many and completing few. Paper and pencil work is deadly for the SP. Verbal and visual work are far more appealing and will hold his interest so that he learns. Lectures, Socratic questioning, workbooks, answer-the-questions-at-the-back-of-the-chapter—all these leave the SP disinterested. Assigning homework to the SP is more than likely a futile gesture and only provides an arena of conflict between SP student and teacher and SP child and parents.

SJ Learning Style: The child who has the SJ combination hungers for belonging, especially to the family group and, later, when he enters school, to his classroom group. *Responsibility, dependability, duty,* and *service* are words associated with the SJ student.

Since about two-thirds of teachers are themselves SJs, the SJ student generally finds in the traditional classroom a place he understands and can relate to. The SJ student usually wants to please the teacher because he is the teacher, the authority figure without which it is difficult to create a unit to belong to. The values of the teacher are accepted as good values. Good study habits, doing homework as assigned and on time, learning one's lessons as directed are seen as worthwhile. The SJ, better than any of the other styles, fits into the classroom as it is frequently designed and maintained.

SJ students usually do well with workbooks. They like and need structure and do best when lessons are presented sequentially in increments that make sense. The SJ student is conscientious and will attempt to do his best as long as he receives clear directions so that he knows how to proceed with the task. The SJ is not apt to rely on "winging it," as might an SP or an NF. He is most comfortable if he has studied and is prepared for the daily recitations.

The SJ student can do well in a classroom arranged in rows and columns where the main interaction is between teacher and student. He does respond, to some degree, to negative criticism and will try to do better if what he has already done is not up to the teacher's standards. The SJ does not thrive on long-term, independent projects, as might an NT. The SJ does not always enjoy discussion groups, as does the NF. The SJ would prefer that a question-and-answer session be conducted, led by the teacher. The Socratic method of instruction has appeal for an SJ, and he learns well in this mode.

Although the SJ may not have the language facility of the NF, he usually does well in responding in writing to questions posed by the teacher or posed by the text. These generally do not seem a waste of time to the SJ student.

The SJ child is usually obedient and conforms to the standards of classroom conduct set down by the teacher. The SJ child can tolerate sarcasm far better than can the NF or the NT, but he does take it seriously, unlike the SP. The SJ is likely to belong to school clubs and takes great interest in these. As long as what he is studying are facts or procedures, he is comfortable; but ask of the SJ child that he speculate, invent, guess, or improvise and his studious dependability may dissolve. The SJ child takes report cards seriously, and these are important to him. The SP is likely to forget to take his home, the NT views this card as a curiosity (since he tends continuously to sit in judgment of his own performances), and the NF sees it as personal judgment on him, signifying personal recognition by his teacher; but of all types, the SJs value and respect the report card most.

The SJ child thrives on stability. He takes responsibility well. He learns from traditional instructional technology, including demonstration. He usually enjoys school, and is at home there if the teacher is consistent and stable.

NT Learning Style: Children who have the NT combination hunger for competency. They must know all they *should* know, and their lists of *should-knows* are endless. Building, architecting, inventing, and commanding describe the NT child. He looks for whatever will enable him to understand, explain, predict, and control. He is the little scientist.

The NT tends to collect rules and principles and loves to give structure to his cognitive world. He enjoys tracking the ideas of others and developing his own ideas. He seeks to know how an idea was conceived, how it was put together, what contradictions can be uncovered, what are unanswered questions, *why* things are. He is ordinarily filled with intellectual curiosity and will focus on technology from an early age, especially if he is male. Female NTs often find cultural pressures turning them in more "feminine" directions.

The NT tends to be an independent learner and likes to pursue his inspirations, tracking down the information until his desire for understanding is satisfied. This characteristic can cause him, at times, to neglect other areas that may then suffer failing grades.

The NT is comfortable with a logical, didactic presentation of material to be learned and usually can independently follow up through reading. He tends not to have the writing facility of the NF and may put off recording his findings on paper, preferring to acquire new information rather than waste his time communicating to his mentors that he knows something. Thus he may fail to complete homework assignments.

The NT may be a loner in the classroom, especially the introverted NTs. The introverted NTs are prone to this loner nature partly because they find no others like themselves as they move through school—there being only one introverted NT per average class. The NT is, however, interested in sharing his ideas with those he respects and considers his intellectual peers. He often seeks this kind of communication only with the teacher, which can increase his isolation from his peers. In the higher ranges of intelligence, the NT can be an intellectual snob, and he may need help in appreciating other qualities besides intellectual capabilities, for example, social skills. The NT himself often does not have well-developed social skills and needs coaching in this area. Since he is relatively imperturbable and not easily moved to emotional display, he may have difficulty understanding how others are more easily aroused and quicker to discharge their feelings. Being thus somewhat oblivious to others' feelings, he may occasionally offend.

The NT student needs help in establishing priorities. He has such a hunger to know everything that he has difficulty coming to terms with the fact that he *cannot* know everything. He can become a grind and fail to develop necessary recreational skills. Play may be seen as a waste of time for the NT student, who wants to get on with the business of learning.

The NT student tends to be fairly self-sufficient, but he does respond to feedback concerning the visibility of his competency and his accomplishments, if that feedback comes from some-one he considers competent. He is turned away by manufac-tured compliments. Generally, the NT is of serious mien. He is vulnerable to serious personality hurt if he has too many fail-ure experiences. The NT, by nature, has a built-in self-doubting system and needs constant success experiences to counter-act this. Working against frequent success is the NT's tendency to push himself just a bit beyond what is comfortable, what he has almost mastered. Each day he may escalate his standards.

NT children give the appearance of having a psychological wall built around them, so they often seem cold and unfeel-ing. Physical punishment for the NT child is always unwise. He will tend to have a keen sense of justice on the one hand and a strong need to remain in control on the other hand. Phy-sical assault by an elder both violates his sense of justice and destroys his feeling of control. He may resent such unjust (in his eyes) assault bitterly over a long period of time. The NT responds well to verbal, logical, well-reasoned dialogue. Once he understands the reason for a situation, the NT child usually accepts it and goes along with whatever accommodations are necessary.

NF Learning Style: Children who have the NF (intuitive-feel-ing) combination hunger for an ever-increasing sense of self. The search for self begins early and is a life-long quest. The NF child wants to "be himself" as well as "somebody." With-in this group are found the charismatic, the empathic, the dramatic, and the idealist, seeking ever to establish an identity and to feel complete and undivided.

The NF child seems to have a built-in desire to communicate in a personal way with others. He is almost hypersensitive to hostility and conflict, at times becoming physically ill from being exposed to this kind of tension. To subject an NF child to sarcasm or ridicule is unwise and cruel. He thrives on recognition, caring, personal attention, two-way exchanges, and recognition of his emotional attitudes.

It is important to the NF child that his teacher know him by name and that he be recognized, known, and acknowledged. He needs personal feedback on the papers he produces, and the personal note written on a composition can be a powerful motivator to the child, as long as the comments are positive. A negative reaction can well provoke the NF child into rebellion or inaction.

The NF student enjoys interaction. He works well in a democratically-run classroom, and participates enthusiastically in group decisions. He is able to work independently for a time, but he does better if periodically he receives feedback through dialogue. The NF learns from the discussion method, role-playing, dramatic play, and through fiction. It is the NF who usually shows early talent in communication skills. He enjoys reading, especially fiction and fantasy. The NF child's spoken vocabulary often is far beyond his ability to capture his thoughts on paper. Often the composition placed on audio tape provides a way of expressing the NF's richness of creativity and content.

The introverted NF child (at best one per classroom) often is painfully shy and needs encouragement to socialize with his classmates. Being hypersensitive to rejection, he may hold back, remain unnoticed, uninvolved, lonely, and apart if he is not given help in developing friendship skills. Most NF children tend to have vivid imaginations and may be over-stimulated by violence and horror. They tend to carry imagery in their minds for a long time and often are subject to nightmares.

Cooperation rather than competition speaks to the NF child. He identifies strongly with others so that he suffers the pain of the loser at the same time he himself may be the winner. Competition with himself, and opportunities to share the improvement of his own achievement level do motivate the NF, who always needs constant positive feedback on his efforts.

The NF child is apt to prefer subjects which focus on people to subjects which are more abstract, e.g., science or business processes. He is apt to choose liberal-arts majors over science and technology. The NF learns in face-to-face dialogue, enjoys participating in the decision-making of a democratic classroom, enjoys giving pleasure to others, is sensitive to his own and others' emotions, and thinks in terms of social interactions. He has a built-in drive to better the social situation, to make it more pleasant and more nourishing. As he seeks to

perfect himself, so does he seek to perfect the social environment, at home and in the classroom.

The NF child can be particularly responsive to teachers who
are accepting and nourishing, who verbalize recognition of
feelings, who individualize their instruction, who use lots of
small group interaction, who genuinely respond to and accept
the ideas and opinions of class members, and who avoid sarcasm and ridicule as a means of class control.

V
TEMPERAMENT
IN
LEADING

A leader is a leader only insofar as he has followers. If we want our subordinates to do something and they do not do it, then, plainly, they have not followed our lead. Likewise, if we want our charges to accomplish something, quite apart from how they go about it, and they do not accomplish it, then, again they have not followed our lead. Now these are the only two ways that we can be leaders: we can want certain *actions* and we can want certain *results*. *The degree in which we get what we want is the measure of our leadership.*

A follower is a follower only insofar as he does what a leader wants in order to please the leader. Whatever our temperament, we are all social creatures, and so want to please the boss (or displease him—we are not indifferent on this issue). Work is done for the boss. We grow for our parents, learn for our teacher, win for our coach. Even the most independent among us presents his work as a gift to the boss, which makes the boss rather imprudent if he fails to say, in some manner, "Thank you."

Is not the paycheck and the satisfaction of doing a good job enough? Apparently not. This is not to say that pay and self-esteem are not important; clearly, they are. Rather, it is to say that they are not enough. We all want appreciation, and we want it from the person in charge.

We not only want to be thanked for our contribution, we also want the appreciation to be proportional to our achievement.

The greater the achievement the greater the hunger for appreciation. The high achievers have more appetite for appreciation than the low achievers!

Watch a creative person. He does his thing. When the boss fails to notice, our achiever hightails it over to his private appreciator that he has stashed somewhere close by in the organizational bushes. His appreciator gives him his needed "warm fuzzies" in a manner precisely fitting his conception of achievement; his thirst is assuaged. He returns to work with renewed energy.

Watch an achieving person whose boss fails to give him strokes and who has no private stroker. He soon leaves the job in search of a place where he is appreciated.

Since leadership is getting people to do what the leader wants them to *because* the leader wants them to, and since achievement *creates* a hunger for appreciation *by the leader*, then it follows that *the primary job of the leader is appreciation*. Other tasks the leader may have must be regarded as trivial in comparison to this. The leader has got to learn how to notice achievement and thereupon to thank the follower for his gift.

Imagine that! Thanking someone for doing something he's *supposed* to do! That sticks in the craw. Even so, the leader damn sure better swallow this or his team is going to lose, and the owner is going to get a new coach (as well he should).

Even if the leader swallows the bitter pill there's a catch to it. One man's meat is another's poison, even in the domain of appreciation. To thank a person for something he does not consider accomplishment is to at least miss him, and at worst insult him. And here the temperament of the leader predisposes him to awareness of achievement *he* values and obliviousness to achievements valued by other temperaments. So, even if he grants that thanking his subordinates for their work is his main task, he is very likely to botch it by unconsciously imposing his own style onto his subordinates and thanking them for doing things they regard as irrelevant and valueless.

So if a leader accepts the primacy of appreciation he then has the task of learning about his own temperament and that of his subordinates. Let us therefore review in brief what sorts of appreciation might be relevant to the four temperaments.

Appreciation

Appreciating the SP: SPs appreciate recognition of the clever, facile ways they work. Commendation for the grace and flair of their actions is more important to them than note of how much work was done. The SP is process-oriented, not product-oriented. If the work entails risks and taking chances, this should be commented on. When the risks pay off, he needs companionship in celebrating the results. When they do not, he needs support and encouragement, expressions of comfort that this was merely a temporary setback. Boldness, bravery, endurance, cleverness, adaptation, and timing—these are what SPs pride themselves on and so feel appreciated when these qualities are noted by the leader.

Appreciating the SJ: Caution, carefulness, thoroughness, and accuracy of work are valued by the SJ, for he is *product*-oriented. An SJ enjoys comment about whatever he produces, especially if these comments recognize how well the product meets the standards set forth. He appreciates being recognized as a responsible, loyal, and industrious person, which is not difficult, for those three adjectives can readily be applied to most SJs. SJs need an abundance of appreciation, although they will have difficulty in showing their pleasure when recognition is given.

Appreciating the NT: NTs want to be appreciated for their ideas. They want an intelligent listener who will take the trouble to follow the complexities of the NT's conception. Seldom does an NT enjoy comments of a personal nature; rather he responds to recognition of his capabilities. Appreciation by management of a routine task well done would not only *not* delight an NT, but might even make him suspicious of the manager. The qualifications of the person rendering appreciation are vital to an NT. The fact that the person holds a high office signifies nothing if he does not also possess intellectual competency in the area he is appreciating. NTs have difficulty appreciating others verbally and, as with the SJs, have difficulty accepting appreciation.

Appreciating the NF: NFs value expressions of appreciation which are more personal than those valued by NTs. NFs want

to be recognized as unique persons making unique contributions and need an awareness of this stated by their subordinates, peers, and superiors. The other three styles can handle
negative criticism more easily than can the NFs, who become
immobilized and discouraged when met with negatives. It is
important to an NF that his feelings as well as his ideas are
understood by others and he wants constant feedback concerning both as verification.

The styles differ in what irritates them at work. SPs resent
being told how to work. They want to be free to "fly by the
seat of their pants." Standard operating procedures make
the SPs restless and impatient. SJs, in sharp contrast, are
irritated by others who do not employ standard operating
procedures. The SJs value order, and simply do not understand
people who do not follow the rules and regulations. Deadlines
for the SJs are important, and they are impatient when these
deadlines are violated. NTs become irritated when asked to do
something that is illogical, or violates reason or principle. The
NT insists on getting maximum effect with least effort and is
bothered when rules, traditions, or biases get in his way. NFs
become irritated when treated impersonally, as if they were
only their job or office. They do not wish to "hide behind their
uniform" any more than they wish to be confined by it. Whatever is done is done by them personally, not by their office,
badge, or warrant, and is so to be seen.

In the working situation, ways the styles are apt to irritate one
another can also be suggested. For example, the SPs are most
apt to annoy others by not following through on agreements
and failing to inform others that they have not. They also may
be careless about details and this may irritate others. The SPs
can be unprepared at times when preparation is indicated,
can over-praise when such approval is not earned, and can
spring the unexpected on colleagues perhaps too frequently.
At times they make commitments for others without consul-
tation, an act which understandably can upset the person on
whose behalf a commitment was made.

SJs can irritate by too frequently communicating a "doom and
gloom" position and failing to speak in positive ways. SJs can
also hurt with sarcasm and sharp criticism, perhaps even
ridicule. They may reward only the most productive and fail
to notice minor contributions of others. SJs can fail to smile

or laugh and can transmit an attitude of fatigue and worry which can be catching.

NTs also can hurt with sarcasm and ridicule, but the source of this is usually doubt about the capabilities and comprehension of others. NTs also can irritate by what seems to others an unwarranted insistence on splitting hairs in making distinctions so that others forget the point at issue. NTs are sometimes seen as using a vocabulary which their listeners find pretentious and pedantic.

NFs may irritate others by playing favorites and by being particularly charmed with one person, only tomorrow to turn to another, abandoning the first without an explanation. NFs may give offense by insisting on comments regarding emotional reactions in situations where the ideas are more appropriate for exploration. They can take the side of a supposed underdog and in the process imply that others present are hardhearted and unsympathetic to the needs of others. NFs also can be over-helpful, giving too much help that is neither wanted nor needed.

It is not enough for a manager to appreciate and understand the temperaments of his subordinates; he also must know how his own temperament affects his leadership. And he needs to know what he can expect from his superiors and associates, given a knowledge of their temperament styles.

The following pages provide a description of four management styles, using the same dimensions as previous chapters. A profile of the SP Management Style is followed by descriptions of the SJ, the NT, and the NF. The strengths, possible weaknesses, pressure points, characteristic ways of dealing with colleagues, stroking patterns, effective management teaming, placement within an organization, use of time, and institutional deficits if this style is not present are described.

SP Manager at Work

This managerial style negotiates with ease and has, of all the types, the highest sense of reality. He is a natural negotiator, but other titles which might capture this style are "Troubleshooter," "Diplomat," and "Beachmaster." This leader is good at putting out fires, at unsnarling messes, and at responding to crisis situations in a way which none of the other types can match without great effort. Running through this style is a note of expediency: Whatever needs to be done to solve a problem situation is done. Ties to the past and ties to the future are expendable.

Some large corporations make efficient use of the talents of this group when they buy another company which is in the "red," but which they want, perhaps, for patents and tax write-off. The larger corporation sends in an SP Trouble-shooter to take over the smaller company, with directions to straighten it out, that is, incorporate it into the body of the mother company. The Troubleshooter is empowered with the authority to do whatever has to be done to make this new arrival a part of the parent organization. And this will happen rather quickly, for somehow this leader has a talent for getting people to cooperate with him and with each other on the basis of expediency. There is an attitude of sureness and damn-the-torpedoes, full-speed-ahead that causes others to be fully confident in the negotiator's decisions and directions. If this leader experiences self-doubt, he does not transmit it to those around him.

Some of this confidence seems to stem from the Trouble-shooter's strong sense of reality. Somehow this temperament has more realism than the others, who go into a situation with several sets of glasses firmly placed over their views of that situation. They filter the situation through the lens of policies, or the lens of traditions, regulations, sacred cows, and through the lens of mandating to themselves that certain persons must be there, or the lens of a belief system that because something happened in 1910, it must continue to happen. These lenses that other temperaments wear serve as a filter which obscures vision of what is immediate, what is right here, and what is right now. The troubleshooting SP wears none of these glasses. He goes into a situation, not like a babe in the woods, but more like a wolf in the woods, with a sharp nose for opportunity. He is not saddled with rules, regulations, policies, traditions, contracts, and old relationships. Putting it in other terms: To the Negotiator everything—and everybody—is negotiable!

When the Negotiator goes into a situation with the intent of getting warring factions to compromise, he does not consider anything which either side owns as non-negotiable. Most representatives of opposing factions reserve the things they own or the things they have done as non-negotiable. They take their places at the conference table with a tiny bit of something in mind which they intend to negotiate. They plan to give up a pittance in exchange for whatever they can get. The Negotiator, however, goes back and looks in closets, and says, "Hey, look at all that gold. Let's bring it out and negotiate it!" This extraordinary sense of reality gives this type not an edge, but an entire plane over everybody else. He makes everybody else look like amateurs when it comes to negotiation.

The Negotiator also makes everyone else look like amateurs when it comes to troubleshooting. Consider the beachmaster, who functions in a shooting war. He is the leader who goes in with the first wave which attacks an island, or a continent. All the men and material are on the beach. The beachmaster is given absolute authority to shove anything into the sea. No one can say one word to him about what goes and what does not. His objective is one thing—to get the men off the beach and into the bushes. Beachmasters have to have a split-second sense of timing, an overwhelming sense of what is right here, right now, and in seconds decide what has to be pushed into the ditch or into the sea, or under the ground. So when a commander has men stacking up on a beachhead and he needs a beachmaster, he does not send in someone who is laden with traditions and the rules of warfare, or who is acutely aware of the future, or the penalties of failure, or who is acutely aware of the meaning of death in the lives of the men on the beach. Survival is the issue. All other considerations are expendable. Nothing counts on that beachhead but getting off the beach and into the bushes—surviving to attack and secure the objective.

The Beachmaster brand of leadership is not restricted to war. This type is outstanding in rising to any crisis situation. An SP Beachmaster of tremendous ability was sent into a sick high school which had been ailing for a long time. This high school was a graveyard for principals. A principal would be assigned to that school and the faculty would "kill" him off in a few months. The faculty was made up of two warring factions, each battling the other; but each side knew how to dismantle a principal, and did so with unerring regularity. No one could deal with the situation, which got worse and worse. The faculty became more and more at odds. The students were learning less and less. Parents were up in arms. Finally, the Superintendent took his lieutenant and said, "Get over to that school and straighten it out." In three months the war had ceased,

and the school was a harmonious unit, with harmonious transactions. Needless to say, the Troubleshooter was an SP, and
he had an unerring instinct for getting people to cooperate
with each other right here and now. If there had been a different staff at that school, in all probability he would have
been able to function just as effectively. This type is so realistic, so unfettered with things of the past, that they can see
the opportunity current in each situation.

This kind of manager tends to be impatient with theories, concepts, goal statements, and statements of philosophy. They get
restive with these issues, seeing them as exercise in futility.
They themselves are the very essence of flexibility, flexible
with themselves and flexible in their expectancy of others.
They are open-minded and can change positions rather easily.
They love to take risks, love to gamble, love to solve problems
in crises. When the Negotiator is getting a school out of
trouble, rescuing a business from going under, or getting an
industry out of the "red," he is excited and enthusiastic.

But consider the situation if the Negotiator/Troubleshooter is
asked to stay and consolidate that school, or industry, or business. Suppose he is asked to head up the business that is now
in the black? Suppose he is asked to *maintain* an organization,
establishing human and data systems. What is he going to do?
He is going to make mischief. He is going to give himself activities which fit his preferences. He is going to go around
setting fires so that he can put them out. That is the penalty
of having a Troubleshooter stay on as stabilizer. He does not
get his jollies from stabilizing. He feels he's not earning his
keep, has nothing worthwhile to do, is bored—and so he goes
out looking for trouble. The moral of this story is, for an organization of any size, Negotiators are needed on a staff so
that they can solve crisis situations. They should not be required or allowed to stay in a situation once it is unsnarled.
This is a disservice to the Negotiator and to the organization.
This sort of leader needs to be kept mobile and used in the
manner for which he is suited.

Managerial Strengths: The Troubleshooter/Negotiator is practical in every sense of the word. He deals with concrete problems in an expeditious manner. He can observe a system and
see how it actually works, can find where breakdowns and
errors occur, and can figure out the corrections needed very
rapidly. Under the SP leader, change will be easy, for he can
adapt easily to new situations. He welcomes and seeks change.

As a leader, more than any other, this type will know what is going on in an organization, for he has acute powers of observation regarding the environment. Under his leadership things happen with an economy of motion. The SP leader does not fight the system but uses what is there and available to solve problem situations. He does not use his energies needlessly in worrying about changing what cannot be changed. Things that *can* be changed—personnel, procedures, policies—are all negotiable in the crisis.

Possible Weaknesses as a Manager: The SP leader might be reluctant to pay attention to theory and may be impatient with abstractions. He does not like the unfamiliar and may react negatively to change that he himself has not wrought. He lives so fully in the immediate moment that he may have difficulty remembering commitments and decisions of the past. Yesterday is quickly gone and just as fast forgotten. Current demands preempt anything else. This belief leaves the SP leader in a position of being somewhat unpredictable to his colleagues and subordinates. When there is nothing to troubleshoot, the Troubleshooter/Negotiator leader can become rigid.

Characteristic Ways of Dealing with Colleagues: The SP manager easily responds to the ideas of others if they are specific. He is flexible, patient, open-minded, and adaptable in working with others, who generally find the SP leader easy to get along with. He is not threatened by the possibility of failure in himself or others, so will take risks and encourages others to do the same. He changes his position easily as new facts and new situations arise—seldom finding this shift in position a threat to his self-esteem. He is willing to take orders from superiors and will not fight those above him, although he may not always carry out their directives. The SP leader is matter-of-fact about things as they are and does not chafe about what might have been. He does not judge his fellow workers and accepts their behaviors as matter-of-factly as he does situations. He does not trouble himself or others seeking to understand underlying motives or hidden meanings. The SP leader verbalizes appreciation easily and often voices approval before the accomplishment or achievement in order to encourage others.

Contributiions in a Management Team: An SP leader can spur action to a management team as can no other type. Things are sure to happen with this type around. The SP probably will be at his best in verbal planning and decision making. He may not enjoy or be good at producing written documents. He can spot trouble spots in an organization while they still are minor and can prevent small problems from becoming large ones because of inattention. Operations are apt to run smoothly with an SP aboard, since he will detect early signs of trouble in these operations. Productivity is apt to be high, and he usually will be aware of the comfort and working conditions of employees. The SP leader is not likely to allow unnecessarily bad working conditions to exist for employees without attempting to do something about them.

The SP leader needs the support of a thoroughly organized support staff who will provide reminders of scheduled appointments, who will schedule "unpleasant" jobs and remind the SP manager concerning these, and who will see to it that long-term issues are given closure. He needs support services that will help in setting priorities and will capture the endless flow of projects in writing for future reference.

SJ Manager at Work

The SJ manager might be called the Traditionalist, Stabilizer, or Consolidator. His focus is on the organization as a body, and he nourishes and cares for that social organism. The SJ manager's abilities lie in establishing policies, rules, schedules, routines, regulations, and hierarchy. He is good at drawing up lines of communication, at following through. He is patient, thorough, steady, reliable, orderly. He values policies, contracts, and standard operating procedures. This sort of manager can be relied on to arrange the environment so as to bring stability to an organization. He enjoys the process of stabilizing, feels he is most useful and earning his keep in such a process. People under the SJ manager know that they can count on things when he is in charge. They know that supplies, personnel, and an orderly way of conducting business will be there. Things will be settled and the organization will be stabilized.

The Traditionalist leader, in keeping with the name, carefully preserves the traditions of the organization, knowing that these give comfort, a sense of belonging, and a sense of permanence to employees and clients alike. Should the organization be lacking traditions, the SJ leader is likely to ensure that they are created. He is likely to move quickly to establish a basic fund of rites, rituals, and ceremonies, realizing as he does their function in the solidification of the social organism. There appears to be a theme of sentimentality running through the administrative structure led by an SJ manager, which can be exemplified by the retiring septegenarian receiving his gold watch, the official welcome rites provided for new employees, the traditional office Christmas party, the Fourth of July picnic for employees and their families, and so on.

The SJ leader has a very special sense of social responsibility. He wants to know where his duty lies and then quickly get at it. The desire to keep busy with the discharge of his obligations is strong in the SJ. This sort of industriousness is also something he values in his subordinates, colleagues, and superiors. The hard worker is much admired by the SJ.

Stabilization is a necessary stage in the life of any organization, but there is a tendency, after a time, for stability to go too far. And this style of management, of all the managerial types, is most subject to Parkinson's Law (1957), the law of domination of means over ends. This law implies that over a period of time, in any organization, the number and cost of procedures will increase with constant or even declining outcomes. The SJ manager is particularly vulnerable to the law, interested as he is in stabilizing the organization. This manager can find himself developing new procedures for the sole purpose of maintaining old procedures. He can find that he has generated means that in turn generate more means. He can find that he has allowed personnel and materiel to expand, to consume the available resources, without a clear picture in his head of the results which are to be delivered by this expansion. Organizations only too quickly become immobilized in procedural strait jackets (the name for which is *Bureaucracy*) when too much stabilization, too many traditions, too much consolidation takes place. Change can be brought to a grinding halt, and people will be doing things solely because they were done previously. The SJ manager more than others can become the victim of this hegemony of means over ends without realizing what has happened.

The stabilizer manager has a tendency to resist change and so must monitor his own behavior to insure that, in his zeal for policy, regulations and standard procedures, he does not overshoot the mark and attain too much stability. If he does, he may be a roadblock to necessary and healthy organizational growth, wasting much of his own and others' efforts. His employees will be dully doing things just because they did them last year and doing them slavishly, in a certain way, because that is the way they were done last year. A budget item, for example, might be adopted only because it was justified on a previous budget. Though operational costs are carefully watched, results costs are examined little, if at all. This bureaucratic disease is not limited only to SJ managers, of course; but the traditionalist is particularly vulnerable here. He should, therefore, periodically take a look at the effects of procedures of his organization to eliminate operations that have long been without worth but are continued, just because they are there, codified in procedural handbooks. The SJ manager can nourish and maintain an organization in an outstanding manner if he will keep a sharp eye out for the dangers of bureaucracy.

The appreciation behaviors of management are, as we said, the primary tools of management. How, then, does an SJ manager tend to behave in his appreciation role? How does he stroke? How does he give feedback to his employees (and superiors) that he has noticed what they are doing and knows about what they have contributed?

Here a phenomenon arising out of temperament can be observed. The SJ has a hunger to serve, to be needed, to do his duty. He feels a sense of responsibility and obligation, intrinsically believing that he always must earn his keep, each and every day. He feels that, somehow, he is indebted to society and must always work at paying what he owes. He tends to project that need onto others, with the result that only the person most worthy is seen as deserving plaudits. Since people must always *earn* their keep, that is, *earn* appreciation, only those who have been most worthy should be appreciated. Only the winners get the ribbons. Otherwise, the unconscious belief dictates, employees might become less productive. Giving credit where credit is not most deserved would be bad for morale; therefore, only the winner can receive the grand prize. Those in second and third place may receive a blue and green ribbon, but no other player gets anything!

To be most effective, the SJ manager must train himself to pay attention to the least achievement and systematically reward those achievements just because they were achieved. The manager who has this basic need to stabilize would do well to examine his implicit belief that only the *truly* deserving may be shown appreciation, and that the truly deserving can be only the outstanding few. He would do well to experiment with finding something, no matter how trifling, the least productive employee has contributed and expressing appreciation for that.

Managerial Strengths: The SJ manager easily does those things which create stability in the system. He is decisive, and he enjoys the decision-making process. He understands the values of an organization as they exist and tries to conserve these values. He understands policy and honors its intent. He is persevering, patient, works steadily with a realistic idea of how long a task will take, seldom makes errors of fact, tends to be outstanding at precision work, and can be counted on to follow through on commitments. Before he takes action, he will weigh the consequences and will try to see the practical effect of the decision. He possesses and admires common sense. He is himself orderly and admires this in others. He will be on time and on schedule.

The SJ manager is best when he can plan his work and follow through on the plan. He likes to get things clear, settled, and wrapped up; he may be restless until a decision is reached on materiel, personnel, and upcoming events. Others with whom he works will know where he stands on issues.

The Traditionalist leader is an applied thinker and wants an organization to be run on "solid facts." He is able to absorb, remember, manipulate, and manage a great amount of detail within a system. He is a superdependable leader who is an extraordinarily hard, steady worker. A good day's work for a good day's pay makes sense to the SJ manager. The superiors of this leader can count on him, as can his subordinates, to know, respect, and follow the rules, expecting them to apply equally to all.

The SJ manager will run efficient meetings, will be most comfortable with a well-ordered agenda. He will establish a formal, impersonal style in dealing with colleagues until he is well acquainted. He enjoys established routines and is a painstaking worker. The SJ manager is thorough about the business of the organization, is loyal to its purposes and personnel, and is usually briefed to the last detail.

Possible Weaknesses as a Manager: The SJ manager may be somewhat impatient with projects which get delayed by complications. He may be inclined to decide issues too quickly and, at times, may not notice new things which need to be done. He is excellent at preserving the effective procedures of an organization, but also may preserve less successful rules and regulations, not taking time to examine them for results. He may not be as responsive to the changing needs of an organization, which would be desirable, especially in times of rapid change.

The SJ leader is likely to hold that some people are good and some people are bad—and that the latter should be punished. From this position, the SJ manager can fall into relationships that create tensions, caused by his being, at times, blaming, denigrating, and negative. He may find himself responding to the negative elements of people as he becomes overtired and under pressure. If he does not make a conscious effort, he may slip without awareness from "this is a bad act" to "this is a bad act and, therefore, this is a bad person."

A sensitive pressure point for the Traditionalist may exist in his possible tendency to be overconcerned with the possibility of dire happenings. It is he, after all, who invented Murphy's Law. He may exaggerate the probability of things going wrong and thus may find himself using energies anticipating crises which never occur. An additional element of the Traditionalist's belief system is the notion that people can make something of themselves if only they work hard enough and long enough. This can pressure the SJ into being highly competitive and using his energies in pursuit of the perfect organization —thereby setting himself up for failure.

Characteristic Ways of Dealing with Colleagues: The SJ manager wants his colleagues to get to the point and stick to the point. He wants the facts and likes stable, sensible, reliable people. He believes that he is a realist, which in fact he is, when dealing with data systems. When he deals with human systems, however, he may not always be accurate in his perceptions of interpersonal transactions.

The SJ leader will be clearcut in his dealings with his colleagues and, if he feels that they are not observing agreed-upon procedures and policies, will call this to their attention; but he may do this before others rather than privately, or with words which are unnecessarily critical and harsh. He may find it easier to comment on his own and others' weaknesses than their strengths, tending to take his own and others' strengths as obvious and expected—and therefore not needing comment.

The Traditionalist manager may withhold strokes unless he believes they are fully deserved and may have difficulty in accepting strokes from others—thereby transmitting an attitude of rejection which is unintended. The SJ leader may find the giving of symbolic strokes, such as honors, trophies, appointments to coveted positions, titles, and so on, more comfortable than the giving of verbal or contact strokes.

Contributions in a Management Team: The Traditionalist/ Stabilizer leader particularly complements an NF leader, who brings strong focus onto people as people, while the SJ leader supplies an effective, smooth-running system. The SJ manager is excellent at plan-execution and operationalization. He can maintain an excellent data flow upward and downward so those around him are kept well informed. If an organization does not have an SJ manager on the management team, important details may be missed. Plant utilization may be poor. There may be poor control of materiel and personnel procedures, and far-reaching decisions may be made at inappropriate levels—by clerical personnel, for example. Time and materials waste may occur without management's notice. A system without a traditionalist leader may find itself in a constant state of change without a base of policy and regulation.

NT Manager at Work

The Traditionalist leader feels good when he is setting up rules, regulations, and procedures and feels he is thus earning his salary and serving the organization well; the Troubleshooter leader feels good when he is putting out fires, and feels guilty when he is not; the NT leader has to be conceptualizing something to feel good about himself within the organization. He must *design*, and so is called the Visionary leader. He is inspired and energized by being asked to do some kind of architectural or engineering job. Then and only then does he feel that he is worth his salary. He prides himself on his technical knowhow (including managerial technology) and wants to use his intellect to figure out complexities, to get models onto paper, to rise to challenges of design for increased effectiveness and efficiency. When asked to design something, the NT manager goes happily to work. When asked to put something together for the first time—a prototype—he is all the more happy, since he is doing that which is most worthwhile. He is not interested in maintenance or in consolidation, and he abhors unsnarling messes. It does not make much sense to him that crises should even exist, and to the Visionary things have to make sense. This leader can be adamant and stand on principles against all antagonists, no matter what the price. He cannot bear for either himself or others to make the same mistake twice. One error is forgivable; a second occurrence of the error, unthinkable. The Visionary seeks and enjoys complexity; he avoids redundancy. He expects a great deal from himself and only a little less from others.

Even though it is the Visionary leader who can envision how an organization might look ten years hence and blueprint that ten-year goal, he may have difficulty communicating the details of those goals and the plans to reach them. People follow this leader because they find his visions of the future contagious; but they sometimes get lost because of his tendency to avoid redundancy. The NT prefers not to say anything twice and assumes understanding; that is, if something is only implied, that suffices. The NT does not believe it necessary to verbalize this implication. He exercises an economy of communication, being reluctant to state the obvious lest he appear naïve or insulting to his listeners. Thus the Visionary, the architect of systems, may have a communication problem. Although he has the capacity to conceptualize and communicate his models, he tends to become too technical and terse in the way he talks, may present ideas too involved in details, and may present too much complexity in too short a time. Very often, therefore, his audience loses sight of the forest while trying to comprehend the trees.

As a manager, the Visionary is not a natural appreciator, and part of his problem in the arts of appreciation stems from his reluctance to state the obvious. He unwittingly assumes that if a person has done a good job, then this is obvious—obvious to him and obvious to all others, and therefore he, the NT leader, need not say anything. If he does, the person who made the contribution and who is the recipient of the appreciation might think, "Why is he saying this? Is it not perfectly obvious that I have done a good job?" And so the Visionary is reticent to express appreciation for fear of being seen as manipulative. At least that is his rationalization. Probably part of the truth is that he himself is embarrassed by being told by somebody when he has done a good job, and is likewise embarrassed when he tells others about his appreciation for their contributions. So with these rationalizations—that the receiver of the appreciation would find the verbalizations manipulative and devious—he tends not to say anything to his subordinates or superiors about their efforts and achievements.

Yet in his head he has firm grasp of the concept in human transactions that was so well articulated in the group therapy movement: *If people are not told overtly and clearly that they are appreciated, they will conclude the opposite.* People, regardless of type, never take for granted that they are appreciated unless they are told that they are. If an employee is accomplishing something, be it ever so small, he needs to be told *by the manager* (for which there is no substitute!) that his accomplishments are recognized, are confirmed, that they matter. The fact that the employee is paid in dollars for this accomplishment is beside the issue. If the organization is to get all the employee's commitment, the employee will have to be paid in currency over and above dollars, currency which responds to the basic need of that employee's type. The concept stressed here is that the leaders, and only the leaders, are in a position to express officially appreciation in the name of the organization. Another way of stating this principle of management is that only the administrator can officially express appreciation. Thus, if an employee is to be made aware that the organization, the corporate body, is appreciative of his efforts and contributions, then the spokesman for that organization, the voice of the corporate body, must be the one who holds the office of manager. Only the leader of an organizational unit can officially activate the motor of achievement. The Visionary manager may have difficulty with this interaction and should study particularly the behavior of an NF leader in this area.

Managerial Strengths: The Visionary leader is the architect of change. He is interested in the principles on which the organization is built or is to be built. If the SJ is the pessimist, the NT is the skeptic. He questions everything and bases answers on laws and principles. He is able to see the dimensions and axes of systems as if he had x-ray vision, and so can plan and construct capably. Characteristically he is able to see how the needs of the immediate system he serves interlock with those of other systems within the total structure. He sees the interworkings of the system itself and the long- and short-range implications of events which occur and behaviors which people display.

The NT manager's focus is on possibility. What exists presently can be changed, as it should be, since it is a mere remnant of the past. When he moves into an organization, he is likely to discern immediately the power base and power structure, and from an impersonal point of view. This managerial type is often intellectually ingenious and can pioneer in technical or administrative areas.

Possible Weaknesses as a Manager: When the Visionary manager is involved in the creative process, he has enormous drive; but once his castle is designed, he is more than willing to allow someone else to take over execution and construction. As a result, he may find that his designs and plans were not carried out to his satisfaction. He seldom blames others for this failure, only himself—but he will tend to repeat his premature loss of interest in the next situation. This is particularly true with NTPs. NTJs are apt to do the same thing but usually at a later stage.

Because the focus of the Visionary leader is on principles, he may, at times, be unaware of the feelings of others and be equally oblivious to their hurts and joys. People, therefore, may find him cold and distant and may have difficulty in approaching him. Colleagues may not feel comfortable in commenting on the homely events in their lives, and thus the NT manager can become isolated from the other-than-business activities of people within the organization. As a result, the NT manager often finds himself at a loss for small talk in social or semi-social situations.

The NT manager is apt to be intellectually oriented and may unknowingly communicate an attitude on his part that he does not value subordinates (or superiors) who are not intellectually gifted. He may find difficulty in his interpersonal transactions because of his projections onto others that they (also) should be thoroughly competent, adequate, and achieving in all possible respects. The Visionary leader expects a great deal of himself and others, often more than can be delivered, and he might do well to remind himself that people with great strengths also have great weaknesses. Because the NT leader tends to escalate standards for himself and others, he typically feels restless and unfulfilled. This restlessness sometimes takes the form of verbalized impatience by the NT manager with snarls and errors, and, at times, an impatience with finding it necessary to cover ground already discussed.

Characteristic Ways of Dealing with Colleagues: The NT manager typically tracks the thought processes and ideas of others rather easily and enjoys doing so. He is responsive to the new ideas of colleagues and enthusiastic about his own. He enjoys solving problems and, when faced with a colleague's problem, will be stimulated rather than weighed down by the prospect of solving the problem. He has the courage of his convictions and is willing to stand alone against the crowd if he believes that he is right.

The Visionary/Architect/Builder likes to make decisions, particularly the NTJs, yet colleagues will know where the Visionary leader stands on issues *only* if they ask! The NT assumes that his position is obvious and, therefore, it would be redundant to verbalize it; but he can be counted on to be frank if his opinion is solicited. When others speak for him concerning his position, he can become inwardly annoyed, although he usually does not allow this reaction to show. And, as often as not, when others do speak for his position, they are wrong.

The NT manager may, at times, be too nonconforming and ahead of the crowd to have public acceptance or a devoted, dedicated following. He tends to be on the growing edge of change and seldom looks back over his shoulder to check if others are close behind. His "self-power awareness" causes him to be noncompetitive. Seldom does the NT believe that he must get ahead at the expense of others. Seldom does he demonstrate a need to minimize the contributions of colleagues.

The Visionary manager is an excellent decision maker and can be counted on to remember and to honor decisions, even when under great pressure. In an organization, the Visionary is the "portrait painter of ideas." Because he can so easily conceptualize the results that staff members suggest as their contributions, he is comfortable in a management system that focuses on results rather than on procedures.

The NT, manager or producer, may quickly leave an organization (either physically or psychologically) if his talents are not used.

Contributions in a Management Team: If an organization does not have a Visionary/Architect/Builder on the management team, planned change may be minimal, and sooner or later deterioration will occur. The status quo will continue, perhaps to obsolescence. The NT manager can contribute theoretical structure and develop useable alternatives for actions being considered. And the structures the NTs develop are apt to take into consideration the benefits for the entire system as well as the immediate system being developed. NTs contribute a belief and enthusiasm in possibilities of ideas which are often contagious to others. They can be as supportive and enthusiastic about the ideas of another as their own and ordinarily are as good at following as leading, being able to do either as the circumstances demand. An NT team member may want to spend too much time planning and delay execution, but an SP team member can provide the proper stimulus.

NF Manager at Work

The final type of leader is called the Catalyst leader because of his talent for being personal and personable. The NF leader has the capability of drawing out the best in people, and he is first and foremost people-oriented. His focus is not on the organization, that is, instrumental, in the way of the NT and SJ, but is transactional, a characteristic he shares with the SP manager. That is, his focus is on the individuals within the organization. He is very, very personal in his transactions and tends to become deeply committed to the progress of those around him, forever alert for their possibilities in both career development and personal growth. In this he is like a chemical catalyst that, when put into a chemical mixture, acts as a reagent, catalyzing or actuating otherwise latent potentials. The individual in encountering such a leader is "drawn out" and "activated."

When the NF manager is around others, he demonstrates an interest in developing their possibilities, and thus his focus is primarily on the potentialities of his staff, with the development of the organizational system being secondary. The NF is the natural democratic leader and the natural participative. His forte is a smooth, people-oriented process, with documents and products a fallout rather than a primary target. The Catalyst leader is comfortable working in a democractic climate, and is sympathic to his people, generous with his willingness to listen to their troubles, and sincerely concerned with their personal problems. Sometimes the Catalyst leader can find that this involvement takes too high a toll of his energy, so that he has little left for himself.

The NF manager, with his verbal fluency, can be an enthusiastic spokesman for his organization. As an appreciator, he is outstanding. He is always and forever looking for and reacting to the best in others and communicates the fact that he is seeing this goodness. The Catalyst listens carefully, intently, and with an abundance of verbal and nonverbal feedback, so that the receiver is aware that he is being carefully and completely attended—and that he is valued. The Catalyst, with his gift of language, seems to know somehow how to say the right things at the right time to express appropriate appreciation.

The Catalyst leader, focusing as he does on people growth, values approval—approval for himself and for his administrative unit. He can, in the process, subordinate his own wishes and wants to the wishes and wants of others, sometimes to the degree that he leaves little for himself: The values and priorities of others have almost erased those he holds. Other people's priorities can very quickly take over because of the Catalyst leader's tendency to place the needs of others before his own. Like the SJ manager, the NF manager can then get overtired and come to a point where he finds little personal reward in his work. The obvious way to avoid this, of course, is for the NF leader to review periodically *his* goals, *his* priorities, *his* purposes to see if he is moving in a desired direction.

The NF leader includes the ENFJ, who is the natural leader of this type, and the ENFP, INFP, and INFJ, who will have to work a little harder at their leadership. Their primary hunger is for a search for self, through achieving identity and integrity. They are marked by idealism, are often charismatic, are superbly empathic, and have a flair for dramatizing the mundane events of living into something special.

Managerial Strengths: The management style of the Catalyst leader is marked by personal charisma and commitment to the people he leads. He usually has a tongue of silver and communicates through speech his caring and enthusiasm. He is sometimes gifted in seeing the possibilities of both the institution and the people with whom he works, focusing intuitively on their strengths. He excels in working with and through people and, as the head of a democratically-run organization, allows the contributions of all members of that organization to surface. He usually is comfortable in unstructured meetings. More often than not, he is accurate about the organizational climate. He tends to be patient with complicated situations and can wait for the right time to move forward. The Catalyst can be extraordinary as the head of an organization, the visible leader who speaks well for the organization itself and for the people in it. He often has an unusual store of energies, although these seem to come in bursts powered by a new enthusiasm. Yesterday's projects, at that point, may not receive needed attention.

The NF leader has, when he is at his best, the talent, more than any other temperament, for seeing how a liability can be turned into an asset, particularly when dealing with people problems. He forgets very easily yesterday's negative, disagreeable events and tends to remember the agreeable, tending to be a romantic about both the future and the past—always the optimist in his public presentation of self. Generally he hides his pessimistic moments, wanting to spare others any discomfort that might arise from these "down" times.

The Catalyst manager tends to be the best and most abundant giver of appreciation. He uses enthusiasm, listening, and approval as he works with people. Because he gives so much, he himself needs replenishment through having others give to him, in turn, expressions of enthusiasm, listening, and approval. If he receives this support he can continue contributing at his very high degree of productivity. If he does not, if he is met with continual disapproval, he can become discouraged and may look outside the organization for this kind of recognition. He values words of appreciation from his colleagues, his superiors, and his subordinates and can appreciate the intentions of the giver even when the approval is oblique. The Catalyst manager tends to be motivated himself by positive comments rather than negative ones, tends to see the positive in others and events.

Possible Weaknesses as a Manager: The NF leader may find that other people's priorities eat up much of his time because he is so responsive to interpersonal transactions—and, indeed, seeks them out. The Catalyst tends to be very generous with his time, even to the point of neglecting his obligations outside the organization and neglecting necessary recreational time.

He sorely needs to schedule renewal time for himself if he is not to have his energies drained to the point where he is unproductive and immobilized.

The Catalyst manager may find himself making administrative decisions on the basis of his personal likes and dislikes, rather than on the basis of what might be best for the organization. He may also find himself torn frequently between the needs of his subordinates and the request of his superiors, as he is so sensitive to the situation of the former. He can find himself viewed as the champion of two opposing groups because he has listened to both sympathetically and has communicated understanding. Both factions conclude, only too often, that the NF, because of his empathic feedback, subscribes to their position. In truth, the NF is so in tune with the feelings of others that he is vulnerable to finding himself wanting to please all of the people all of the time. If his unit is under criticism from superiors or if things do not go well within his unit, he may too quickly lose self-confidence, internalizing what may be the failures of others as *his* failures.

The NF manager is able to create a climate where people in his administrative unit have freedom, autonomy, and initiative. This usually causes healthy growth for the unit, but, at times, as a result of this freedom, autonomy, and initiative, mandated operations do not get carried out; the NF leader has to accept the brunt of this—which does not always lead to the best career development situations for him. Another hazard for the NF leader is that he has a tendency to avoid unpleasantness, perhaps hoping that, if he can delay facing these difficulties, they may somehow disappear. Sometimes, then, he finds that he has taken what was a temporarily easy way out, only to find that larger problems have resulted, both institutional problems and interpersonal problems. He may find himself rescuing "victims" of the system and this may lead him into conflicts with his loyalty to the institution and loyalty to individuals in the system. In spite of his best efforts to avoid this, the NF manager may find himself creating dependency relationships. Others will tend to lean on him for support, seek direction, perhaps unduly, and generally drain his energies by bids for attention. Usually the Catalyst will be at a loss as to how this happens, and mystified how to prevent the situation from developing again and again with a variety of people.

Characteristic Ways of Dealing with Colleagues: The Catalyst

leader relates well and is popular with his colleagues. He hungers for personal contacts and goes out of his way to seek these, especially the extraverted NF. He is sociable and enjoys being with his staff, whether socializing or working. He touches base frequently with his staff and knows a great deal about their problems, their feelings, and their pleasures. He tends to seek close, interpersonal relationships with his colleagues and find his work a source of social satisfaction as well as a place to be productive in work.

Contribution in a Management Team: The Catalyst leader will add a personalized, people-centered point of view to a management team and can speak to the social consequences of a ploy in a way other types may not. If an organization does not have an NF leader on a team, members of the organization may find the environment cold, sterile, inhuman, joyless, dull, and complain about the absence of companionship. Esprit de corps may be low and enthusiasm minimal. Although excellent data systems may exist, the people in the system may not be used as effectively as they might. Many a troubled water can be stilled when a Catalyst is present to pour on the necessary oils.

The Catalyst is outstanding in public relations, is excellent as spokesman for an organization, for he has the facility of communicating his enthusiasm. He works well with all types of people and can "sell" an organization to its clients. The people who work with him usually feel good about the organization and about their place in it. If the Catalyst is given freedom to create and to manage, he can move; conversely, if he has too many standard operating procedures to follow, he may become frustrated. Those around the Catalyst may tend to be loyal to him personally, at times at the expense of seeing organizational needs, priorities, and issues.

On a management team, other team members are apt to enjoy working with the NF and find him supportive and attentive to their points of view. He has the characteristic, as does the SP, of being able to make business a pleasure.

Each style of leadership has its own unique contribution to make to the working situation. SJs lend stability and confidence. SPs make excellent problem-solvers and lend excitement. NTs provide vision and theoretical models for change.

NFs lubricate the interpersonal fabric of an organization and can predict the social consequences of the NT's theoretical models.

Knowing one's own management style is essential if strengths are to be used productively. But leadership style is only half of interaction. Follower style represents a critical dimension in the effectiveness of a leader. This has been described in detail in Chapter II in terms of the four styles and in the portraits of the sixteen types. Some additional considerations might be useful at this point, however. We shall discuss the observations of Seeland (1976), who has analyzed the constraints to change inherent in each of the four styles and has suggested strategies for winning the support for change from each of the four styles.

Constraints to Change—NFs: Spokesmanship in groups under management may be largely from the NF group (especially ENFP and ENFJ), characteristically persuasive, verbal, and outspoken, appealing to their colleagues through emotion-laden positions. NFs tend to identify themselves and their colleagues as capable, highly-trained professionals concerned with the needs of humanity in general and the "clients" of the institution served in particular. They do not always cast management in this same role. Self-determination is viewed as a crucial feature in the NF's work environment. Autonomy is highly valued as an earmark of unique identity. They are extremely sensitive to even a hint of imposed structure, to the notion of authoritarianism, or, in fact, to any move on the part of management that could be interpreted as circumscribing individuality. It is unlikely that any institution-wide change can occur without its being supported by the NFs.

Given that NFs need recognition of their individuality, and their personal worth, and given that they are dedicated to democratic processes, involving NFs in decision (as in participative management) is likely to elicit their support. If a wanted change can be described in terms of human values, of better meeting the individual needs of employees and clients, then NFs are likely to see such change as desirable. They need an abundant opportunity to discuss possible change long before it is to be implemented. Change for NFs should never be sudden, but be implemented slowly. The time-honored management rule of "no surprises" applies in full force to the NFs.

Constraints to Change—SJs: As with the NFs in follower groups, SJs are apt to be highly influential. They are characteristically outspoken and ready to voice opinions, but in a manner somewhat different from the NFs. The SJs tend to focus on procedural matters, ways of doing things, rather than on human values. They are not so sensitive about lines of authority as are the NFs. SJs like the security provided by clearly-defined lines of authority, and frequently are vaguely uncomfortable with the positions articulated by their NF colleagues. SJs tend not to be as dramatic as the NFs and are thus more frequently influenced by the NFs.

Strategies for winning SJ support for change need to give consideration to the SJ's need to be responsible and to serve, to uphold tradition, and to deal with the status quo. Providing SJ with *facts* to support a desired change may help to engage their cooperation. Furthermore, if the desired change can be described in terms of a more efficient way of getting things done, in terms of a better procedure, the SJs will be likely to react positively in the degree the change makes sense to them. In contrast with the NFs, who need verbal discussion, the SJs need to have written documents describing the change. In fact, they tend to become rather impatient with discussions, particularly repetitive or lengthy discussions. If the SJs can be involved in writing a procedural manual involved in the change, they are apt to be delighted and are also apt to produce a thorough and sensible document.

Constraints to Change—NTs: NTs usually comprise a respected minority among a follower group. They are not often constrained to exert visible leadership but are often powerful forces behind the scenes. They gain the respect of their colleagues through their mastery of the technical and pragmatic aspects of the enterprise. They are logical and seldom are resistant to change the pragmatics of which can be specified. NTs readily accept the ideas of others and do not find long discussion periods necessary before accepting change, as do the NFs. Nor are the NTs either threatened or impressed by designated authority, as might the SJs be. Titular power means little to them; power by virtue of competency does, and this applies to the competency of the manager. NTs often hold themselves aloof from the positions taken by their NF colleagues, and will not often fight for issues. They will fight against issues which violate the common reason.

Strategies for winning NT support for change require a recognition of the NT's need for competency and to be seen as competent. Their support can best be engaged through appeal to their intellect. One way to effect this is to give the NTs opportunity to design the model for change. Changes in which the NT has had a hand in devising are heartily endorsed by the devisor.

Constraints to Change—SPs: SPs tend to ignore the rules of any system they are in, preferring to march to their own drums as independent free spirits. They seldom seem involved with insitutional concerns and are, therefore, rarely influential either as a positive or as a negative force for change. Only when a crisis occurs do the SPs mobilize for action and thus their involvement with change must, by definition, be unplanned. There can be no strategies for winning SP support for *planned* change; they can be counted on to lend excitement to unplanned change and are very likely to be unilaterally involved in pursuing their own impulses to change.

Temperament in Teaching

Many school districts in California[5] show a rather consistent distribution of teacher and administrator types (a few small districts vary from this when they have NT administrators):

	School Personnel	Pupils & General Population	Difference
SJ........	56%	38%	+ 16%
NF.......	36%	12%	+ 24%
NT.......	6%	12%	− 6%
SP	2%	38%	− 36%

This distribution seems to affect the behavior of individual teachers and administrators. First, neither the SJ teachers nor the SJ administrators feel any need to defend their views on instruction or administration, even if it occurred to them to do so. Belonging to so massive a majority, the SJ educators unconsciously assume their views to be the norm and are continuously surprised when colleagues take issue with them on

[5]Contact the Center for Application of Psychological Types, University of Florida, Gainesville, for data on schools in other states.

"basics" and "fundamentals." Most of their views are met with general agreement, not only from their colleagues and superiors, but also from the parents (the SJ parents, much more frequently than others, faithfully attend PTA meetings).

But the NF contingent in schools, which far exceeds NF frequency in the general population, is very outspoken (albeit self-consciously, since the NFs are very much aware of the solid majority position held by the SJs). NF teachers believe in the "search for self" and they will never back down or keep quiet about it. Occasionally, of course, an NF can be alone on a faculty surrounded by SJs; in such a situation he does keep quiet, since he gets no encouragement for his views.

The one or two NTs in the school (if any) stand on the sidelines of this idealogical tug-of-war, amused, puzzled, skeptical, and detached, wondering how these people got so mixed up and why they don't get on with the "real business of school," which is, of course, "intellectual development."

The single SP (and in most schools there isn't even one) doesn't even stand on the sidelines. He hasn't the faintest notion of there even being a tug-of-war; he is off doing his thing, oblivious to the regulations as well as the course of study.

We may note that school districts periodically (by the calendar) "go back to basics"; meaning, of course, that the SJs are in the driver's seat and are intent upon reversing the inroads made by the NF's "self-actualization" curriculum. And so it goes, through the decades, an eternal sine wave:

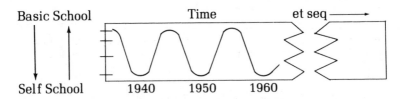

So our SJ educators, quite sure of the reason for their school, step into classrooms of 32 children who are to be their Pygmalion Project (encountered elsewhere in the domains of mating and parenting). They must change these formless beings into their own image. Let us review the extent of their problem, stated in Chapter IV:

ESFJ	ESFJ	ESFP	ESFP	ENTP	INTP
ESFJ	ESFJ	ESFP	ESFP	ENTJ	
ESFJ	ESTJ	ESFP	ESTP	ENTJ	
ESTJ	ISFJ	ESTP	ISFP	ENFP	
ESTJ	ISTJ	ESTP	ISFP	ENFP	
ESTJ	ISTJ	ESTP	ISTP	ENFJ	INFJ

In passing, we might reflect on the impact that J. L. Moreno's book *Who Shall Survive?* (1934) should have had on our SJ pedgagues—but didn't. Sociometry, the measure of social relationship in the classroom (Moreno's invention), is brought out every 20 years or so, dusted off, and used for awhile, only to be jettisoned when the school inevitably returns to "fundamentals."[6]

Coming back to the teachers' problem: How are they to turn all of these kids into savers or spenders, skeptics or believers, i.e., whatever the *teachers* are? We can be quite certain that, if the temperament hypothesis means anything, they are going to fail, as they should. The problem, as it is posed, cannot be solved. We cannot change another's character any more than a leopard can change his spots. But it is well that we cannot. The real pedagogical problem is not how to *change* temperament, but how to *utilize* one's own temperament in establishing and maintaining a facilitative relationship with the differing temperaments of students.

This is not easy, entailing as it does an understanding of teaching and learning styles. We've discussed learning styles in Chapter IV; let us, then, turn our attention to teaching styles.

Teaching in SP Style: SP teachers are interested in the development of freedom and spontaneity in their students. In pursuit of this the SP teacher can be counted on to do the unexpected. It seems a pity that this group are so seldom drawn to the profession of teaching (about 2 percent), preferring to go

[6]There is some variance in what is held to be "fundamental." Mostly it is the "3 R's," which is to say, clerical skills. Now and then, however, the fundamentals edge (ever so slightly) into the NT domain of philology, epistemology, and logic (the latter including mathematical reasoning).

into more action-oriented occupations, for the SP teacher has
a unique and valuable style. It is, however, understandable
why they do not go into this field, desiring as they do the
unfettered life. Yet their focus on the immediate, on living the
good life, taking enjoyment where it can be found, reacting
with spontaneity to new situations, and taking time for play
can make the SP teacher especially attractive to students.
They thrive on performance and more often than not their
teaching presentations is an entertaining, attractive show or
contest that teaches.

Unfortunately, SPs tend to abandon formal education in greater
numbers than any other style. As was pointed out in the chapter on children, the SP student is the one most apt to show
discrepancies between scores on academic ability tests and
grade point average. The usual classroom simply is not man-
aged in a way that appeals to the style of the SP learners;
thus, they move on to other ways of using their time as soon
as they legally can. Relatively few SPs stay around higher
education long enough to obtain the necessary credentials to
teach, and their unique style is largely lost to educational
systems and other occupations that demand prolonged formal
studies.

When SPs do decide to go into teaching, they can be exciting
mentors. They also are apt to be somewhat unpredictable,
and students seldom know what might happen from day to
day. If absolutely forced, SP teachers may turn in their plans,
but they are not likely to follow them with any regularity.
They value too much their freedom to respond to whatever
impulse strikes them on a given day or at a given moment.

The interaction of the SPs with their students is curiously
like that of the SJ teachers with their students; that is, focus
is on communication student to teacher rather than student
to student. SPs' enjoyment of performing induces them to be
the star of the classroom; this, of course, requires an audience.
And students enjoy every minute of this. They may or may not
learn the prescribed curriculum, but they will look forward to
their classroom experience under SPs and are likely to hold
them in great affection. The relationship can better be compared with that of an admired older sibling with a younger
brother or sister rather than that of child to surrogate parent.

The notion of being accountable for outcomes does not speak
to SP teachers, for their strength is in providing a variety of

action experiences for the student. Something is always happening in the classroom, which is usually noisy, filled with what seems a jumble of objects. Students get engaged enthusiastically in project after project and activity after activity—some of which may be completed and some not. SP teachers often teach through construction play, letting students manipulate tools and use up materials. They like to use films, filmstrips, video tapes, and the like as part of their instructional program. Asking students to answer questions listed at the end of a chapter is shunned by SP teachers. If they give homework assignments at all, little distress is voiced if students fail to turn the assignments in. Nor are the SP teachers apt to feel pressured to correct and return these assignments, whether produced in or out of class.

SP teachers can add a dimension to a teaching team which other styles do not naturally employ. SPs may not always, however, have the regard and admiration of their teaching team members, because of the SPs' tendency to follow impulses which may not fit in with the well-laid plans of the team. SPs are not burdened with the belief that learning is its own reward nor with the companion belief that extrinsic rewards for learning are bad. Hence, SPs are more likely than the other styles to make learning incidental to competing in some sort of contest. SPs have no built-in constraint against letting children risk themselves, fight, and get excited.

Teaching in SJ Style: SJ teachers are interested in developing the usefulness and place of students in society.

Three out of five teachers are likely to be SJs, and their interest in preserving and passing on the cultural heritage within the context of socially recognized institutions explains this percentage. Responsible, dependable, contributing to the needs of others, and creating and preserving social harmony—are all terms that characterize the SJ teachers.

SJ teachers are apt to have well-established classroom routines. Their work is more than likely to be well laid out, planned in advance, sequential in presentation, and clear in articulation. SJ teachers are usually firm and fair disciplinarians who expect students to obey the rules of the classroom and institution. SJs themselves present such a model of comportment.

SJ teachers are somewhere between the NF and NT teachers in psychological distance which is placed between student and teacher. SJs are not as empathic (and, therefore, not as vulnerable) with the students as are the NFs nor are they as distant as the NTs. SJ teachers are apt to prefer the obedient students and are willing to devote endless energy to helping those students learn. The SJs may be less patient with non-conforming students, such as an SP who is disruptive.

SJ teachers usually are excellent in teaching by the Socratic question. They generally can be observed encouraging student-to-teacher interaction and minimizing the time spent in student-to-student interaction. SJ teachers see running the classroom as their responsibility; giving this over to students does not seem appropriate to them unless this is defined as a lesson in management.

SJ teachers are thorough in providing criticism of perfor-mances and reports to the students so that the students have knowledge of results. On the other hand, the SJ is somewhat reluctant to point out the ways and degrees in which student performances are correct—a tactical error, especially for NF students. NT students can put off the SJ teachers through the NTs' independent attitudes and tendency to follow their own intellectual interests. The message the NT sends to the SJ teacher, albeit unwittingly, is that the teacher is not needed. The fact that NT students do very much need their mentors, but in their own particular way, is not always apparent to SJ (or NF, or SP) teachers.

SJ teachers can be even more put off by SP students who are interested in action and adventure, and who resist every effort to force "good study habits" into their repertoire. The SP stu-dents react to this disapproval by acting up, which further stimulates the teacher's disapproval and an unhealthy cycle is created—which the SPs always lose and, in the process, also often lose their formal education, since they solve the conflict by leaving school as soon as they can.

NF students may lean on SJ teachers in a way which gives annoyance, always seeking the approval so necessary for the NF to build identity. The NF's offer of help is seldom really helpful to an SJ teacher and eventually causes the teacher irritation, especially when the NF often is busy at the "help-ing" activity rather than working at assignments.

The 38 percent of students who are SJs tend to harmonize with the climate established by SJ teachers, a climate which is nurturing but which expects that lessons be done on time and in an orthodox manner.

SJ teachers work well in the organizational structure. They may voice criticism of the administration of the school and district, but they remain loyal and supportive when outside forces assault the institution or the people in that institution. SJ teachers understand and encourage school loyalty, work well with school activities and student government. They usually support the athletic program, the recreational program, and the parent organizations. SJs lend stability to a school, are themselves responsible representatives of society, and expect both their students and their colleagues to be the same.

Teaching in NT Style: NT teachers are interested in the development of intelligence. They seek answers to nature's enigmas and inspire their students to do likewise. They focus on relationships and complexity components and try to lead their students to do likewise. NT teachers tend to be impersonal in their approach to their students, taking it for granted that students want to learn. At times NT teachers can be oblivious to the emotional climate of a classroom and may continue a planned lesson when the students would benefit more from another sort of experience. NT teachers are aptly described as subject-centered.

NT teachers often enjoy designing and building new curricula, although they are not always willing to be involved in the implementation of their ideas, especially when clerical details are involved. Preferring not to teach the same material over and over, NT teachers will seek new tactics even if dealing with the same content area. This type of teacher can become disinterested once a subject content is understood, and it is no accident that the majority of NT teachers are in higher education where, presumably, intellectual demands are the greatest. In high schools, NTs tend to be in the sciences and mathematics while few teach happily in the business, industrial arts, or humanities.

NT teachers carefully track the thought processes of their students, especially those students who are interested in their own intellectual growth. If a good debate ensues, the NT teachers are most pleased. They like to share intellectual discoveries of their students and enjoy inspiring them to stretch intellectual muscles. If a student wants to follow his or her own curiosity, an NT teacher generally is encouraging, given that the project is rational. Predictably, NT teachers are good at using a problem-centered discussion approach in instruction, although they can become impatient with class dialogues which drift off the subject or if the learning process seems to be moving too slowly.

NT teachers may have to discipline themselves to introduce more redundancy into their teaching, fighting the tendency to state a principle or fact once and then expect students to have gained that knowledge once and for all. Because of their dread of boring the students, NTs have a tendency to move too rapidly for all but a few. NTs are better at teaching technical subjects than clerical, historical, or artistic subjects. They are usually not interested in teaching slower-moving students and are generally more comfortable with the rapid learner.

With their high standards for students, NT teachers tend to escalate performance standards, and an outstanding class may be the yardstick against which all succeeding classes are held and found wanting. Thus students in the classes of NT teachers may not have a sufficient number of success experiences to balance their misses or failures. NT teachers usually value knowledge of subject matter (as vehicle for intellectual development) over development of social and aesthetic skills, which is just the reverse with the NF teacher.

Students of an NT teacher are likely to know where the teacher stands as far as discipline and expectations for achievement are concerned. Seldom can an NT teacher be persuaded through emotional appeal to shift a position which is well-reasoned and, in the NT teacher's view, just and equitable. For example, an NT teacher does not often give in to administrative or parental pressure to change a grade which the NT believes has been accurately assigned to a performance. NTs do have difficulty communicating to their students that their efforts are appreciated, believing that this is obvious, which, unfortunately for the students, is not the case. Students often believe that they are judged inadequate by the NT teacher when, in fact, their performances were most satisfactory. As in other settings, in teaching the NT needs to make conscious effort to verbalize appreciation for the contributions of students in their efforts to learn. NT teachers may have to work hard to create a positive climate in their classrooms, because of this obliviousness to others' need for appreciation and the NTs tendency to see only a few students as doing work "up to standard" while the majority are seen as "marginal" and "inept." Yet the NTs are the most likely of all the temperaments to devise tasks for their students fitted to the growing edges of each student. Since their primary mission is the development of intelligence in each child, they are more likely to be aware of *variations* in intelligence both between children and within children. They are less likely than others to make the mistake of assuming that because a child does poorly or well in a given task he therefore will do poorly or well on another, different task. Also, it is the NT teacher who is more likely than others to be sensitive to the student's self-concept in the domain of competence. Since he's always feeling his own intellectual pulse, the NT can see how the child views his repertoire of capabilities.

On a teaching team, an NT almost always works well with another NT, but the inclusion of an NF can provide an element which is not offered by the NTs. NF teachers are apt to be sensitive to the emotional climate of a classroom in a way which others are not. NTs generally are supportive of the institution and supportive of their team members, but they expect a high degree of competency from both other teachers and the administration—who find that NTs have little patience for redundant or needless paperwork or for unproductive meetings. NTs are apt to lose interest in attending meetings which contain content better delivered in written form.

NT's are apt to continue to improve their professional skills in their chosen field, and, as a group, apt to have more than their share of advanced degrees. They are likely to be well read in professional literature and invest heavily in professional books. As a group, their voice will be heard in support of rigorous academic standards, and seldom do they subscribe to the position that learning must always be pleasant, easy, and comfortable. They themselves are appreciative of inservice opportunities if the presentations are directed toward relevant, academically rigorous content.

Teaching in NF Style: The teaching style of the NFs is marked by personal charisma and commitment to the students they teach. NF teachers are genuinely concerned about all aspects of the welfare of their students, their social as well as their intellectual development. They tend to relate to each student on an individual basis and often attempt to individualize instruction. Under the NF's leadership, students often find that they have talents previously unrecognized.

NF teachers themselves often are talented in conducting a democratic classroom. They want to involve their students in the decision-making process and are willing to abide by the group decision. They also are more willing than other types to allow student-to-student interaction and do not see themselves as the source of all wisdom. NF teachers usually have the courage to permit students to fail at times and are there to provide encouragement when needed.

NF teachers are much in touch with the climate of their classrooms and are willing to change a well-planned lesson if students seem to need other experiences at a given time. The NF teachers can plan and operate a "three-ring circus" in their classrooms, for they have a great tolerance for a multitude of simultaneous activities as long as they are productive. They use large group, small group, and individualized instructional modes with equal comfort, reluctantly using workbooks and manufactured tasks and projects, preferring to create their own curriculum materials.

NFs can be unconventional in their teaching and can handle the unconventional in students. If appropriate to the curriculum, NF teachers use instructional materials directed toward social development with ease. "Values" curricula and experiences often appeal to them.

NFs interact individually with each student in their classrooms; at times, this creates an emotional overload for these teachers who, as is typical of NFs, are empathic and in touch with the emotions of others as well as their own feelings. This makes them vulnerable to negative as well as positive input. Relating to over 100 students in a multi-class situation may place a strain on the emotional well-being of an NF, and it is vital that sufficient recreation time is arranged.

The belief that they must be caring and be cared about by all those they lead and teach may harm the effectiveness of an NF teacher. If they dislike a student, the NFs may suffer until they figure out the reason for the dislike and then are apt to struggle to quell this dislike, even though in the perceptions of others it may be well justified. NFs can cast an administrator into an authority-figure role and project onto him or her old reactions to primary relationships, for example, the NF's relationships with father and mother. It is difficult, sometimes, for NFs to be as accepting of superiors in general as the NFs are of students and fellow teachers. This is quite understandable in view of the NF's hunger for integrity and unique identity, but nonetheless can be quite destructive to working relationships.

NF teachers may put off paperwork until it reaches crisis level. They also may put off facing unpleasant relationships or situations, always hoping that these will disappear if ignored. NFs, however, relate well to others and tend to be popular and strong leaders among faculty. Although tending to say positive things about others, if their dislike is incurred, NFs can be quite critical. Where the SJ is apt to be critical of institutional procedures and ways of doing things, the NFs are more apt to direct remarks to people in particular and their particular behaviors—at times when the person being criticized is not present. This can extend to discussing inappropriate details concerning students and their parents in the teachers' faculty room. In general, however, NF teachers are apt to be more nourishing than toxic in their relationships with those about them. They tend to be enthusiastic about their career and to enjoy teaching. They are willing to devote all the time necessary to do what needs to be done and enjoy opportunities to participate in inservice experiences if relevant to their interests. They are apt to prefer interactional workshops to lectures, and small group experiences to large group presentations. They tend to keep up on professional literature in a somewhat cursory manner, although they always are interested in anything which is innovative and new. The NF teachers are apt to invest in classroom materials that enhance their instruction, where the NT spends the same resources on professional books.

Teaching Style—Summary: On the following page a summary of the characteristics of each of the four styles is given: the prime value in education, the percentage of teachers of each style and their likely length of service, their favored subject areas, and their favored instructional techniques.

TEACHING IN STYLE—SUMMARY

	PRIME VALUE IN EDUCATION	PERCENTAGE OF TEACHERS AND LENGTH OF SERVICE	FAVORED TEACHING AREAS		FAVORED INSTRUCTIONAL TECHNIQUES	
SPs	Growth of Spontaneity and Freedom	4% Short stay in Teaching	Arts Crafts Sports	Drama Music Recreation	Projects Contests Games	Demonstrations Shows
SJs	Growth of Responsibility and Utility	56% Long stay in Teaching	Agriculture Clerical Business Sports Social Sciences	Political Science Homemaking History Geography	Recitation Drill Composition	Tests/Quizzes Demonstration
NTs	Growth of Knowledge and Skills	8% Medium stay in Teaching	Philosophy Science Technology	Communications Mathematics Linguistics	Lectures Tests Compositions	Projects Reports
NFs	Growth of Identity and Integrity	32% Long stay in Teaching	Humanities Social Sciences Theatre Music	Foreign Languages Speech Theology	Group Projects Interaction Discussion	Shows Simulations Games

Finale

What has been said? Well, everybody's different and everybody's OK in their style as is. Let's face it, most of us are strangers to each other. I have my desires, you have yours. You keep yours and I'll keep mine because what each of us wants is good. What's more, you have your talent and I have mine and I can admire you for yours. I hope you will reciprocate.

It is simply not true that you and I go through the same stages to become mature. Maybe you had an identity crisis or two, but I didn't, and it's not because I'm immature or fixated at some stage, passage, or season of my life. I'm just not into identity, never have been, never will be. I've other fish to fry.

Well, stranger, there isn't any way you can really understand me, but if you stop trying to change me to look like you, you might come to *appreciate* me. I'll settle for that. How about you?

APPENDIX: THE SIXTEEN TYPES

Portrait of an ENFJ:

ENFJs are outstanding leaders of groups, both task groups and growth groups. They have the charming characteristic of seeming to take for granted that they will be followed, never doubting that people will want to do what they suggest. And, more often than not, people do, because this type has unusual charisma. ENFJs place a high value on cooperation from others and are most willing to cooperate themselves.

Found in only about 5 percent of the general population, ENFJs place people as being of highest importance and priority. As a result, ENFJs may find themselves feeling responsible for the feelings of others to an extent which places a burden on the relationship. An ENFJ communicates caring, concern, and a willingness to become involved. Thus people turn to ENFJs for nurture and support, which an ENFJ is usually able to deliver. At times, however, these kinds of demands can overwhelm ENFJs, who find at this point that they lack the skills to dissociate. ENFJs do not seem able to turn away from these demands even when they become unreasonable. Or, if forced to let go of the burden through sheer unavailability of time or energy, ENFJs experience a guilt all out of proportion to the realities of the commitment made to the relationship.

ENFJs are especially vulnerable to idealizing interpersonal relationships, raising these relationships to a plane which seldom can sustain the realities of human nature. Because of this tendency to raise interpersonal relations to the ideal, ENFJs may unwittingly overpower their friends, who believe that they cannot possibly live up to an ENFJ's perception of them. The fact is, ENFJs are extraordinarily tolerant of others, seldom critical, and always trustworthy.

ENFJs take communication for granted and believe that they are understood and that their communications are accepted. Just as they themselves are accepting, so do they assume that others are the same. When ENFJs find that their position or beliefs were not comprehended or accepted, they are surprised, puzzled, and sometimes hurt. Fortunately, this does not happen with high frequency, as ENFJs have a remarkable fluency with language, especially in speech; they are particularly adept when communicating face-to-face as opposed to communicating in writing. They are influential, therefore, in groups, having no hesitation about speaking out, no matter how large or small the group may be.

ENFJs have an unusual ability to relate to others with empathy, taking into themselves the characteristics, emotions, and beliefs of others. This can pose a danger for ENFJs, because they can unconsciously over-identify with others and pick up their burdens as if they were their own. In the process, ENFJs may risk their own sense of identity. They have a natural ability to mimic because of this highly developed ability to empathize by introjection. They are likely to be very concerned about the problems of those close to them, but they also may get as deeply involved in the problems of those *not* so close and may find themselves over-extended emotionally.

ENFJ's would do well to follow their hunches, for their intuition tends to be well developed. Decisions made purely on the basis of logic may not be so sound, and checking with a person who has a strong T preference might be at times advisable for the ENFJ. In the framework of values, however, the ENFJ is on certain ground. Generally, they know what they prefer and can read other people with outstanding accuracy. Seldom is an ENFJ wrong about the motivations or intent of another, hidden or not.

ENFJs are socially adept and make excellent companions and mates. They also are deeply devoted to their children, yet tend not to be domineering to either the children or a mate. In fact, the ENFJ is so even-tempered that he or she can be victimized by a mate who might have become more and more demanding.

ENFJ mates always try to please and feel personally responsible when home life does not go smoothly. They are tireless in their efforts to see that it does, providing generously from available income, time, and energy. This dedication often exists, however, side by side with an ENFJ's dream of the perfect relationship—a characteristic of all NFs, but one which is particularly strong in an ENFJ. Thus an ENFJ has that longing for the ideal that results in a vague dissatisfaction with whatever is in the way of relationships, mating as well as friendship.

This longing for the perfect carries over into the careers of ENFJs, who experience some degree of restlessness whatever their jobs. And, as with ENFPs, ENFJs have a wide range of occupations which offer success. Being verbally adept, ENFJs contribute to an unusual level when dealing with people, particularly face-to-face; the media, the ministry, and the stage and screen are populated with successful ENFJs. They make superior therapists, charismatic teachers, excellent executives, and personalized salespersons. Areas that would not permit utilization of the interactional talents of ENFJs, for example, accounting, should be avoided; otherwise, almost any people-to-people occupation where personal, sustained contact is involved capitalizes on the personality of an ENFJ.

ENFJs like to have things settled and organized. They prefer to plan both work and social engagements ahead and tend to be absolutely reliable in honoring these commitments. ENFJs are very much at home in complex situations which require the juggling of much data. At the same time, they can handle people with charm and concern. ENFJs are usually popular wherever they are. Their ability to be comfortable either leading or following makes them easy to have around, whatever the situation. A well-developed ENFJ group leader can provide, almost endlessly, activities for groups to engage in with almost no preplanning and can find adequate roles for members of the group to play. In some, this can amount to genius which other types find hard to emulate. In this ability to organize without planning there is a certain similarity to an ESFJ, but the latter acts more as a master of ceremonies than as a leader of groups. The ESFJ is more of a recreational leader, who insures that each member has fun at a party and that the right things are expressed at social occasions, especially institutional social occasions such as weddings, funerals, parties, and the like. ENFJs, just like the ESFJs, value harmonious human relations above all else; but ENFJs are not so easily

crushed by indifference as are ESFJs and are more independent of others' valuations.

Portrait of an INFJ:

INFJs focus on possibilities, think in terms of values and come
easily to decisions. The small number of this type (1 percent)
is regrettable, since INFJs have an unusually strong drive to
contribute to the welfare of others and genuinely enjoy helping their fellow men. This type has great depth of personality;
they are themselves complicated, and can understand and
deal with complex issues and people.

It is an INFJ who is likely to have visions of human events
past, present, or future. If a person demonstrates an ability
to understand psychic phenomenon better than most others,
this person is apt to be an INFJ. Characteristically, INFJs have
strong empathic abilities and can be aware of another's emotions or intents even before that person is conscious of these.
This can take the form of feeling the distress or illnesses of
others to an extent which is difficult for other types. INFJs
can intuit good and evil in others, although they seldom can
tell how they came to know. Subsequent events tend to bear
them out, however.

INFJs are usually good students, achievers who exhibit an
unostentacious creativity. They take their work seriously and
enjoy academic activity. They can exhibit qualities of over-
perfectionism and put more into a task than perhaps is justified by the nature of the task. They generally will not be visible
leaders, but will quietly exert influence behind the scenes.

INFJs are hard to get to know. They have an unusually rich
inner life, but they are reserved and tend not to share their
reactions except with those they trust. Because of their vulnerability through a strong facility to introject, INFJs can be
hurt rather easily by others, which, perhaps, is at least one
reason they tend to be private people. People who have known
an INFJ for years may find sides emerging which come as a
surprise. Not that INFJs are inconsistent; they are very consistent and value integrity. But they have convoluted, complex
personalities which sometimes puzzle even them.

INFJs like to please others and tend to contribute their own
best efforts in all situations. They prefer and enjoy agreeing

with others, and find conflict disagreeable and destructive. What is known as ESP is likely found in an INFJ more than in any other types, although other types are capable of such phenomena. INFJs have vivid imaginations exercised both as memory and intuition, and this can amount to genius, resulting at times in an INFJ's being seen as mystical. This unfettered imagination often will enable this person to compose complex and often aesthetic works of art such as music, mathematical systems, poems, plays, and novels. In a sense, the INFJ is the most poetic of all the types. Just as an ENTJ cannot *not* lead, so must an INFJ intuit; this capability extends to people, things, and often events, taking the form of visions, episodes of foreknowledge, premonitions, auditory and visual images of things to come. INFJs can have uncanny communications with certain individuals at a distance.

INFJs often select liberal arts as a college major and opt for occupations which involve interacting with people, but on a one-to-one basis. For example, the general practitioner in medicine might be an INFJ, or the psychiatrist or psychologist. As with all NFs, the ministry holds attraction, although the INFJ must develop an extraverted role here which requires a great deal of energy. INFJs may be attracted to writing as a profession, and often they use language which contains an unusual degree of imagery. They are masters of the metaphor, and both their verbal and written communications tend to be elegant and complex. Their great talent for language usually is directed toward people, describing people and writing to communicate with people in a personalized way. INFJs who write comment often that they write with a particular person in mind; writing to a faceless, abstract audience leaves them uninspired.

INFJs make outstanding individual therapists who have the ability to get in touch with the archetypes of their patients in a way some other types do not. The INFJs are also the most vulnerable of all the types to the eruption of their own archetypal material. As therapists, INFJs may choose counseling, clinical psychology, or psychiatry, or may choose to teach in these fields. Writing about these professions often intrigues an INFJ. Whatever their choice, they generally are successful in these fields because their great personal warmth, their enthusiasm, their insight, their depth of concentration, their originality, and their organizational skills can all be brought into play.

At work as well as socially, INFJs are highly sensitive in their handling of others and tend to work well in an organizational structure. They have a capacity for working at jobs which require solitude and concentration, but also do well when in contact with people, providing the human interaction is not superficial. INFJs enjoy problem-solving and can understand and use human systems creatively and humanistically. As employees or employers, INFJs are concerned with people's feelings and are able to provide in themselves a barometer of the feelings of individuals and groups within the organization. INFJs listen well and are willing and able to consult and cooperate with others. Once a decision is made, they work to implement it.

INFJs are generally good at public relations and themselves have good interpersonal relations. They value staff harmony and want an organization to run smoothly and pleasantly, themselves making every effort to contribute to that end. They are crushed by too much criticism and can have their feelings hurt rather easily. They respond to praise and use approval as a means of motivating others, just as they, the INFJs, are motivated by approval. If they are subject to a hostile, unfriendly working condition or to constant criticism, they tend to lose confidence, become unhappy and immobilized, and finally become physically ill.

As mates, INFJs are usually devoted to their spouses, but may not always be open to physical approaches. They tend to be physically demonstrative at times, but wish to choose when, which is when they are in the mood. This may be quite confusing to an extraverted mate. Often an INFJ's expressions of affection will be subtle, taking a humorous, unexpected turn. INFJs need and want harmony in their homes and find constant conflict, overt or covert, extremely destructive to their psyches. Their friendship circle is likely to be small, deep, and long-standing. As parents, INFJs usually are fiercely devoted. A female INFJ, particularly, is linked to her children in a way different from the other types: with almost a psychic symbiosis. This deep bond can create an overdependency that can be unhealthy for both mother and child. At the same time, INFJs tend to be good friends with their children, while firm in discipline. They usually are concerned about the comfort of a home and most especially the comfort, physical health, and emotional well-being of both mates and children.

Portrait of an ENFP:

For ENFPs nothing occurs which does not have some significance, and they have an uncanny sense of the motivations of others. This gives them a talent for seeing life as an exciting drama, pregnant with possibilities for both good and evil. This type is found in only about 5 percent of the general population, but they have great influence because of their extraordinary impact on others. ENFPs strive toward the authentic, even when acting spontaneously, and this intent is usually communicated nonverbally to others, who find this characteristic attractive. ENFPs, however, find their own efforts of authenticity and spontaneity always lacking, and tend to heap coals of fire on themselves, always berating themselves for being so conscious of self.

ENFPs consider intense emotional experiences vital; when they have these, however, they are made uneasy by a sense of being there but with a part of themselves split off. They strive for congruency, but always see themselves in some danger of losing touch with their real feelings, which ENFPs possess in a wide range and variety.

ENFPs exercise a continuous scanning of the external environment, and nothing out of the ordinary is likely to escape their attention. They are keen and penetrating observers and are capable of intense concentration on another individual while aware of what is going on about them. Their attention is never passive or casual, never wandering, but always directed. At times, ENFPs find themselves interpreting events in terms of another's "hidden motive," giving special meaning to words or actions. This interpretation tends to be negative and, more often than not, inaccurately negative. In the process, an ENFP may find that he or she has introduced an unnecessary, toxic element into the relationship. While ENFPs are brilliantly perceptive, they can make serious mistakes in judgment, which works to their discomfort. These mistakes derive from their tendency to focus on data which confirm their own biases. They may be absolutely correct in their perceptions but wrong in their conclusions.

Because they tend to be hypersensitive and hyperalert, they may suffer from muscle tension. They live in readiness for emergencies; because they have this facility, they assume this is true for others. They can become bored rather quickly with both situations and people, and resist repeating experiences. They enjoy the process of creating something—an idea or a project—but are not as interested in the follow-through. They are typically enthusiastic, and this is contagious. People get caught up and entranced by an ENFP. Yet this type is marked with a fierce independence, repudiating any kind of subordination, either in themselves or in others in relation to them. They do tend to attribute more power to authority figures than is there and give over to these figures an ability to "see through" them—which also is not apt to be there. While ENFPs resist the notion of others becoming dependent or having power over them, their charisma draws followers who wish to be shown the way. ENFPs constantly find themselves surrounded by others who look toward the ENFP for wisdom, inspiration, courage, leadership, and so on—an expectancy which, at times, weighs rather heavily on an ENFP.

ENFPs are characteristically optimistic and are surprised when people or events do not turn out as anticipated. Often their confidence in the innate goodness of fate and human nature is a self-fulling prophecy.

ENFPs have a remarkable latitude in career choices and succeed in many fields. As workers, they are warmly enthusiastic, high-spirited, ingenious, imaginative, and can do almost anything that interests them. They can solve most problems, particularly those dealing with people. They are charming and at ease with colleagues; others enjoy their presence. ENFPs are outstanding in getting people together, and are good at initiating meetings and conferences, although not as talented at providing for the operational details of these events. They enjoy inventing new ways of doing things, and their projects tend to become a cause, quickly becoming personalized. They are imaginative themselves, but can have difficulty picking up on ideas and projects initiated by others. They must make these ideas and projects their own if ENFPs are to lend their energy and interest. Once people or projects become routine, ENFPs are likely to lose interest; what *might be* is always more fascinating than what *is*. ENFPs make extensive use of their intuitive powers. They usually have a wide range of personal and telephone contacts, expending energy in maintaining both career and personal relationships.

ENFPs make excellent salespeople, advertising people, politicians, screen or play writers, and in general are attracted to the interpretative arts, particularly character acting. People-to-people work is essential for ENFPs, who need the feedback of interaction with others. ENFPs may find it difficult to work within the constraints of an institution, especially in following rules, regulations, and standard operating procedures. More frequently, institutional procedures and policies are targets to be challenged and bent by the will of an ENFP. Colleagues and superiors sometimes find themselves in the position of having to accommodate and salvage. At times, ENFPs demonstrate impatience with others; they may get into difficulty in an organization by siding with its detractors, who find in an ENFP a sympathetic ear and a natural rescuer. In occupational choice, ENFPs quickly become restless if the choice involves painstaking detail and follow-through over a period of time. Variety in day-to-day operations and interactions best suits the talents of ENFPs, who need quite a bit of latitude in which to exercise their adaptive ingenuity.

As mates, ENFPs tend to be charming, gentle, sympathetic, and nonconformist. They are not likely to be interested in the less-inspired routines of daily maintenance and ever will be seeking new outlets for their inspirations. As parents, ENFPs are devoted although somewhat unpredictable in handling their children, shifting from a role of friend-in-need-rescuer to stern authority figure. They may not always be willing to enforce their impulsive pronouncements, but leave it to their mates to follow through. A mate of an ENFP can expect charming surprises: extravagant generosity punctuated by periods of frugality. Independent actions regarding money on the part of an ENFP's mate are not ordinarily welcomed, and the mate may find him or herself in an embarrassing situation of having to return purchases. ENFPs generally are the ones in charge of the home, and a conflict-free home is desired, almost demanded. When he or she is in charge of economic resources, the ENFP's home may contain extravagant luxuries, while necessities may be missing. They are not always interested in saving for the future and may be casual in giving consideration to such things as life insurance, savings accounts, and even a ready cash supply for mate and children.

ENFPs are characteristic in their pursuit of the novel, their strong sense of the possible, and outstanding intuitive powers. At the same time, they have warmth and fun with people and generally are unusually skilled in handling people. Their extraverted role tends to be well developed, as is their capacity for the novel and the dramatic.

Portrait of an INFP:

INFPs present a calm, pleasant face to the world and are seen
as reticent and even shy. Although they demonstrate a cool
reserve toward others, inside they are anything but distant.
They have a capacity for caring which is not always found
in other types. They care deeply—indeed, passionately—about
a few special persons or a cause. One word that captures this
type is *idealistic*. At times, this characteristic leaves them feeling isolated, especially since INFPs are found in only 1 percent of the general population.

INFPs have a profound sense of honor derived from internal
values. The INFP is the Prince or Princess of mythology, the
King's Champion, Defender of the Faith, and guardian of the
castle. Sir Galahad and Joan of Arc are male and female pro-
totypes of an INFP. To understand INFPs their cause must be
understood, for they are willing to make unusual sacrifices
for someone or something believed in.

INFPs seek unity in their lives, unity of body and mind, emotions and intellect. They often have a subtle tragic motif running through their lives, but others seldom detect this inner
minor key. The deep commitment of INFPs to the positive and
the good causes them to be alert to the negative and the evil,
which can take the form of a fascination with the profane.
Thus INFPs may live a paradox, drawn toward purity and
unity but looking over the shoulder toward the sullied and
desecrated. When INFPs believe that they have yielded to an
impure temptation, they may be given to acts of self-sacrifice
in atonement. The atonement, however, is *within* the INFP,
who does not feel compelled to make public the issue.

INFPs prefer the valuing process over the purely logical. They
respond to the beautiful versus the ugly, the good versus the
bad, and the moral versus the immoral. Impressions are gained
in a fluid, global, diffused way. Metaphors and similes come
naturally but may be strained. INFPs have a gift for interpreting symbols, as well as creating them, and thus often write in
lyric fashion. They may demonstrate a tendency to take de-
liberate liberties with logic. Unlike the NT, they see logic as
something optional. INFPs also may, at times, assume an unwarranted familiarity with a domain, because their global,
impressionistic way of dealing with reality may have failed to
register a sufficient number of details for mastery. INFPs may
have difficulty thinking in terms of a conditional framework;

they see things as either real or fancied, and are impatient with the hypothetical.

At work, INFPs are adaptable, welcome new ideas and new information, are well aware of people and their feelings, and relate well to most, albeit with some psychological distance. INFPs dislike telephone interruptions and work well alone, as well as with others. They are patient with complicated situations, but impatient with routine details. They can make errors of fact, but seldom of values. Their career choices may be toward the ministry, missionary work, college teaching, psychiatry, architecture, psychology—and away from business. They seem willing and usually are able to apply themselves scholastically to gain the necessary training for professional work, often doing better in college than in high school. They have a natural interest in scholarly activities and demonstrate, as do the other NFs, a remarkable facility for languages. Often they hear a calling to go forth into the world to help others; they seem willing to make the necessary personal sacrifices involved in responding to that call, even if it means asking others to do likewise. INFPs can make outstanding novelists and character actors, for they are able to efface their own personalities in their portrayal of a character in a way other types cannot.

As mates, INFPs have a deep commitment to their pledges. They like to live in harmony and may go to great lengths to avoid constant conflict. They are sensitive to the feelings of others and enjoy pleasing those they care for. They may find it difficult to reconcile a romantic, idealized concept of conjugal life with the realities of everyday living with another person. At times, in fact, INFPs may seem fearful of exuberant attainment, afraid that current advances may have to be paid for with later sacrifices. The devil is sure to get his due if the INFP experiences too freely of success, or beauty, or health, or wealth, or knowledge. And thus, INFPs guard against giving way to relaxing in the happiness of mating. They may have difficulty in expressing affection directly, but communicate interest and affection indirectly.

For INFPs, their home is their castle. As parents, they are fierce in protection of home and family and are devoted to the welfare of family members. They have a strong capacity for devotion, sympathy, and adaptability in their relationships, and thus are easy to live with. They are loyal to their family and, although they may dream of greener pastures, if they stray into those pastures they soon locate the nettles. The almost preconscious conviction that pleasure must be paid for with pain can cause a sense of uneasiness in the family system of an INFP, who may transmit an air of being ever-vigilant against invasion. In the routine rituals of daily living, INFPs tend to be compliant and may even prefer having decisions made on their behalf—until their value system is violated! Then INFPs dig in their heels and will not budge from ideals. Life with an INFP will go gently along for long periods, until an ideal is struck and violated. Then an INFP will resist and insist.

Portrait of an ENTJ:

If one word were used to capture ENTJ's style, it would be *commandant*. The basic driving force and need of ENTJs is to lead, and from an early age they can be observed taking over groups. This type is found in approximately 5 percent of the total population. ENTJs have a strong urge to give structure wherever they are—to harness people to distant goals. Their empirical, objective, and extraverted thinking may be highly developed; if this is the case, they use classification, generalization, summarization, adduction of evidence, and demonstration with ease. They resemble ESTJs in their tendency to establish plans for a task, enterprise, or organization, but ENTJs search more for policy and goals than for regulations and procedures. An ENTJ's introverted thinking (analysis and conservation) may be less well developed than the extraverted thinking processes, and the ENTJ leader may turn to an ENTP or INTP to provide this kind of input. ENTJs are similar to INTJs except that the former places greater trust in empirical thought than in intuition; it is the ENTJs' own intuitive sense of coherence, however, that augments and supports their empirical thinking.

Although ENTJs are tolerant of established procedures, they can abandon any procedure when it can be shown to be indifferent to the goal it seemingly serves. Inefficiency is especially rejected by ENTJs, and repetition of error causes them to become impatient. For the ENTJ, there must always be a reason for doing anything, and people's feelings usually are not sufficient reason. When in charge of an organization, ENTJs more than any other type desire (and generally have the ability) to visualize where the organization is going and seem able to communicate that vision to others. They are the natural organization builders, and they cannot *not* lead. They find themselves in command and sometimes are mystified as to how this happened. As administrators, ENTJs organize their units into a smooth-functioning system, planning in advance, keeping both short-term and long-range objectives well in mind. They seek and can see efficiency and effectiveness in personnel. They prefer decisions to be based on impersonal data, want to work from well-thought-out plans, and like to use engineered operations—and they prefer that others follow suit. ENTJs will support the policy of the organization and will expect others to do so.

ENTJs will usually rise to positions of responsibility and enjoy being executives. They are tireless in their devotion to their jobs and can easily block out other areas of life for the sake of work. They will be able to reduce inefficiency, ineffectiveness, and aimless confusion, being willing to dismiss employees who perpetuate such behaviors. ENTJs tend to work in organizational structures of some sort, tend to be in charge administratively, and rise to top levels of responsibility, whether in the military, business, education, or government.

ENTJs take charge of the home. When an ENTJ is present, there will be little doubt as to who is in command. Because their work is so important to them, however, they can become increasingly absent, especially if male. Male or female, ENTJs expect a great deal of their mates, who need to possess a strong personality of their own, a well-developed autonomy, many and varied interests, and a healthy self-esteem. A career wife, however, may not be appealing to an ENTJ male, who is apt to view his home and family as a part of his professional background, a resource, and adjunct to his own career development.

As a parent, an ENTJ will be thoroughly in charge, and the children will know what is expected of them—and will be expected to obey. When this does not occur, an ENTJ parent is not apt to make a scene; rather, there is more likely to be a low-key, firm issuance of reprimand and a taking-for-granted of immediate obedience. While both mating and parenting are roles of importance to the ENTJ, they are to some degree preempted by the ENTJ's strong career interest. The romantic dream and the quest for the ideal mate is usually not a characteristic of this type. ENTJs generally do, however, expect a home to be attractive, well-ordered, with meals served punctually and maintenance accomplished on schedule—all these in the service of the larger goal of creating a family system where children can be reared to be productive and healthy and establishing a devoted, harmonious relationship between man and woman. An ENTJ male might expect his mate to be active in civic and community affairs, to be socially sophisticated, and as well-educated as he. The ENTJ female may find it difficult to select a mate who is not overwhelmed by her strong personality and will.

Portrait of an INTJ:

INTJs are the most self-confident of all the types, having "self-power" awareness. Found in about 1 percent of the general population, the INTJs live in an introspective reality, focusing on possibilities, using thinking in the form of empirical logic, and preferring that events and people serve some positive use. Decisions come naturally to INTJs; once a decision is made, INTJs are at rest. INTJs look to the future rather than the past, and a word which captures the essence of INTJs is *builder*— a builder of systems and the applier of theoretical models.

To INTJs, authority based on position, rank, title, or publication has absolutely no force. This type is not likely to succumb to the magic of slogans, watchwords, or shibboleths. If an idea or position makes sense to an INTJ, it will be adopted; if it doesn't, it won't, regardless of who took the position or generated the idea. As with the INTP, authority per se does not impress the INTJ.

INTJs do, however, tend to conform to rules if they are useful, not because they believe in them, or because they make sense, but because of their unique view of reality. They are the supreme pragmatists, who see reality as something which is quite arbitrary and made up. Thus it can be used as a tool— or ignored. Reality is quite malleable and can be changed, conquered, or brought to heel. Reality is a crucible for the refining of ideas, and in this sense, INTJs are the most theoretical of all the types. Where an ESTP sees ideas as the pawn of reality, an INTJ sees reality as the pawn of ideas: No idea is too far-fetched to be entertained. INTJs are natural brainstormers, always open to new concepts and, in fact, aggressively seeking them.

INTJs manipulate the world of theory as if on a gigantic chess board, always seeking strategies and tactics that have high payoff. In their penchant for logic, the INTJs resemble the INTPs. The logic of an INTJ, however, is not confined to the expressably logical. Unlike INTPs, INTJs need only to have a vague, intuitive impression of the unexpressed logic of a system to continue surely on their way. Things need only *seem* logical; this is entirely sufficient. Moreover, they always have a keen eye for the consequence of the application of new ideas or positions. They can be quite ruthless in the implementation of systems, seldom counting personal cost in terms of time and energy. Theories which cannot be made to work are quickly discarded by the INTJs.

To understand INTJs, their way of dealing with reality rather than their way of dealing with ideas should be observed closely. Their conscious thought is extraverted and empirical. Hence, they are better at generalizing, classifying, summarizing, adducing evidence, proving, and demonstrating than are the INTPs. The INTJs are somewhat less at home with pure reason, that is, systemic logic, where principles are explicit. In this respect they resemble the ENTJs. The INTJs, rather than using deductive logic, use their intuition to grasp coherence.

INTJs have a drive to completion, always with an eye to long-term consequences. Ideas seem to carry their own force for INTJs, although they subject every idea to the test of usefulness. Difficulties are highly stimulating to INTJs, who love responding to a challenge that requires creativity. These personality traits lead INTJs to occupations where theoretical models can be translated into actuality. They build data and human systems wherever they work if given even a slight opportunity. They can be outstanding in scientific research and also outstanding as executives who generate a plethora of implementations of ideas. Teamed with an INTP who is the architect of systems, the INTJ provides a dimension to an organization which insures that the work of the INTP does not gather dust on library shelves.

INTJs can be very single-minded at times; this can be either a weakness or a strength in their careers, for they can ignore the points of view and wishes of others. INTJs usually rise to positions of responsibility, for they work long and hard and are steady in their pursuit of goals, sparing neither time nor effort on their part or that of their colleagues and employees.

INTJs live to see systems translated into substance; an INTP, by way of contrast, is content to design the system. In both these types, however, coherence is the master. Both internal and external consistency are important, and if an INTJ finds that he or she is in a working situation where overlapping functions, duplication of effort, inefficient paper flow, and waste of human and material resources abound, the INTJ cannot rest until an effort is made to correct the situation. Cost-effectiveness is a concept which has a strong imperative for INTJs, who frequently select occupations in engineering, particularly human engineering. They also can be found in the physical sciences, in roles which require development, such as curriculum building, and, in general, any job which requires the creation and application of technology to complex areas.

Fellow workers of INTJs often feel as if the INTJ can see right through them, and often believe that the INTJ finds them wanting. This tendency of people to feel transparent in the presence of the INTJ often results in relationships which have psychological distance. Thus colleagues find the INTJ apparently unemotional and, at times, cold and dispassionate. Because of their tendency to drive others as hard as they do themselves, INTJs often seem demanding and difficult to satisfy. INTJs are high achievers in school and on the job. On the job, they take the goals of an institution seriously and continually strive to respond to these goals. They make dedicated, loyal employees whose loyalties are directed toward the system, rather than toward individuals within the system. So as the people of an institution come and go, the INTJs have little difficulty—unlike the NFs, who have their loyalties involved more with persons than offices. INTJs tend, ordinarily, to verbalize the positive and eschew comments of a negative nature; they are more interested in moving an institution forward than commiserating about mistakes of the past.

As mates, INTJs want harmony and order in the home and in relationships. They are the most independent of all the types. They will trust their intuitions about others when making choices of friends and mates, even in the face of contradictory evidence and pressures applied by others. The emotions of an INTJ are hard to read, and neither male nor female INTJ is apt to express emotional reactions. At times, both will seem cold, reserved, and unresponsive, while in fact INTJs are almost hypersensitive to signals of rejection from those for whom they care. In social situations, INTJs may also be unresponsive and may neglect to observe small rituals designed to put others at their ease. For example, INTJs may communicate that time is wasted if used for idle dialogue, and thus people receive a sense of hurry from an INTJ which is not always intended. In their interpersonal relationships, INTJs are usually better in a working situation than in recreational situations. They do not enjoy physical contact except with a chosen few.

As parents, INTJs are dedicated and single-minded in their devotion: Their children are a major focus in life. They are supportive of their children and tend to allow them to develop in directions of their own choosing. INTJs usually are firm and consistent in their discipline and rarely care to repeat directions given to children—or others. Being the most independent of all the types, they have a strong need for autonomy; indifference or criticism from people in general does not particularly bother INTJs, if they believe that they are right. They also have a strong need for privacy.

The most important preference of an INTJ is *intuition*, but this is seldom seen. Rather, the function of *thinking* is used to deal with the world and with people. INTJs are vulnerable in the emotional area and may make serious mistakes here.

Portrait of an ENTP:

ENTPs wish to exercise their ingenuity in the world of people and things. Found in about five out of every hundred people, ENTPs extravert intuition; thus they deal imaginatively with social relationships as well as physical and mechanical relations. They are very alert to what is apt to occur next, and always sensitive to possibilities.

ENTPs are good at analysis, especially functional analysis, and have both a tolerance for and enjoyment of the complex. Usually enthusiastic, ENTPs are apt to express interest in everything, and thus are a source of inspiration to others, who find themselves caught up by the ENTP's enthusiasm. This type is delighted over many things and so is easy to please, often showing the effervescence of their NF counterpart, the ENFP. The ENTP is the most reluctant of all the types to do things in a particular manner just because that is the way things always have been done. They characteristically have an eye out for a better way, always on the lookout for new projects, new activities, new procedures.

ENTPs are confident in the value of their pursuits and display a charming capacity to ignore the standard, the traditional, and the authoritative. As a result of this open attitude, they often bring a fresh, new approach to their work and their lives. The ENTP is a keen judge of the pragmatics of both the social and the mechanical, and may become expert at directing relationships between means and ends.

Where the introverted NTP sees design as an end in itself, the extraverted NTP sees design as a *means;* the end is the invention that works, the prototype that is replicable. Ideas are valuable when and only when they make possible actions and objects. "It can't be done" is a challenge to an ENTP and elicits a reaction of "I can do it." They are not, however, the movers of mountains as are the INTJs. Rather, the faith of the ENTPs is in their ability to improvise something, and they display an unusual talent for rising to the expediency of a situation. Superficially, ENTPs resemble ESTPs in their derring-do. But the focus of the ENTP is on competency and the sense of power this gives, rather than on the feeling of freedom of action experienced by the ESTP.

ENTPs can be fascinating conversationalists, able as they are to follow the complex verbalizations of others. They may deliberately employ debate tactics to the disadvantage of their opponents, even when the "opponents" are close associates and valued friends. ENTPs are the most able of all types to maintain a one-up position with others. They value adaptability and innovation and thus respond quickly and adeptly to another's shifting position. They may even be several jumps ahead. The ENTP, talkative and motivating, is often the life of an enterprise. The ENTP can be an entrepreneur and cleverly makes do with whatever or whoever is at hand, counting on ingenuity to solve problems as they arise, rather than carefully generating a detailed blueprint in advance. A rough draft is all that an ENTP needs to feel confident and ready to proceed into action, counting on the ability to improvise as a situation develops. Because of this tendency to depend on ingenuity and improvisation, they may neglect very necessary preparation at times. After repeated failures in situations where improvising has met with defeat, the ENTP may develop ways of avoiding such situations as a substitute to thorough preparation.

ENTPs can succeed in a variety of occupations, as long as the job does not involve too much humdrum routine. At this point, they become restless. If a project in which they are engaged is no longer challenging, they tend to lose interest in that project and fail to follow through—often to the discomfort of colleagues.

Seldom are ENTPs conformists. ENTPs enjoy outwitting the system and use rules and regulations within the system to win the game—whatever it may be. They understand well the politics of institutions and deal with these realities very well, always aiming to *understand* the people within the system rather than to judge them. ENTPs are good at innovative projects and can administer them well if dull routine is not involved. They usually are outstanding teachers, continuously devising new participative ways to make learning exciting for the students. As an employee, an ENTP may work against the system just for the joy of being one-up. For ENTPs, to be taken-in, to be manipulated by another, is humiliating; this offends their joy in being masters of the art of oneupmanship. ENTPs are the natural engineers of human relationships and human systems. Their good humor and optimistic outlook tend to be contagious, and people seek out their company.

As mates, ENTPs tend to create a lively living environment. They are gregarious, laugh easily and often, and are typically in good humor. Orderliness in the routines of daily living is not apt to inspire them; they usually solve this problem by mobilizing those around them. Tom Sawyer illustrated this talent when he solved the problem of getting his Aunt Polly's fence whitewashed. Life with ENTPs is likely to be a daring adventure; they can lead families into physical and economic dangers. ENTPs improvise to remain unaware that they do not have the necessary knowledge of the situation to ward off such dangers.

If the mate of an ENTP is not competitive, he or she is likely to find the one-up/one-down transactions somewhat wearing. If the mate is competitive, the result might be conflict. Although usually good providers of economic necessities, ENTPs at times engage in brinkmanship with their careers, placing them in jeopardy and behaving as if unaware of the consequences; they may thus offer unnecessary challenges to those who have power over their professional success. When challenges elicit negative responses from superiors, ENTPs are apt to react with delight at having an opportunity to improvise a solution to the crisis—and, more often than not, they succeed in doing so.

ENTPs are likely to have all sorts of hobbies and to be experts in unexpected areas, but they are not apt to share these hobbies with their mates or children in the sense of teaching them. In fact, ENTPs may be very inconsistent in the attention given to offspring. Usually, it is feast or famine. ENTPs have a lively circle of friends and are interested in their ideas and activities. They are usually easy-going, seldom critical or nagging. At their worst, they can show undependable, fickle characteristics and may be rather easily discouraged.

Portrait of an INTP:

INTPs exhibit the greatest precision in thought and language of all the types; they tend to see distinctions and inconsistencies in thought and language instantaneously. The one word which captures the unique style of INTPs is *architect*—the architect of ideas and systems as well as the architect of edifices. This type is found in only 1 percent of the population and therefore is not encountered as frequently as some of the other types.

INTPs detect contradictions in statements no matter how distant in space or time the contradictory statements were produced. The intellectual scanning of INTPs has a principled quality; that is, INTPs search for whatever is relevant and pertinent to the issue at hand. Consequently, INTPs can concentrate better than any other type.

Authority derived from office, position, or wide acceptance does not impress INTPs. Only statements that are logical and coherent carry weight. External authority per se is irrelevant. INTPs abhor redundancy and incoherence. Possessing a desire to understand the universe, an INTP is constantly looking for natural law. Curiosity concerning these keys to the universe is a driving force in this type.

INTPs prize intelligence in themselves and in others, but can become intellectual dilletantes as a result of their need to amass ideas, principles, or understanding of behavior. And once they know something, it is remembered. INTPs can become obsessed with analysis. Once caught up in a thought process, that thought process seems to have a will of its own for INTPs, and they persevere until the issue is comprehended in all its complexity. They can be intellectual snobs and may show impatience at times with others less endowed intellectually. This quality, INTPs find, generates hostility and defensive behaviors on the part of others, who may describe an INTP as arrogant.

For INTPs, the world exists primarily to be understood. Reality is trivial, a mere arena for proving ideas. It is essential that the universe is understood and that whatever is stated about the universe is stated correctly, with coherence and without redundancy. This is the INTP's final purpose. It matters not whether others understand or accept his or her truths.

The INTP is the logician, the mathematician, the philosopher, the scientist; any pursuit requiring architecture of ideas intrigues this type. INTPs should not, however, be asked to work out the implementation or application of their models to the real world. The INTP is the architect of a system and leaves it to others to be the builder and the applicator. Very often, therefore, the INTP's work is not credited to him or her. The builder and the applier gains fame and fortune, while the INTP's name remains obscure. Appreciation of an INTP's theoretical work frequently comes posthumously—or the work may never be removed from library shelves at all and thus lost.

INTPs tend not to be writers or to go into sales work. They are, however, often excellent teachers, particularly for advanced students, although INTPs do not always enjoy much popularity, for they can be hard taskmasters. They are not good at clerical tasks and are impatient with routine details. They prefer to work quietly, without interruption, and often alone. If an organization is to use the talents of an INTP appropriately, the INTP must be given an efficient support staff who can capture ideas as they emerge and before the INTP loses interest and turns to another idea.

INTPs take their mating relationship seriously and usually are faithful and devoted—albeit preoccupied at times. They are not likely to welcome constant social activity or disorganization in the home. In all probability, the mate of an INTP will initiate and manage the social life. If left to his or her own devices, the INTP mate will retreat into the world of books and emerge only when physical needs become imperative. INTPs are, however, willing, compliant, and easy to live with, although somewhat forgetful of appointments, anniversaries, and the rituals of daily living—unless reminded. They may have difficulty expressing their emotions verbally, and the mate of an INTP may believe that he/she is somewhat taken for granted. As a parent, the INTP is devoted; they enjoy children, and are serious about their upbringing. The home of an INTP parent is usually calm, low-key in discipline, but well run and ordered.

INTPs deal with the environment primarily through intuition, and their strongest quality, the thinking function, remains relatively hidden except in close associations. Therefore, INTPs are often misunderstood, seen as difficult to know, and seldom perceived at their true level of competency. They are inclined to be shy except when with close friends, and their reserve is difficult to penetrate. They are very adaptable until one of their principles is violated. Then INTPs are not adaptable at all! They may have difficulty in being understood by others because they tend to think in a complicated fashion and want to be precise, never redundant in their communications. Because their feeling qualities may be underdeveloped, they may be insensitive to the wants and wishes of others, often quite unaware of the existence of these wants and wishes.

Portrait of an ESTJ:

ESTJs are very much in touch with the external environment. They know their community and usually are pillars of strength. The best adjective to describe ESTJs would be *responsible*. They represent about 13 percent of the general population.

ESTJs are outstanding at organizing orderly procedures and in detailing rules and regulations. They like to see things done correctly. They tend to be impatient with those who do not carry out procedures with sufficient attention to those details, prescribed by those with the most experience, that will get the job done right.

ESTJs are comfortable in evaluating others and tend to judge how a person is doing in terms of standard operating procedures. They may, at times, be abrupt with those who do not follow the rules correctly. ESTJs are realistic, matter-of-fact, and more curious about new devices and processes than about new principles and theories.

ESTJ's generally are loyal to their institutions, work, and community and make excellent, faithful mates and parents. They see where their duty lies and are not likely to shirk the doing of that duty, even when this requires considerable sacrifice on their part. They frequently rise to positions of responsibility in their jobs, in the community, and in their religious affiliations. They very often belong to several civic clubs and support them both through steady attendance and through their spoken attitudes. ESTJs themselves are punctual and expect others to be also.

ESTJs may not always be responsive to points of view and emotions of others and may have a tendency to jump to conclusions too quickly at times. They may not always be willing to listen patiently to opposing views; they are especially vulnerable to this tendency when in positions of authority. They may need to make special effort to remain open to input from others who are dependent on them—their children, spouses, and employees.

ESTJs are so in tune with the established, time-honored institutions and ways of behaving within those institutions that they cannot understand those who might wish to abandon or radically change those institutions. They follow routines well at home and at work, tending to have a place for everything and wanting everything in its place. They are usually neat and orderly at work and at play.

They approach human relations through traditions and rituals, promoting harmony and contentment in their relationships through creating well-worked-out routines and procedures. Family traditions have meaning for ESTJs, and they willingly participate in observing these. They enjoy opportunities to see friends, former colleagues, and relatives at functions such as retirement dinners, annual picnics, Thanksgiving gatherings, and weddings. ESTJs are relatively easy to get to know; they do not tend to confuse people by sending double messages. They are dependable and consistent, and what they seem to be is what they are.

Portrait of an ISTJ:

ISTJs are characterized by decisiveness in practical affairs, are the guardians of time-honored institutions, and, if only one adjective could be selected, *dependable* would best describe this type which represents about 6 percent of the general population. The word of ISTJs is their bond, and they experience great uneasiness by thoughts of a bankrupt nation, state, institution, or family.

Whether at home or at work, this type is rather quiet and serious. ISTJs are extraordinarily persevering and dependable. The thought of dishonoring a contract would appall a person of this type. When they give their word, they give their honor. ISTJs can be counted on to conserve the resources of the institution they serve and bring to their work a practical point of view. They perform their duties without flourish or fanfare; therefore, the dedication they bring to their work can go unnoticed and unappreciated.

ISTJ's interest in thoroughness, details, justice, practical procedures, and smooth flow of personnel and materiel leads this type to occupations where these preferences are useful. For example, ISTJs make excellent bank examiners, auditors, accountants, or tax examiners. Investments in securities are likely to interest this type, particularly investments in blue-chip securities. ISTJs are not likely to take chances either with their own or others' money.

ISTJs can handle difficult, detailed figures and make sense of them. They communicate a message of reliability and stability, which often makes them excellent supervisors of, for example, a ward in a hospital, a library, or a business operation. They would be capable of handling the duties of a mortician, a legal secretary, or a law researcher. High-school teachers of business, home economics, physical education, and the physical sciences are ISTJs, as are top-ranking officers of the Women's Army Corps. Often this type seem to have ice in their veins, for people fail to see an ISTJ's vulnerability to criticism.

ISTJs are patient with their work and with procedures within an institution, although not always patient with the individual goals of people in that institution. ISTJs will see to it that resources are delivered when and where they are supposed to be; materiel will be in the right place at the right time. And ISTJs would prefer that this be the case with people, too.

As a husband or wife, the ISTJ is a pillar of strength. Just as this type honors business contracts, so do they honor the marriage contract. Loyal and faithful mates, they take responsibilities to children and mate seriously, giving lifelong commitment to these. *Duty* is a word the ISTJ understands. The male ISTJ sees himself as the breadwinner of a family, although he can accept a working wife—as long as responsibilities to children are not shirked. The male ISTJ's concept of masculinity is patriarchal, and both female and male ISTJs make steady, dependable partners. The female ISTJ may abandon the frivolous for the sensible and may not always deepen her sensuality.

As parents, ISTJs are consistent in handling children, and the rules of the family are made clear. A rebellious, nonconforming child may have a difficult time, however, with an ISTJ parent—and vice versa. As a child, the ISTJ is apt to be obedient and a source of pleasure to parents and teachers.

Although ISTJs are outstandingly practical and sensible, they can marry people who are thoroughly irresponsible, with the marriage developing into a relationship more parent-to-child than adult-to-adult. The ISTJ fluctuates from being rescuer to reformer of the wayward mate. The marriage then becomes a lifelong game: On one side, there is Irresponsibility, Promise of Reform, Brief Period of Reform, and Irresponsibility again; on the ISTJ's part, the cycle is Disapproval, Rescue, Scolding, Forgiveness, Acceptance of Promise To Do Better, and on and on. This pattern often is seen when an ISTJ marries an alcoholic and enters a life of caretaking punctuated by periods of anger and rejection. Somehow, although ISTJs can accept periodic fickleness and selfishness in significant others, they do not see this kind of behavior as acceptable in themselves.

ISTJs have a distaste for and distrust of fanciness in speech, dress, or home. The ostentacious is abhored, and a neat, orderly, and functional home and work environment is preferred. Durability of furnishings are of primary concern, esthetics given slim consideration. The clothes of an ISTJ tend to be practical and durable rather than in the latest style or luxurious. "No nonsense" in both food and clothes seems characteristic of this type who tend not to be attracted by exotic foods, beverages, or places.

The male ISTJ may enjoy stag, men-only parties and use a different sort of language when only men are present. The yearly hunting or fishing trip as a male ritual is often a part of recreation for an ISTJ. More than the female, the ISTJ male is apt to be involved in community service organizations that transmit traditional values to the young, such as Boy Scouting. They understand and appreciate the contributions these groups make in preserving the national heritage. Along with the SJs, the ISTJ takes particular delight in festive occasions held in the context of rituals, for example, weddings, holiday feasts, and birthdays. At work, the ISTJ is apt to see the holiday office party as a necessary nuisance and would be likely to participate and enjoy these events.

Portrait of an ESFJ:

ESFJs, the most sociable of all types, are energized by interactions with people, tending to idealize whatever or whoever they "admire. *Harmony* is a key to this type, which is represented in about 13 percent of the general population.

ESFJs are the great nurturers of established institutions such as the home, the school, the church, and civic groups. Wherever they go, they promote harmony and harmonious relationships. They are outstanding hosts or hostesses, able to call people by name, usually after one introduction. At a social gathering they can be observed attending to the needs of others, trying to insure that all are comfortable and involved. Social ties matter to the ESFJs, and their conversations often drift to nostalgic recounting of past memories. Traditions are developed, supported, and carefully observed by the ESFJ.

ESFJs are hurt by indifference and need to be appreciated both for themselves and for the abundance, typically in the form of services, they give to others. They are conscious of appearances and take the opinions of others regarding social standards very seriously. Values in an ESFJ may take the form of *shoulds* and *should nots* and may be freely expressed. Conscientious and orderly, ESFJs may become restless when isolated from people.

Career selection by ESFJs may lean toward service occupations. They have such outgoing personalities that they are outstanding at selling, being an invariable winner in sales contests. They are apt to have seniority in any sales group within an organization. Observation of ESFJs at work in a sales transaction will demonstrate how this type personalizes the sale: The customer is not buying the product; he or she is buying personally from the ESFJ. This same characteristic causes ESFJs to be good in teaching, preaching, supervision, administration, coaching, and, in general, people-to-people jobs. They seldom become a source of irritation to their superiors, for they respect and obey the rules and regulations, are duty- and service-oriented. They are loyal to their bosses. ESFJs are likely to be aware of and enjoy discussing events and problems in the lives of their colleagues; but when conversations turn to abstractions of philosophy or science, the ESFJ may become restive. Analysis of the complex—for example, an attempt to find an explanation of events through an analysis of principles —does not excite their interest, as it does the NTs'.

ESFJ mates have a set of values which contain clear *shoulds* and *should-nots*, and they expect their family to abide by these. They are conscientious about home responsibilities, are orderly about the home, and prefer that other occupants be the same. They enjoy socializing and entertaining. ESFJs want family decisions settled efficiently and quickly and want family living routinized, scheduled, and correctly executed. They do not rebel against routine operations, are devoted to the traditional values of home and hearth, respect their marriage vows, and are the most sympathetic of all types. They tend to be dependent on their mates and may marry to insure that they have a proper place in the social strata. They enjoy the rituals connected with serving of good food and beverages, thrive on festive occasions, respect and accumulate a goodly store of material possessions. They take their role in the community seriously and are sensitive to the acknowledged, official decision-makers and identify with them. They are aware of status, and often depend on higher authority as the source of opinions and attitudes.

ESFJs wear their hearts on their sleeves and are outgoing in their emotional reactions. They need to be needed, loved, and appreciated and may spend much energy reassuring themselves that this is the case. They can become melancholy and depressed and even suicidal if they take the blame for whatever might be wrong in their institution or their personal relationships—as they are prone to do.

ESFJs usually respect and revere their parents, and as children were responsive and obedient pupils. They seem able to express the right feeling for a given situation. They are soft-hearted, sentimental, and usually observe with gusto and a flourish birthdays, anniversaries, and the like, making of the event a delightful, important occasion. At the same time, however, ESFJs can cause others undue tension by expressing anticipations of gloom and doom, exhibiting a bent toward the pessimistic that can be contagious. They need to control their fears that the worst is sure to happen and suppress their tendency toward crepe-hanging and anticipating disasters.

The children of an ESFJ are seen as an extension of the family, and all they do reflects on the ESFJ. If things do not go well, the ESFJ may be critical, even carping toward his or her mate and children. This type may marry alcoholics or others who are particularly needy. If a female ESFJ is married to a mate who is not a good provider, she can become nagging and brood over a comparison of her possessions and status with that of others. ESFJs, male or female, live in terms of people and things rather than in terms of ideas and principles. They enjoy the process of decision-making, particularly when focus is on the *usefulness* of things and people.

Portrait of an ISFJ:

Six out of every one hundred people are ISFJs. Here the primary desire is to be of service and to minister to individual needs. ISFJs carry a sense of history, a sense of continuity with past events and relationships. Traditions and the conservation of resources are valued highly. The least hedonistic of all types, ISFJs believe work is good, play must be earned. ISFJs are willing to work long, long hours. When they undertake a task, it will be completed if at all humanly possible. Adhering to an established way of doing things and doing them well is valued and respected. The efficiency and effectiveness of an established procedure is not often questioned. Procedures dictated by handbooks are law. If others violate or ignore these standard operating procedures, ISFJs are annoyed and irritated, although they may not always display this reaction. Usually, such irritation is turned inward and may be experienced as fatigue and muscle tension.

ISFJs are super-dependable and seldom are happy working in situations where rules are constantly changing. Their major need to be of service to others leads them into occupations such as nursing, teaching, secretarial work, medical practice (especially general practice), librarian work, and middle-management administrative jobs. They relate well to people who need them, for example, the sick, the ignorant, students, and the "boss." Much satisfaction comes to them when they are taking care of the needs of another and they render the service gently and helpfully. When the recipient is no longer in need, the relationship may change its character, the ISFJ becoming disinterested. They enjoy assisting the downtrodden and can handle better than other types servility in others. If a situation calls for such behavior on their part, they will show "due respect." ISFJs have an extraordinary sense of responsibility and an outstanding talent for executing routines which call for repeated, sequential procedures; for example, ISFJs make extraordinary secretaries, highly efficient nurses, and dedicated teachers. Speculation and theory do not intrigue ISFJs, who would rather leave the less practical matters to others while remaining themselves practical and down-to-earth.

ISFJs tend to be devoted and loyal to a boss and tend to identify personally rather than institutionally. They expect others, including the boss, to follow procedures and are distressed and embarrassed when people do not behave as they are supposed to behave. ISFJs often seem to feel personally responsible for seeing to it that people in an institution or business carry out established rules and routines. They often are aware of status given by titles, environment, offices, and the like and can use this to advantage. They are aware of the value of material resources and abhor the squandering or misuse of these resources. To save, to put something aside against an unpredictable future, to prepare for emergencies—these are important actions.

ISFJs may experience some discomfort when placed in positions of authority over others and may tend to try to do everything themselves rather than insist that others do their jobs. As a result, ISFJs are frequently overworked.

ISFJs are devoted to mate and family and usually are excellent homemakers. The home of an ISFJ is likely to be well kept inside and out. Interior and exterior are meticulously maintained and appointed in the traditional manner. As a parent, the ISFJ expects the children to conform to the rules of society and has a feeling of personal responsibility to see to it that these rules are honored. An ISFJ is apt to find the putting on of airs as offensive and tends to prefer modest, quiet friends rather than more boisterous ones. For the ISFJ, people should behave according to their position in life, and the ISFJ may be annoyed by others who act either above or below their social or economic station.

The ISFJ female often displays a flair for making the interior of the home attractive in a time-honored style, provides attractive, nourishing meals, and maintains the environment in a neat and orderly state. To the ISFJ male and female, the home territory is important to own and to preserve.

While ISFJs are super-dependable, they may be fascinated by and attracted to the irresponsible, the lush, the glutton. Many ISFJs marry alcoholics and then proceed to conduct a rescue-rejection game without end, with the rescuing phase taking the guise of an attempt to reform. Occasionally an ISFJ mother may reveal a tendency to find humor in the "waywardness" of a son, while raising her daughters to respect traditions and to do the Right Thing at the Right Time—always.

ISFJs are frequently misunderstood and undervalued. Their contributions often are taken for granted, and the ISFJ as well is too often taken for granted. This can cause an ISFJ to harbor feelings of resentment, and this bottled up emotion can gnaw inwardly, causing the ISFJ much undeserved suffering.

Portrait of an ESTP:

ESTPs are men and women of action. When someone of this personality is present, things begin to happen. The lights come on, the music plays, the game begins. And a game it is for the ESTP, the outstanding entrepreneur, the international diplomat, the conciliator, and the negotiator *par excellence*. Approximately 13 percent of the general population are of this extraverted, sensing, thinking, perceiving type, and if only one adjective could be used to describe ESTPs *resourceful* would be an apt choice.

Life is never dull around ESTPs. Their attractive, friendly style has a theatrical flourish which makes even the most routine, mundane event seem exciting. ESTPs usually know the location of the best restaurants, and headwaiters are likely to call them by name. ESTPs are socially sophisticated, suave, and urbane and are master manipulators of the external environment.

ESTPs are uncanny at observing people's motivations, somehow hypersensitive to minimal nonverbal cues which other types might miss. And they are masters at using these observations to "sell" the "client." The eye of the ESTP is ever on the eye of the beholder, and all actions are directed toward this audience. Witty, clever, and fun, ESTPs seem to possess an unusual amount of empathy, when in fact this is not the case; rather, they are so acutely aware of minimal signals from others that they are usually several jumps ahead in anticipation of another's position. And ESTPs can use information gained to the ends they have in mind—apparently with nerves of steel, engaging in what seems to others to be suicidal brinksmanship. Other types may find this exhausting, but ESTPs are exhilarated by working close to the edge of disaster. ESTPs are ruthless pragmatists and often offer the ends as justification for whatever means they see as necessary—regrettable, perhaps, but necessary. Usually, however, ESTPs do not care to justify actions, but prefer instead to get on to the next action.

ESTPs are outstanding as initiators of enterprises that bring people together to negotiate. They make invaluable itinerant administrators who can pull troubled companies or institutions out of the red very quickly, and with style! They can sell an idea or project in a way no other type can, but won't follow through on the tedious administrative details of a project. This characteristic often causes ESTPs to be unappreciated for the extraordinary talents they have, for people lose sight of the idea contributed and focus on the details left undone, becoming critical of ESTPs' weaknesses rather than appreciating their strength. Few enterprises which are institutionally based use ESTPs as they should be used. When they strike out on their own, however, they do not always succeed, for their unwillingness to bother with follow-up details may cause an otherwise excellent project to fail. ESTPs need to be sure they have someone who will take care of follow-up if at all possible.

If the promotional, entrepreneural capabilities of ESTPs are used to constructive ends, an institution is fortunate for their presence. If their desire for excitement is not met constructively, however, these energies may be channeled into destructive, antisocial activities such as those of the confidence rackets— counterfeiting, bad-check artistry, safe-cracking, and swindling. A movie of the early 1970's which caught this use of the ESTP's talents was *The Sting*.

ESTPs live in the immediate moment and as mates lend excitement—and unpredictability—to the relationship. The ESTP mate is usually extremely attentive in public and smooth in social rituals. They carry on amusing repartee, and laughter surrounds them as they recount from their endless supply of clever jokes and stories. Charm radiates from ESTPs. Nothing is too good for their friends, although family responsibilities may, at times, be given second priority. The ESTP's mate may in time come to feel like an object—the female a chattel and the male a negotiable commodity. Deep commitments do not always occur in the lives of ESTPs, although they are always popular and know many, many people by name. Relationships usually are conditional, and the condition is the consideration of what the ESTP has to gain from the relationship. Anything gained, however, is shared freely and generously with the mate. The unexpected gift, the impulsive trip to Paris, the extravagant surprise at Christmas—all these an ESTP brings to a mate. Fun, excitement, laughter, and that element of unpredictability are characteristic of their relationship. The ESTPs have a low tolerance for anxiety and are apt to avoid or leave situations that are consistently filled with interpersonal tensions. ESTPs are usually somewhat of a mystery to their mates and to others. Few people comprehend this unique personality. ESTPs themselves understand well the maxim, "He who travels fastest, travels alone." Still, ESTPs are not likely to be lonely for long. ESTPs meet life with a hearty appetite for the good things of the world, searching out excitement, perhaps as a warrior, an athlete, an adventurer, or as a professional gambler, but always seeking the thrill of courting Lady Luck in one fashion or another. A theme of seeking excitement through taking of risks runs through the lives of ESTPs.

Portrait of an ESFP:

ESFPs radiate attractive warmth and optimism. Smooth, witty, charming, clever, voluble, and open to the environment—this describes ESFPs who, like ESTPs, represent about 13 percent of the general population. They are great fun to be with and are the most generous of all the types. *Performer* would be the word which best describes an ESFP.

ESFPs will avoid being alone and seek the company of others whenever possible. ESFPs easily find company, for others are usually highly entertained by the presence of an ESFP. ESFPs love excitement and create it wherever they are. Their joy of living is contagious and generally they wear happy faces. Often outstanding conversationalists, their flowing banter is amusing in its wit. ESFPs have an air of sophistication and are likely to be dressed in the latest fashion, displaying an enjoyment of all the good things of life: dress, food, physical comfort, and happy times. ESFPs create a mood of "eat, drink, and be merry" wherever they go, and around them life can have a continual party-like atmosphere of gaiety.

ESFPs make exciting, if somewhat unpredictable mates, which may give quieter type mates some anxiety and tension from living on the edge of adventure. The home of an ESFP is likely to be filled with people all having a good time. Problems will not be allowed to make their appearance. The ESFP accomplishes this by taking an attitude of "walking by the graveyard whistling," refusing to recognize doom and gloom.

ESFPs can be generous to a fault. What is theirs is yours, and what is yours is yours still. They give assistance to one and all without expectation of a return, just as they love freely without expecting something in return. ESFPs seem to view life as an eternal cornucopia from which flows an endless supply of pleasures that require no effort on their part to insure.

ESFPs' talent for enjoying life can make them more subject to temptations than are other types. They are inclined to be impulsive, and thus both male and female ESFPs are vulnerable to psychological seduction, if not physical seduction, with an ESFP giving in easily and agreeably to the demands of others. As a parent, the ESFP will be entertaining, a friend, and a source of fun and excitement. When there is sickness, or trouble, however, ESFPs may become impatient and may want to absent themselves.

ESFPs' tolerance for anxiety is the lowest of all the types. Anxiety is avoided by ignoring the dark side of a situation as long as possible. They are inclined to be somewhat self-indulgent, but, rather than make an outward show of resistance or make waves, ESFPs will give apparent compliance—and then go their own way to what they enjoy.

ESFPs prefer active jobs and should not be given lonely, solitary assignments. Outstanding in public relations, they love working with people. Decisions are made with personal warmth, based on personal reference or reference to significant others. This type relies heavily on their personal experiences and generally show good common sense.

The gregarious sociability and adaptability of ESFPs make them a source of warmth to others. They do not mind telephone or personal interruptions and are verbally facile in both situations. They can be counted on to have accurate data about the people around them, gaining these data through effortless and continuous observations.

ESFPs are not deeply interested in scholastic pursuits, wanting knowledge only for immediate utility. They avoid science and engineering, gravitate toward business, and are adept at selling, particularly selling tangibles. They can be effective in education, especially elementary school teaching, and can enjoy nursing for its drama. They are good at working with people in crisis, a facility which often leads ESFPs into social work. They also enjoy entertaining people and are thus drawn to the performing arts, thriving on the excitement of being in the limelight.

Portrait of an ISTP:

Just as impulsive as other SPs, the ISTP's life is artful action—and action is end in itself. Action for the ISTP is more gratifying if it is born of impulse rather than of purpose. If the action is in the service of an end or aim, let the aim look out for itself; it cannot be allowed to influence execution. The act is self-directed, self-leading, containing its own imperatives which cannot be suborned to mere rules, regulations, or laws. ISTPs are egalitarian and can be fiercely loyal to "brothers," but they can also be fiercely insubordinate, seeing hierarchy and authority as unnecessary and even superfluous. It is not so much a matter of going against regulations as it is simply ignoring them. The ISTP must do his or her thing, free to vary each next move. And ISTPs are, or want to be, proud of their ability to make the next move skillfully.

ISTPs are often fearless, risking themselves more than other types, despite (even frequent) injury. Of all the types, ISTPs are most likely to pit themselves, or their technique, against chance, odds, or fate. They thrive on excitement; they crave some excitement each day, in the form of fast motion—racing, sky diving, or surfing, for instance. This hunger for action makes them more subject to boredom than any other type, their urge driving them to faster pace. Strangely, however, they are not bored while doing their thing, even though there may be long stretches when nothing happens, as during travel, surfing, hunting, or fishing.

The ISTP nature is most easily seen in their mastery of tools, tools of any kind, from microscopic drill to supersonic jet. From an early age, they are drawn to tools as to a magnet; they must manipulate them, and tools fall into their hands demanding use. Many pilots knew by the age of five that they were going to be pilots. ISTPs tend to take up activities that allow them to use tools: driving, steering, operating. And if a given tool, whether scalpel or earthmover, is operated with a precision that defies belief, that operator is likely an ISTP. Others use tools, of course, but not with the virtuosity of the ISTP. Indeed, we must call ISTP's the tool artisans, for they above all others command the tool and bend it to their impulse. But again, ISTPs—personified in Michaelangelo and Leonardo—work (or better, play) with·their tools on personal impulse and not on schedule. If an externally imposed schedule coincides with impulse, fine; if not, so much the worse for the schedule.

One tool especially attractive to the ISTP is the weapon. Should ISTPs turn against society (for whatever reason), they wield their weapons with lethal genius to support their rejection. The hit man of today, the gunslinger of the American West, and the duelist of 18th Century Europe, may be seen as virtuosos of precision homicide. Hit man, gunslinger, and duelist alike took pride in their prowess. Fortunately they face their own kind in battle, the good warriors of the land: soldier, marshal, police, intelligence agent. This is not to say that all warriors, good or bad, are ISTPs, or that ISTPs are all weapons experts; rather that the weapon virtuoso is more frequently ISTP than not.

ISTPs also play on impulse, taking off at any time just because they "feel like it." (We are advised not to try to stop the ISTP who "feels like" doing something.) The neurosurgeon does crop dusting on the side and rides a motorcycle to the airport, and the financier goes on a hunting trip in the middle of an audit (i.e., SJ scrutiny). There can be no end to the ways ISTPs seek thrills in play. Although they may have the appearance of loners in their work, they nonetheless hang around their own kind in play. The climbers, racers, flyers, hunters, and in general, movers, flock together. The companionship is mediated through the tool, and conversation is sparse and terse.

Like the ISFPs, ISTPs communicate through action, and show little interest in developing verbal skills. Indeed, this lack of interest in communication may be mistaken for what well meaning but misguided medics and educators call "learning disability" or "dyslexia," both preposterous notions when meant as explanations. Let ISTPs get near a tool of any complexity and power and see how fast they pass up everybody in *learning* to use it and how precise their *lexicon* in talking of its features.

Despite their egalitarianism, insubordination, and love of freedom, they can be leaders, even great ones. But they must be
"up front," sword in hand, leading the charge. That is to say,
ISTPs can be very successful as battle leaders, for instance, no
matter how large or small the force under their command.
Their supreme realism, timing, and sense of expediency allows
them to seize the moment and fully exploit whatever resources
can be gotten (theirs or others) and capitalize on deficits and
mistakes of their opponent. Theirs is an expediency or exploita-
tive leadership, based on a special kind of intelligence which
may be called artistic concreteness. Yes, for the ISTP battle
leader, combat is an art, an intellectual game, not in the sense
of strategy (that is for NTs), but rather using whatever is at
hand to defeat the other with the least injury. Battle leaders
are duelists. Patton was such a leader, and we must credit
Marshall (an NTJ strategist) for seeing beneath that flamboy-
ant, impulsive, insubordinate, and reckless exterior a peerless
warrior. The same credit goes to Grant (another NTJ) for selecting Sheridan (STP), and to Hitler (ENFJ) for selecting Rommel
(ISTP). Patton, Sheridan, and Rommel were cut from the same
cloth and showed the same artistic espionage and rapier-like
tactics.

Glory is a pre-20th Century concept better understood by the
ISTP than by others. Or at least the ISTP is more interested in it
than most others. In battle there is glory, for it is in battle that
one can exercise one's lethal skills with positive sanction. The
Seven Samurai were glorified and so have been duelists down
through the ages. Foss, Boyington, Fonck, and von Richtoffen,
all virtuosos of the winged machine gun, are still glorified
heroes. But there are hundreds of warriors just like them in
nature. One can test one's mettle in lethal duel, there's glory in
it, as the film *The Great Waldo Pepper* showed most poetically.

The education and intelligence of the ISTP is worth special
comment. Possessed of artisan intelligence, ISTP is not in the
least interested in the clerical, interpretive, and "science"
curricula that abound in the 20th Century school. The other
SPs, equally bored by the school, will at least act as if they're
trying to learn, but not ISTP. ISTP will stare coldly into the eyes
of the teacher and not even say no. No amount of cajoling, brib-
ing, rewarding, punishing, or threat will get them to do their
school work. School work, quite apart from being irrelevant to
the talents of SPs, is, after all, mere preparation for something
the ISTPs figure they're never going to do anyway. SPs do not
wish to prepare—for anything—and ISTPs are careful to make

this clear to their would-be instructors. What is there to *do, now,* that is *worthwhile?* ISTP will not sit still (literally) for the trivial fare dished out (sanctimoniously, in the eyes of the ISTP). Most seem to agree that ISTPs "should" do their school work. But why? The arguments are piddling and incoherent, warranting the scorn they get from the unshakable ISTP. ISTPs are not "minimally brain damaged," or "hyperactive," or "dyslexic"; they *are* active, and they are stubbornly insistent upon getting to do, in school, some things that allow them to test their intelligence and their mettle. Name-calling and pill-pushing won't change them, other than destroying their self confidence and perhaps creating a stimulant addict now and then. Give them a tool-centered curriculum and watch their speed.

Behaviorally the ISTP is more like the ESTP than any other type, and the older they get, the greater the resemblance. When young, ISTPs may look very much like ISFPs, but as their confidence and pride increase this resemblance recedes. Jungians think ISTPs are just like INTPs with only minor differences, but this is based on the definition of ISTPs as "introverted thinking types." INTPs are logicians, philologists, and architects in the way they think, but ISTPs are completely disinterested in these pursuits. Even a cursory observation of a few clear-cut ISTPs will show how striking the contrast, and how trivial the resemblance.

Still, the most important thing about the ISTPs is their communality with the other SPs. We might think that there would be some resemblance to the ISTJ, having as they do, "IST" in common. But no, their behavior is antithetical in almost every dimension of comparison. One is pessimistic while the other optimistic; one is parental, the other, fraternal; one saves, the other spends; one believes in rules, the other is instinctually insubordinate and recalcitrant to rules; and so on. ISTPs have infinitely more in common with the very different ESFP than they do with any NT or SJ; besides the above, their mood is one of good cheer, they are loyal to their equals, they want no obligations, duties, or confining promises, are uncomplicated in their desires, and are trusting, receptive, and generous.

Portrait of an ISFP:

Although all SPs (Sensuous Performers) are artisans in their nature, they usually do not pursue their artistry with the same devotion to grace and adornment as the ISFP. For whatever reason, the ISFP seems more inclined to the "fine arts" than the other SPs; so when an especially gifted composer, painter, or dancer shows up, he or she, more frequently than not, possesses the character of the ISFP. Beethoven, Toscanini, Rembrandt, and Nijinski, as shown by typohistorical research, were clear-cut ISFPs. But the ISFP temperament is very difficult to observe, even in the great artists, and so ISFP is probably the most misunderstood of all the types.

A major source of misunderstanding is the tendency of ISFPs not to express themselves directly, but through action. If they find a medium of expression, some art form, then the character is expressed in some degree via the medium. If not, it simply doesn't come out, and no one knows them, this social reticence making the character all but invisible. Of course, in those rare cases where remarkable skill is achieved, such as in the virtuoso, ISFPs become celebrites, but their nature is still far from visible. Harpo Marx, a brilliant comedic actor, may well be seen as prototype, in his simultaneous celebrity and mute invisibility.

On close observation, these relatively infrequent SPs (5 percent of the population is ISFP, as compared to 15 percent ESFP) are just as hedonic and impulsive as the other SPs. Here is no NF search for significance, nor for that matter any fascination with science (NT) or commerce (SJ). ISFPs live Epicurean lives in the here and now, and as gracefully as possible. They do not plan and prepare. Submergence in their artistry is not preparation for something later; rather they experience intensely, now. ISFPs do not wait, for to wait is to see their impulse wither and die; they want and value their impulses and see them as the center of their lives. Nor are ISFPs devoted or committed to artful play; rather they are caught, as by a magnet or a whirlwind. So then the long hours of "practice" the virtuoso "gives" to artistry is not practice at all and it is not given; it is *doing* and it is taken from the (willing) ISFP by the performance itself. The act is ISFP's master, not the reverse, so we must abandon any notion of ISFPs as careful and devoted planners and of dutiful preparation and rehearsal. They paint, or sing, or toot, or dance, or run, or skate, or pot, or whatever, simply because they must: the mountain is climbed *because it is there.*

Because the ISFP is always caught up, so to speak, in whatever actions are underway, rather than practicing toward some distant goal, there is no question of the ISFP noticing fatigue, pain, or danger. They are usually quite oblivious to these accompaniments of many of their favorite activities. It is not that ISFPs are inured to them as much as it is that, wholly engaged by an action, they simply do not notice them. In this ISFP is similar to other SPs and different from all other types.

ISFP, like other SPs, has a special kind of intelligence. Please recall that intelligence is defined in this book as doing things well under varying circumstances. This particular category of intelligence might be called "artisan concretization." Such talent differs radically from that possessed by NFs, NTs, and SJs (granting, of course, that they too have their own unique and inherent abilities). This artisan concretization somehow keeps the ISFP more closely in touch with the very real. While the ISTP is attuned to the tool, so to speak, the ISFP is attuned to color, line, texture, shading—touch, motion, seeing, and hearing in harmony. The senses of the ISFP seem more keenly tuned than those of others. Rembrandt could almost taste colors so great was his discrimination, Toscanini could hear a single false note in the most complex operatic-orchestral score, and Hemingway's words tasted and smelled and felt the waves. This extreme concreteness and specificity seems to come naturally to the ISFP and is embedded "in the warp and woof of the man's make."

The social side of the ISFP character must not be eclipsed by the more spectacular performances some of this group are capable of. The ISFP has to be the kindest of all the types with no near competitors. The kindness is unconditional. Here is sympathy, of which we are all capable, carried to its most extreme form. The ISFP is especially sensitive to the pain and suffering of others and, like St. Francis of Assisi, with sympathetic impulsivity gives freely to the sufferer.

ISFP is usually not interested in developing facility in speaking, writing, or conversation. Speech, after all, is abstract, not concrete, ISFPs preferring to have their fingers on the pulse of life. That pulse must be felt—by touch, in the muscles, in the eyes, in the ears. This insistence on the senses being so closely attuned to reality can, in some ISFPs, occasion a breach with language, and language becomes a barrier to smooth interpersonal relations. So ISFPs are sometimes seen by others as reserved and private, tending to give up rather easily in their attempts to express themselves verbally. But this reluctant speech is not so much a lack of ability as it is disinterest.

Hemingway broke that barrier, a splendid instance of an ISFP entering into the world of words and making apparent inarticulateness into art, changing the face of 20th Century literature.

The number of the great artisans who, upon investigation, were found clearly to have been ISFPs, is truly awesome. The other SPs seem to have contributed far fewer masters to the fine arts. Gaugin and Puccini, both ESTPs, were in this sense exceptional. Music and the dance seems almost the province of ISFP, and surely investigation will show many of the great athletes come from this group.

Of course, all ISFPs have not been and need not be artisans in the narrow sense of the word. Art, broadly conceived, is any action the next move of which is a free variable, and it is art thus conceived that is the forte of SPs in general and the ISFP in particular. Thus ISFPs have a lot of leeway in choice of occupation, especially if they don't drop out of school early (most SPs do, since the school offers little that is of interest to them or that challenges their special brand of intelligence). It is a sad day indeed when the ISFP chooses work wherein the operations are fixed by rule or necessity and not free. To be happy and productive the ISFP must choose variable actions and be rewarded for doing them.

Finally, in many ISFPs may be found an instinctive longing for the natural, the pastoral, the bucolic. They are quite at home in the wilds, and nature seems to welcome them. Some have a remarkable way with animals, even wild animals, almost as if there were a bond of mutual sympathy and trust. In some instances a similar bond may be seen between the ISFP and young children, instant and unstudied.

Perhaps the most important thing to understand about ISFPs is that they are SPs, with much in common with ESFPs especially, often resembling ISTPs, and even sharing some traits with the seemingly very different ESTP. To summarize this communality with other SPs, ISFPs may be seen as optimistic and cheerful; egalitation, fraternal, and insubordinate; tending to ward off obligation, duty, confinement, and fetters; a lover of freedom, easily bored, wanting excitement, risk, chance, and tests of luck; uncomplicated in motivation, trusting, receptive, generous, and in every sense of the word a spender rather than a saver.

ISFPs are misunderstood not only because they are retiring, reserved, and even self-effacing, but because the Jungians have cast them as "introverted feeling types," and therefore very much like the INFPs. Watch a few thoroughgoing ISFPs and you'll find they have very little in common with INFPs. Other types are reminded to guard against the natural tendency to project their own traits of character onto the silent ISFP.

BIBLIOGRAPHY

Adler, A. (1956) *The Individual Psychology of Alfred Adler,* Heinz & Rowena Ansbacher (Eds), New York: Basic Books.

Adickes, E. (1907) *Character und Weltanschauung,* Tubingen,

Apfelfach, H. (1924) *Der Aufbau des Characters.*

Bradway, K. (1964) "Jung's Psychological Types," *Journal of Analytical Psychology.* Vol. 9, Tavistock Publishers, pp. 129–135.

Bulliot, P. (1901) De la classification des caracteres et de la physiologie humaine, IV *Congress International de Psychologie.* Paris.

Freud, S. (1920) *Introductory Lectures to Psychoanalysis.* New York: Boni & Liveright.

Fromm, E. (1941) *Escape From Freedom,* New York: Farrar & Rinehart.

Grant, M. (1962) *Myths of the Greeks and Romans,* New York: World Publishing Company.

Graves, R. (1955) *The Greek Myths,* New York: George Brazieler.

Hamilton, E. (1940) *Mythology,* New York: Mentor Books.

Jung, C. (1923) *Psychological Types,* New York: Harcourt Brace.

Kretschmer, E. (1925) *Physique and Character,* New York: Harcourt Brace.

Levy, A. (1896) *Psychologie der Caracter.*

Maslow, A. (1954) *Motivation and Personality*, New York: Harper.

McKinnon, D. (1944) "The Development of Personality," Chapter 1, in J. McV Hunt (Ed.) *Personality and The Behavior Disorders*, New York: Ronald.

Moreno, J. (1934) *Who Shall Survive?* Washington: Nervous and Mental Disease Publishing Company.

Myers, I. (1962) *Manual: The Myers-Briggs Type Indicator*, Palo Alto, California: Consulting Psychologists Press.

Robach, A. (1927) *The Psychology of Character*. London: Kegan Paul.

Seeland, J. (1976) *Unpublished Paper*, California State University, Fullerton.

Sheldon, W. (1936) *Psychology and the Promethean Will*, New York: Harper.

Spranger, E. (1928) *Types of Men*, Halle, Niemeyer, Verlag.

Sternberg, T. (1907) *Characterologie als Wissenschaft*, Lausanne.

Sullivan, H. (1940) "Conceptions of Modern Psychiatry," *Psychiatry*, Vol. III.

Terkel, S. (1972) *Working*, New York: Pantheon Books, Random House.

Wheelright, J. et. al. (1964) *Manuel for Jungian Type Survey* (Gray-Wheelwright Test, 16th Revision). Palo Alto: Society of Jungian Analysts of Northern California.

Extra Answer Sheet

For the questions that appear on pages 5 through 10, enter a check for each answer in the column for **a** or **b**.

	a	b		a	b		a	b		a	b		a	b		a	b		a	b
1			2			3			4			5			6			7		
8			9			10			11			12			13			14		
15			16			17			18			19			20			21		
22			23			24			25			26			27			28		
29			30			31			32			33			34			35		
36			37			38			39			40			41			42		
43			44			45			46			47			48			49		
50			51			52			53			54			55			56		
57			58			59			60			61			62			63		
64			65			66			67			68			69			70		

```
 1        2  3        4  3        4  5        6  5        6  7        8  7        8
```

```
 1        2     3        4     5        6     7        8
   E  I           S  N           T  F           J  P
```

See page 11 for directions for scoring.

Extra Answer Sheet

For the questions that appear on pages 5 through 10, enter a check for each answer in the column for **a** or **b**.

	a	b		a	b		a	b		a	b		a	b		a	b		a	b
1			2			3			4			5			6			7		
8			9			10			11			12			13			14		
15			16			17			18			19			20			21		
22			23			24			25			26			27			28		
29			30			31			32			33			34			35		
36			37			38			39			40			41			42		
43			44			45			46			47			48			49		
50			51			52			53			54			55			56		
57			58			59			60			61			62			63		
64			65			66			67			68			69			70		

1   2   3   4   3   4   5   6   5   6   7   8   7   8

1   2   3   4   5   6   7   8

E I   S N   T F   J P

See page 11 for directions for scoring.

Extra Answer Sheet

For the questions that appear on pages 5 through 10,
enter a check for each answer in the column for **a** or **b**.

	a	b		a	b		a	b		a	b		a	b		a	b		a	b
1			2			3			4			5			6			7		
8			9			10			11			12			13			14		
15			16			17			18			19			20			21		
22			23			24			25			26			27			28		
29			30			31			32			33			34			35		
36			37			38			39			40			41			42		
43			44			45			46			47			48			49		
50			51			52			53			54			55			56		
57			58			59			60			61			62			63		
64			65			66			67			68			69			70		

1   2   3   4   3   4   5   6   5   6   7   8   7   8

1   2   3   4   5   6   7   8

   E   I   S   N   T   F   J   P

See page 11 for directions for scoring.

Extra Answer Sheet

For the questions that appear on pages 5 through 10,
enter a check for each answer in the column for **a** or **b**.

	a	b		a	b		a	b		a	b		a	b		a	b		a	b
1			2			3			4			5			6			7		
8			9			10			11			12			13			14		
15			16			17			18			19			20			21		
22			23			24			25			26			27			28		
29			30			31			32			33			34			35		
36			37			38			39			40			41			42		
43			44			45			46			47			48			49		
50			51			52			53			54			55			56		
57			58			59			60			61			62			63		
64			65			66			67			68			69			70		

1   2 3   4 3   4 5   6 5   6 7   8 7   8

1   E I   2   3   S N   4   5   T F   6   7   J P   8

See page 11 for directions for scoring.

Extra Answer Sheet

For the questions that appear on pages 5 through 10, enter a check for each answer in the column for **a** or **b**.

	a	b		a	b		a	b		a	b		a	b		a	b		a	b
1			2			3			4			5			6			7		
8			9			10			11			12			13			14		
15			16			17			18			19			20			21		
22			23			24			25			26			27			28		
29			30			31			32			33			34			35		
36			37			38			39			40			41			42		
43			44			45			46			47			48			49		
50			51			52			53			54			55			56		
57			58			59			60			61			62			63		
64			65			66			67			68			69			70		

1   2 3   4 3   4 5   6 5   6 7   8 7   8

1   2
E   I

3   4
S   N

5   6
T   F

7   8
J   P

See page 11 for directions for scoring.

Extra Answer Sheet

For the questions that appear on pages 5 through 10,
enter a check for each answer in the column for **a** or **b**.

	a	b		a	b		a	b		a	b		a	b		a	b		a	b
1			2			3			4			5			6			7		
8			9			10			11			12			13			14		
15			16			17			18			19			20			21		
22			23			24			25			26			27			28		
29			30			31			32			33			34			35		
36			37			38			39			40			41			42		
43			44			45			46			47			48			49		
50			51			52			53			54			55			56		
57			58			59			60			61			62			63		
64			65			66			67			68			69			70		

1   2   3   4   3   4   5   6   5   6   7   8   7   8

1   2
E   I

3   4
S   N

5   6
T   F

7   8
J   P

See page 11 for directions for scoring.